INSIDE DIEGO

I N S I D E
DIEGO

How the Best Footballer in the World
became the Greatest of All Time

Fernando Signorini, Luciano Wernicke and Fernando Molina

First published by Pitch Publishing, 2023

Pitch Publishing
9 Donnington Park,
85 Birdham Road,
Chichester,
West Sussex,
PO20 7AJ
www.pitchpublishing.co.uk
info@pitchpublishing.co.uk

ISBN 978 1 80150 413 3

Typesetting and origination by Pitch Publishing

Printed and bound in Great Britain by TJ Books Limited, Padstow, Cornwall

Contents

Preface: AD 10s, muchacho 9

1. Winter Confessions 11

2. What will become of you? 15

3. Close to the revolution 31

4. Ho visto Maradona 55

5. México lindo y querido 84

6. 'O sole mio 113

7. Un'estate italiana 150

8. Losing control 172

9. The stab in the back 206

10. The comeback 228

Epilogue: Live is life 265

'I don't care what Diego did with his life, I care what he did with mine.' – **Roberto Fontanarrosa**

'Fernando Signorini is a total master, a genius. He not only taught me how to prepare myself, but how to prepare my head.' – **Diego Maradona**

'Oh mamma, mamma, mamma,
oh mamma, mamma, mamma,
sai, perché, mi batte il corazon,
ho visto Maradona, ho visto Maradona,
eh, mamma, innamorato son!'

> – *Neapolitan football stadium song*

Preface: AD10s, muchacho

Note: 'Goodbye, boy', referred to 'Goodbye, boys', famous Argentine tango by Carlos Gardel. 'AD10s' (Good bye) has a double meaning: to use the number 10 from Maradona's shirt as 'i' and 'o', and the presence of the word 'Dios', that in Spanish means 'God'

THE STAB was atrocious, insolent wickedness. The crash, which was heard on the field and, some people swear, even in the stands, sounded like a coda. The last note of the saddest tango of all tangos. *A cruel cold destroyed you, robbed you of all illusions, threw you into a deep low bottom, with an absurd wound.* The assistants put him on a stretcher and covered him with a blanket, drawing a curtain over his heart. Barcelona was beating the champion, Athletic Club, two to zero, but in the stands the wind raised a strange lament. Sadness. Without Diego, the night became a well of shadows. Under a powerless light, Barça would score two more goals, although the show had already ended.

Ominous news said that he would not play anymore. *What lack of respect, what a reason abuse!* he shouted, a mixture of anger, pain, faith, absence. Villa Fiorito's *Pelusa*, reared on maté's herbs drying in the sun, had plenty of courage to continue on the path of dreams. *Even if life breaks you.* He swore that those vain promises would blow away with the wind. Like those things that are never achieved.

9

Brave men risk life for a love, and Diego ventured it. Stubborn, like the thousand times he had crossed Alsina Bridge at Pompeii nights. *First you have to know how to suffer.* He crawled through thorns, blind to his sorrow. With humble hope, that was all the fortune of his heart.

And the return came. *You always go back to first love.* Under the mocking gaze of stars and the indifference of others, he came back. Dressed for a party, with his best colour, inside his chest the heart was asking for free rein. He erased the sadness and calmed the bitterness with goals, in great style and with precision. Many, many beautiful, others not so much. *If you do not steal, you are a dimwit!* He sang victory and consecration came. The kid dream.

He filled the champagne glass to the brim, in a thousand and one nights of revelry and joy. *Yours is your life, yours is your love.* Later, disagreement. *The spider you saved bit you.* All the troupe, screaming, trampled on the brotherly hand that God gave him. They plunged the whole harpoon into him with rancor. The sick body did not hold out any longer. *I want to cry in this grey afternoon.*

Diego, life is a breath. You loved with tenderness, you went for broke, what are you going to do? Sooner or later the walk stops. AD10s, boy. For you, there will be no more sorrows ... nor forgetfulness!

Luciano Wernicke
Buenos Aires, July 2021

Note: This text was originally written with phrases from various tangos, some of them with words from the Argentine 'lunfardo' (dialect).

Chapter 1

Winter Confessions

('Confesiones de invierno' – Argentine pop song)

I REMEMBER it as if it were today. I know it sounds incredible, but I assure you that that moment was etched in my mind in that harsh winter of 1972. In Lincoln, my hometown, there wasn't much to do on a Sunday. You couldn't even watch television, because a transmitting antenna had not yet been installed to bring the capital's channels closer to that town, located about 300km west of Buenos Aires, nor did cable signals exist yet. After the unavoidable siesta, although I could better define it as mandatory, those of us who loved football had only one way to connect ourselves with the First Division championship, which at that time was called Metropolitano: the radio. The ball entered my head through the ears, propelled by the voices emitted by the transistor device. Armed with only the words chosen by the narrator, I tried to imagine the goals, the saves, the magic. A few days later, I used to buy the legendary magazine *El Gráfico* and, through its beautiful photographs, discovered if the plays that I had projected in my mind approximated, albeit vaguely, what had really happened in the unreachable stadiums of Buenos Aires, Avellaneda or Rosario. But what caught my attention that cold June day was not the description of a goal, or a specific action, but a name. I had tuned into Radio Rivadavia to listen to the account of the match between Argentinos Juniors and the leader of the tournament, San Lorenzo. At the end of the first half, the host of the programme, José María Muñoz, gave way to the different chroniclers who had to report what had happened in other coliseums. At that time, all the matches of the date were fulfilled simultaneously. However, after two or three minutes, he interrupted the correspondents, fascinated by what was happening in the central circle of the *Bicho de la Paternal* court: an 11-year-old boy dazzled the fans by juggling a ball.

'Zavatarelli, who is that boy who does such wonders?' Muñoz wanted to know.

'He's a kid from the children divisions of Argentinos Juniors, José María,' replied Dante Zavatarelli, the journalist located next to the lime line.

'What is his name?' asked the commentator.

'Diego Armando Maradona.'

'Diego Armando Maradona,' I repeated in the living room of my house in Lincoln, perhaps to sculpt in my head those words that I had found attractive. While Muñoz had been bewitched by the boy's talent, I had been struck by the sound of his name.

Years later, received as a physical education teacher at the Nuestra Señora de Lincoln School and working as a trainer for the first football team of the Rivadavia Club in the same city, I heard again that trio of words that combined harmoniously so many times that I ended up familiarising myself with it – as it must have happened to millions, I think. First, as the new hope of Argentinos Juniors, although already in the professional team. Then, as the leader of the youth team that won the U-20 World Cup in Japan in 1979, led by coach Cesar Menotti, and finally as the star of the 1981 Boca champion, already on television, because finally a municipal official had thought to place an antenna that would feed the leisure of the *Linqueños*. Thanks to the images on TV, I managed to put a face to the musical name, and also discovered that Muñoz had fallen short with his praise. The boy not only dominated the ball at will, but he was an expert in the art of scam. A youth master of outstanding cunning, of an exquisite mischief that is no longer seen on the courts, or at least I have not seen again. Nobody fools anybody anymore.

In December 1982, after the World Cup in Spain and the disastrous Malvinas War, I had the pleasure of seeing, on a field, that tangle of curls with prodigious feet that had so enraptured me from a distance through a cathode-ray tube. It was at the Camp Nou, on a cold Catalan night. Diego scored the only goal for the *Blaugrana* team with a prodigious touch that outwitted the great Basque goalkeeper Luis Miguel Arconada, defender of the Real Sociedad and the Spanish national squad nets. A very similar touch, almost traced, to the one that Diego himself would draw four years later against Belgian Jean-Marie Pfaff in the World Cup in Mexico, to score the opening goal for the light-blue-and-white team.

Shortly after that first visual, distant and certainly unidirectional contact, destiny —which sometimes acts cruelly but was excessively generous with me – crossed my path with that kid whom everyone in Spain called *Pelusa*, from a fortuitous encounter and a misfortune that, I must admit, turned out to be lucky. From there, we moved forward together for about 14 years. We flew in fast Ferraris on safe highways and stumbled along stony and dangerous trails. We piloted racing boats and paddled in the thick mud. We won and we lost. Today, looking from the distance that time and experience grant, and after so many trips, so many championships, so many anecdotes, I feel that those 14 years were 140.

It is very difficult to chronologically tell the story of one of the most famous guys in the world. Millions have watched him play, heard him speak, read about him, watched one or more of the documentaries that have been produced about his surprising existence. But everyone has seen Maradona, read about Maradona, listened to Maradona, watched documentaries about Maradona. I'm going to tell you about Diego, the kid who trained with ambition, the human being who appeared when the cameras and flashes were turned off, the boy forged in the very poor neighbourhood of Villa Fiorito who travelled to the top of Everest without warm clothes or help from the Sherpas. Maradona … Maradona was another person, with whom Diego only shared his last name.

When Napoli won the first *Scudetto* in its history, in 1987, a fan painted a superb phrase on one of the walls of the Poggioreale cemetery, the main one in the city: 'You don't know what you have lost.' I do not. I have lived it and I am going to tell it so that others do not miss it.

This book is written from affection, although with the rigour of a true friend: the one who accompanies and supports his buddy through thick and thin. The one who says 'yes' but he also says 'no'.

Chapter 2

What will become of you?

('¿Qué va a ser de ti?' – famous Catalonian song)

LIFE IS trial and error, risking, falling and getting up. You learn from experiences. The wise Catalan Joan Manuel Serrat declared a few years ago that 'there is no manual: the world of sensations and relationships is full of unforeseen events'. And Diego had them, yes, a lot. His passage through Barcelona was plagued by unexpected setbacks. At the beginning of December 1982, the joy for having defeated Real Madrid at the Santiago Bernabéu stadium – with two assists from his feet, for Esteban Vigo Benítez and Enrique *Quini* Castro González – and scratching the top of the table was dissipated in just one week on the Camp Nou pitch, when a fierce Real Sociedad defender, Alberto Górriz Echarte, hit Diego with a brutal kick from behind. The blow of the implacable defender from San Sebastian – a dark harbinger of what would happen nine months later, on the same stage and with another Basque executioner – caused Diego a sprain to his right ankle with a partial rupture of ligaments that prevented him from playing for a couple of weeks in the team led by the rough German

15

coach Udo Lattek. But when the injury began to loosen, after the rain downpour, an analysis determined that Diego had contracted hepatitis. 'Hepatitis! Maradona, indefinite leave,' titled with 'Catastrophe' said the Catalan newspaper *El Mundo Deportivo* on 17 December. Nice Christmas gift for the *culés* fans, who had asked Santa Claus for Diego to return to the pitch soon! The *Blaugrana* issued a brief and vague statement that raised more doubts than certainties: 'Diego Armando Maradona is affected by hepatitis of possible viral origin, for which he has been discharged having to rest completely for an undetermined period.' The truth was that Diego missed 13 league games that, during his absence, led to a head-to-head race between Athletic Club of Bilbao and Real Madrid, a race that the Basque team won by a nose.

Diego returned to the team the same day that Barcelona unveiled their new coach, Cesar Luis Menotti, after the departure of Lattek. The No.10 and *El Flaco* (the skinny guy) were old acquaintances: together they had been champions in the U-20 Youth World Cup in Japan in 1979 and they had competed in the 1982 Spanish Cup. By the way, Cesar had also caused Diego one of the greatest sadnesses of his professional life. It happened before the 1978 World Cup in Argentina. Menotti had summoned 25 players to carry out an extensive preseason of almost two months in a country villa called 'Dulce Refugio', located in the town of José C. Paz, about 40km from Buenos Aires. Twelve days before the start of the tournament, Menotti gathered the squad in the centre of the training field to announce the names of the three footballers who would be left out of the official list: Humberto Bravo, Víctor Bottaniz and Diego Maradona, who at that time was 17 years old. Four decades after the thorny determination, the former coach acknowledged a likely error. 'At one point, you have to decide. I left Diego out in '78. If you asked me now if I was wrong, I would say it is probable, it is probable. It is very difficult, this,' he said, and emphasised that the fact was hidden behind the goals of Mario Kempes and Argentina's World Cup triumph.

From the hand of Menotti, *Pelusa* found sports consolation in the final of the Copa del Rey, played at La Romareda stadium in Zaragoza on 4 June 1983. FC Barcelona defeated Real Madrid 2-1, with a goal from a header by Marcos Alonso Peña in the last minute of the match. I remember the date because just that day was a month after my arrival in Spain, more precisely in the capital of Catalonia, together with my wife Carmen.

After working for a decade as a physical trainer for the Rivadavia team in Lincoln, the city of the province of Buenos Aires where I was born on 7 December 1950, I decided to leave my family's company – a processor of livestock by-products derived from fat – and cross the Atlantic to have an experience in European football. The only thing I asked my mother was to pay for our plane ticket to Spain, for me and Carmen, one way only. We travelled with barely $1,100 in our pockets: $800 that we had saved and $300 that three friends gave me, fearful that hunger would overcome me in a couple of weeks. My wife, who was also linked to sport through tennis, as a player and teacher, accompanied me unconditionally. We started in Barcelona because the coach who had convinced me the most, not only because of his game system but also considering his ethical assessment of football was working there: Cesar Luis Menotti. The world-champion coach had hypnotised me with two of his sentences. One: 'Although winning is important, because you compete for that, much more important are the means used to reach a purpose.' Two: 'Football should serve as a great excuse to be happy.' I had planned to spend time in Barcelona to see how Cesar developed his method and modus operandi, and then go to Italy and Germany, countries that at that time had very competitive leagues and excellent teams.

June is not the best month of the year to stand in the morning sun on the edge of the Mediterranean Sea. Much less in front of the main access gate to the interior of the Camp Nou, which did not even have so much as a little tree under which to take refuge from the merciless rays that made the Catalan earth creak. Every day, people from all over the world, although mostly local, crowded in front of the railings to see their idols arrive in their cars, and also try to cross that door into the green Eden where the team trained. I know this because I went there myself, for several days, to ask the guards if they could do me the favour of letting one of Menotti's collaborators know that a physical trainer recently arrived from Argentina wanted to observe some of the training sessions, thirsty for knowledge. Every morning, the guys listened to my plea, nodded their heads without changing their stern faces or moving a finger to satisfy my request. Every afternoon, I would return to the austere hostel where I had settled with Carmen, on Carrer d'Amílcar, fed only with frustration. However, I decided not to give up and returned daily until a miracle paved the way to paradise. A miracle that took shape through my perseverance ... and also by chance. One morning, crushed against the railings by the crowd fighting to get through the gate, I noticed that a young man, who appeared from the bowels of the stadium, had crossed the parking lot to ask something of the guards who jealously protected the access from the outside. The boy, who spoke to them in Spanish with a foreign accent, my own accent, received a brief reply from the head of the defenders, a big man named Benito, after which he turned to go back towards the access door to the changing rooms. Enlightened by what I thought was a unique opportunity, I yelled at Benito, who looked at me and – perhaps pitying the condition of Phoebus's victim, perhaps tired of seeing me there every morning – called the young man, whom I later learned was a friend of Diego's, José Luis Menéndez.

'Hey you! Here's a countryman of yours who wants to see Menotti.'

Menéndez turned around, looked at me and beckoned me to come in, while Benito gave me access and my former companions at the gate gave me tender epithets: 'Come on, you bastard! Why the South American yes and we not? Has he a crown, damn it?'

'Come on, skinny,' Menéndez invited me. 'Come here. Cesar is just here.'

We arrived at an entrance marked with a sign that announced the path to the dressing rooms and we began to go down a spiral staircase. After a few steps, I heard the unmistakable booming voice of Menotti, who was evaluating work issues with his assistant, Rogelio Poncini. Menéndez introduced me and I explained to Cesar what I wanted.

'No problema,' he told me. 'Leave your name to the guards at the entrance and when I leave, I authorise your entry for tomorrow. We are going to train in the afternoon.'

I thanked him and returned to the hostel, eager to come back to the stadium the following afternoon to finally witness a training session for FC Barcelona ... and eager to tell Carmen what had happened. She also arrived at our accommodation with good news: after several days of searching, she had finally found a job as a teacher, at the Club Tennis de la Salut school, managed by the famous Spanish tennis player Manuel Orantes.

The next morning, I headed towards the Camp Nou with a very different expectation. Upon arriving at the gate against which for so many days I had suffered the heat of summer and the cold of uncertainty, Benito received me with a 'Good morning, Mr Signorini. Go ahead,' and a wry face that, I could swear, looked a lot like a wink. I stepped through the gate again, through the many unfortunates that had remained on the other side, and headed toward my cement Mecca. The impact was tremendous. The non-stop journey from a rural field to one of the most gigantic and important stages in the world was as powerful as it was moving. Two situations were chiselled in the marble of my memory: one, the trek through the depths of such a magnificent theatre, full of life-size photographs of the stars of the present and past and display cabinets crammed with cups, jerseys, boots and other football offerings; the second, to enter a sea of seats that surrounded a green island on which Cesar and his players, including the best footballer on the planet, moved to the rhythm of the ball. I felt extremely fortunate to be able to enjoy a unique moment thanks to the generosity of Menotti, who, without knowing me, had facilitated the path to a destination that in Argentina had seemed less than unattainable.

The privilege of being able to witness the training showed me that a super-professional team was preparing with a method quite similar to the one we used in Rivadavia in Lincoln, of course with much more distinguished players. Menotti favoured that most of the efforts were made with the ball, in pursuit of executing imitative movements of the game.

After about ten or 12 training sessions, one day I arrived earlier than usual. The heat was so intense that I had to look for a protective roof to defend me from the midday sun in that huge empty parking lot until the arrival of Menotti and his players, who were going to train for the last game of the season. I remember the date: 28 June 1983. Two days before, on the 26th, Real Madrid and FC Barcelona had drawn 2-2 at the Santiago Bernabéu stadium, and one day later, on the 29th, they had to decide the title a few metres from where I was standing. But I don't remember that date because of that string of *Clasicos* but because that afternoon I spoke for the first time with the best football player I've ever seen, Diego Maradona. I was reviewing my notes when a red Volkswagen Golf extinguished the silence that enveloped the deserted arena. It was Diego, who had arrived, preceded by the roar of his car, prepared to race and show off. He jumped down and in two strides he reached the same door that I had crossed a couple of weeks before with the help of José Luis Menéndez to meet Menotti. Diego turned the knob and pulled, but the door remained tightly closed. He insisted three or four more times, in a frantic way, until he gave in to the immobile and stuck metal mass.

'Did you see, Diego?' I intervened, without detaching myself from the wall that sheltered me from the sun. 'And they say that the early bird catches the worm. (In Spanish, 'Al que madruga, Dios lo ayuda' – ' God helps who gets up early.') He turned and looked to my eyes. His annoyance had turned into curiosity. His teeth had parted and his mouth had broadened into a friendly smile.

'Sure,' I continued before he spoke, 'but you get there first and the door is closed ...'

He took a few steps towards me. His smile widened and he showed me shiny teeth that no longer wanted to bite.

'Can you believe this? How can I be so *green*?' he asked with the naivety of what he was, a 22-year-old boy. A very intelligent and observant kid. He showed it to me immediately, catching me by surprise.

'So you're a *profe*, you?' (Note: 'profe' is short for 'professor', a common and affectionate way of calling someone 'professor' in Argentina.)

He threw me off. How did he know? I suspected that he would have seen me talking to Cesar before or after some practice, or perhaps sitting alone in the stalls, which surely must have spurred his curiosity to the point of asking Menotti who was that strange man sitting alone in the stand.

As soon as I stammered a timid 'yes', Diego sent me to the canvas with a devastating proposal:

'I will play the final tomorrow against Real Madrid and the next day, at night, I am going to Argentina. I will return in 12 days for the preseason in Andorra. When I come back, I want to invite you to a barbecue at my house. With Jorge [Cyterszpiler, his agent], we are thinking of opening a football school in Barcelona and we are going to need trainers.'

I was dizzy. A guy I had never talked to before, whom I barely saw from afar a handful of times while training, who was also the best footballer in the world, was offering me to go eat at his house and work with him ... one minute after meeting me! If there had been someone else in that parking lot in that magical moment, I would have asked them to pinch me. That was an amazing dream that couldn't happen in real life!

Recovered from the surprise, I explained that I had already requested permission from Cesar to witness the preseason of a highly competitive team from the first day of work, and that he had authorised me, so that I would also travel to the principality nestled in the Pyrenees, between Spain and France.

'Well, fantastic. See you there!' He dismissed me with a pout and resumed his way to the locker room through the door that had, at last, been unlocked by a club employee.

The next day, deprived of going to the Camp Nou to watch the game – my meagre budget didn't allow it – I went to dinner with a friend at a pizzeria called Corrientes 348, an address in Buenos Aires mentioned in the tango 'In dim light' ('*A media luz*' in Spanish). I didn't know it, but that restaurant – owned by Jorge Buzzo and Jorge Vallejos, two former Argentine footballers based in Barcelona – was Diego's favourite. A long time after the end of the match, with a *culé* victory by two to one, with a goal from the idol born in Villa Fiorito, we heard a shouting that came from outside the pizzeria. In a few seconds, a large group entered, led by ... Diego! I couldn't believe what was happening. *Pelusa* sat at the end of a long table flanked by his girlfriend Claudia and his mother, *Doña Tota*, with her back to the door that led to the bathroom. At one point, I got up to go to the restroom and, as I passed the group celebrating the Barça victory, Diego recognised me and greeted me:

'*Profe*, what are you doing here?'

'How are you, *Diegucho*! I brought you luck,' I replied, as if to say something.

Upon returning to the dinner room, I noticed that *Doña Tota*'s chair was free – she possibly had also gone to the bathroom – and I sat for a few seconds next to Diego, who made some comments about the game. I got up right away and greeted the diners. He dismissed me with a 'See you in Andorra'.

The trip to the Pyrenees was not easy for me. It involved a great sacrifice, because with Carmen we had just enough money. While I was trying to legalise my title as professor of physical education, I had gotten an informal job at the fairgrounds in Barcelona, setting up and taking down stands, with which I had been able to collect a few *pesetas*, the Spanish currency from the time before the euro. I decided to invest all the money in an adventure that represented a unique opportunity, without certainties but important promises, and my wife understood. I stayed at the hostel Del Sol in Andorra La Vella (The Old) and the first day I showed up at the Communal Stadium in the capital of the principality, a modest pitch with an area for about 400 people seated. At the entrance gate to the interior of the venue, surrounded by a hundred fans and curious onlookers, I ran into two large bodyguards that usually protect the FC Barcelona squad during their trips, whom I did not know. 'Here we go again,' I thought. I appeared before one of them and, with a stony face, I assured him that I was an Argentine physical trainer friend of Cesar and Diego, whom they had invited to watch the training sessions. Not everything was a vile lie: I was a physical trainer …

'Stay here,' the gatekeeper suggested, with a suspicious tone. 'The team hasn't arrived yet.'

Two minutes later the bus appeared, with Menotti sitting behind the driver, on the aisle seat, and Diego placed to the right of him, a corridor in the middle. People were screaming, happy to see their heroes up close. While one of the guards was opening the gate, the vehicle entered and the other custodian, the one who had spoken to me, called me:

'Come here.' He gestured for me to go through the access and, raising his right index finger, he warned me, 'When *El Niño* and the Mister come, we will see if what you say is true.'

I didn't like the threatening expression at all, but I was calm. In fact, the intimidation finally evaporated when, a few minutes later, Cesar and Rogelio Poncini passed by on their way to the field and greeted me with great kindness. Freed from the harassment of the guard, I joined them and we walked together towards the playing field, which was surrounded by a running track.

'*Profe*, how many metres long is the athletics track?' Menotti asked me. 'I'd like to do a job there.'

'If it is regulatory, it is 400 metres in its internal edge,' I answered with confidence.

While Cesar and Rogelio were evaluating the day's exercises, Diego appeared, dressed in training clothes and shoes with untied laces.

'Hey, *Profe*,'- he greeted me happily. 'It is good to see you here!'

I shook his hand and he continued, but he stopped at two steps and turned to me:

'Claudia is on the platform with some friends, drinking maté. Why don't you go?'

I went to the stand, but I was ashamed to disturb Claudia, who was chatting jovially with two people. I greeted her from afar, with a wave of my hand, and walked up the steps to the last row, where I thought I could see the training better. I took a seat, took my agenda out of my backpack, and began to write some notes. So focused was I on what I was scribbling that I only noticed Claudia's close presence when she was a couple of metres away.

'*Profe*, what are you writing down?'

Again I was amazed at the familiarity and affection with which I was treated.

'I'm following that little guy.' I pointed to Diego. 'I think he's going to be fine!'

She laughed and invited me to share the maté with her and her friends.

'I brought a *pastafrola* [quince pie],' she remarked happily.

Pastafrola, my favourite pie! And I was hungry. I could not resist. Until then, my rigourous Andorran diet had consisted of a cappuccino with a croissant for breakfast, two packs of ten chocolate cookies each – one at lunch, one at snack time – and a chicken leg with lettuce salad for dinner. All these delicacies were well accompanied by a very tasty … tap water.

A few days later, after several sessions in which I had learned more than in a year's career, walking through Andorra La Vella, I read a poster in a music house a poster announcing a recital by the Argentine singer Mercedes Sosa in the Plaza del Rey in Barcelona, on Saturday, 20 August. The next day, shortly before a new training session began at the Communal Stadium, I mentioned it to Cesar because I knew he was a great admirer of *La Negra* from Tucuman (a province in the north of Argentina). His eyes widened and, immediately, he asked Poncini until what day they were staying in Andorra. The assistant explained that on the 17th they had a friendly in Alicante against Hercules and then they returned to the Pyrenees until the 21st, because on the 22nd they had to face Nottingham Forest – a very prestigious English team at that time, because they had won the European Cup (now the Champions League) twice in a row, in 1979 and 1980 – in the traditional Joan Gamper tournament, which is held every summer at the Camp Nou. Cesar considered Poncini's words and, after a few seconds, decided to bring forward the end of the preseason.

'Let's change. From Alicante we will travel directly to Barcelona.'

'And the players who stay here, Cesar?'

'They leave for Barcelona on the day of the match.'

'But … what are you going to say to the leaders? And to the press?'

'Something is going to occur to me.'

On 15 August, two days before the meeting in Alicante, Menotti held a press conference at the Hotel President, where the team was staying, in which he announced that the preseason in Andorra would be reduced by a few days.

'Why has the stage been shortened?' consulted one of the journalists who covered the preseason.

'Because we have to train at the Camp Nou before the Gamper Cup,' Menotti answered, with sincerity. A leopard can't change its spots …

Back in Barcelona, I continued working on the assembly of stands at the Barcelona Fairgrounds. My wife had started to teach at the Club Tennis de la Salut, but the economic resources were not enough. For a couple of weeks, I accepted a night-guard post at some kiosks that the *Patronato de Leprosos* (council board to fight against leprosy) had set up on boulevard Passeig de Gràcia, one of the main avenues of the city, in front of Plaça de Catalunya. A Spanish friend had offered me that job which, although it forced me to stay there from ten at night to ten in the morning, was very well compensated: they paid me 10,000 *pesetas* a night, money that today would represent about €250. For me, hungry and undocumented, it represented a fortune! At that time, a common worker earned about 60,000 *pesetas* a month. Of course, not everything was rosy: the Catalan winter is usually very harsh, much more during the early mornings. It was so cold that I grew a beard to protect my face from the icy wind.

At the same time, I kept seeing Diego a couple of times a week because Carmen started giving tennis lessons to Claudia, on the court of the village where they lived in the Pedralbes neighbourhood. Diego and I used to play with them, too. He ran with amazing agility, and he hit the ball very well. He had ability for tennis ... well, almost all sports.

One afternoon, while we were drinking water and sodas to recover from a game, Diego asked me:

'On Sunday at noon, wait for me with Carmen on the sidewalk of the Camp Nou. I'm going to pick you up so we can have a barbecue and chat.'

I told my wife about the invitation while we were riding public transport back home. I remembered that talk in which Diego had told me about his interest in opening a football school and, frankly, I was tired of spending all night awake on Passeig de Gràcia, cold and armed with a wooden stick to protect the donations destined for the hapless lepers from eventual robberies.

I waited for the day of the barbecue, licking my lips, and not precisely because of the delicious taste of the meats that were masterfully roasted by Don Diego, *Pelusa*'s dad. Honestly, I was dying to know what fate would have for us. On Sunday we arrived at the stadium early. We waited a long time until the red Volkswagen Golf reappeared like an exhalation with its now usual roar of greeting. But, to my surprise, instead of being driven by Diego, the steering wheel was in the charge of a friend of the *Ten*, Néstor Varrone. We get into the car and in less than a sigh we reached the Pedralbes mansion, located 1km and a few metres from the stadium. We got out of the Golf and I noticed with some disappointment that the garden was full of family and friends of the hosts, including Jorge Cyterszpiler. I must confess I had imagined a more intimate meal. Don Diego was in charge of the grill, a situation that predicted a succulent lunch. Better than nothing ...

During lunch, my wife commented that a tournament for youth players was being organised at the Club Tennis de la Salut, and she consulted Raul *Lalo* Maradona, who was 16 years old and handled the racket quite well, if he was interested in participating. *Doña Tota* and Don Diego encouraged their second male child, and he accepted. He did not take long to regret it: the draw determined that he had to face the number one in Spain in his category, Fernando García Lleo. On the day of the match, *Lalo* arrived dressed from head to toe in premier Puma clothing, accompanied by a troupe of Argentines, including a boy with a video camera. He looked like the number one and García Lleo a modest ball boy. The match ended 6-0 6-0. I think it lasted less time than it took me to write this sentence. Despite the overwhelming defeat, *Lalo* had a nice second match. The coach of the Belgian team was an Argentine guy. He approached me to ask if Raul had signed up for the doubles championship.

'No, he has no one to play with.'

'I have a kid who wants to participate and was free because we are odd [numbers]. Will he want to accompany him?'

I consulted *Lalo* and he accepted. The next day, Raul and his team-mate won – the Belgian was a remarkable player – and the Argentine group, which had once again taken over the club, celebrated as if the couple had become champions in the Wimbledon tournament. Claudia, who always stood out for her public relations skills and for being an excellent host, announced that Diego was inviting all the members of the Belgian team to a barbecue at the Pedralbes home. The kids couldn't believe it. They were happier to meet Diego than to have won their games!

The very fun meal included some tennis matches in which *Lalo* and Diego fared quite well against the talented Belgian boys. At dessert time, while Claudia was handing out chocolates, Diego asked who wanted to go to the football stadium. Everyone raised their hands except me. I did not want to abuse the generosity of the Maradona-Villafañes. Diego pulled a bundle of tickets out of his pocket for the game that, the next day, would pit FC Barcelona against Athletic Club de Bilbao, the defending league champions, at the Camp Nou. A duel that had begun to be flavoured with fervent rivalry, and would end with the sounds of war. A historic meeting, which marked a before and after in Diego's career. And in my life.

Chapter 3

Close to the revolution

'Cerca de la revolución' – Argentine rock song

I ONCE read in a book, I don't remember which one, that in the Mandarin language the word 'crisis' is made up of two characters that could be written as *Wei* and *Ji* with our Latin letters. *Wei*, it seems, means 'danger' or 'risk'. *Ji*, on the other hand, symbolises a diametrically opposite concept: 'opportunity'. Undoubtedly, the Chinese have an optimistic outlook on life, based on a millenary culture that has gone through hundreds of difficulties, stumbles and falls, but still stands. On Saturday, 24 September 1983, Diego was swept away by a critical tsunami. But instead of surrendering to pessimistic predictions and drifting to the bottom of the sea, he fought hard against the dark torrent until he overcame the whirlpool, beat the waves, and reached the beach of success.

While Argentines and Belgians, and of course thousands of Catalans, enjoyed the passes of Diego and the goals of Miguel Ángel *Periko* Alonso – the father of Xabi Alonso, a world champion with Spain – and Julio Alberto Moreno, I listened to the game on the radio and I wrote a letter (there were no emails or WhatsApp) to a friend from Argentina. Suddenly, the commentator announced that Diego was being removed on a stretcher after a violent kick by one of the Basque defenders, Andoni Goikoetxea. At that time, the journalists in charge of the broadcast were unaware of the severity of the injury, although internally I sensed that something serious was happening. Nobody took that kid off the pitch just like that, much less on a stretcher. After the match, a reporter notified that Diego had been transferred by ambulance to the Asepeyo clinic. Right away, Carles Bestit, the head of the *culé* club's medical services, described that Diego had suffered 'a fracture of the peroneal malleolus of the left ankle, with deviation and tearing of the internal lateral ligament', and assured that it was essential to operate on him immediately. The responsibility of the surgery fell on Rafael González Adrio, a highly prestigious traumatologist who had the support of Cesar Menotti and the former doctor of the Argentine team in the 1978 and 1982 World Cups, Rubén Oliva, whom Diego blindly trusted. Oliva, who was based in Milan, spoke by phone with González Adrio and they both agreed that an urgent operation was necessary because, if not, the bone adhesions that were going to occur could be very serious. Meanwhile, Diego was torn between the pain caused by the break and the uncertain future. Before the anaesthesia sedated him, he implored González Adrio to do everything possible to ensure his return to the pitch. The doctor guaranteed that he would play again in a few months … although, internally, he too had been dominated by uncertainty.

While Diego spent two hours on the operating table and Claudia, on the verge of collapsing, prayed to all the saints for a happy ending, the media became the scene of a pathetic duel. Meanwhile, Cesar Menotti ranted against the ineptitude of the referee Bartolomé Jiménez Madrid, who had not only acted apathetically to the rough play of the Bilbao players but had barely admonished Goikoetxea after his bestial kick. 'For things to change, someone must die,' roared the Argentine coach. His Basque colleague, Javier Clemente, did not honour his surname (note: 'clement'). 'I am proud of my players,' he declared, laconic and defiant, from the visiting dressing room. No one was left in doubt that he was referring exclusively to the vehemence of the 'good guy' Andoni, since his team had just been humiliated with an overwhelming four to zero. The admonished Goikoetxea downplayed his ruthless attack, which he described as 'one more action of the match' for which, in his opinion, he deserved 'no sanction'. The Competition Committee did not think the same: it suspended him for 18 games. After appeal, the sentence was reduced to just seven. Goikoetxea, nicknamed 'The Butcher of Bilbao', kept the boot with which he struck Diego in a glass box and made it the main attraction of a macabre altar erected in the living room of his house. Years later, Diego would reflect that Andoni had attacked him 'in our field, 60 metres from their goal, but the Basque Country declared me *persona non grata*'.

The morning after the fateful game, Carmen and I went to the Asepeyo clinic to greet Diego. We met Jorge Cyterszpiler and some relatives and friends of the *Ten*. The doctors allowed us to see him for a minute and we found him smiling, his hair covered by a white cap and his left leg wrapped in a cast. He told us that the operation had gone very well and that the doctors had placed two nails that would help to weld the broken bones, and that a few weeks later they would be removed with another operation. We gave him words of encouragement and, as we left his room, we also comforted Claudia. Two days later, *Pelusa* was able to return to his house.

During several afternoons, I returned to Pedralbes to visit Diego, interested in knowing how he recovered. One of those days, I found Diego a little dejected. He explained to me that he had heard and read comments that he would not play again, or that he would no longer be the same, and that he was afraid that the injury would keep him from the stadiums forever. 'I don't want to leave football without having been captain of Argentina,' he confessed to me tearfully. I tried to console him, to inject confidence into him. I commented that Oliva was very optimistic, and that there was no real reason to worry. Diego, however, continued to curse his bad fortune. He told me that, a year before, he had met Carlos Bilardo, while he was recovering from the fierce hepatitis that had taken him away from the fields for almost three months. In that meeting, which occurred in a spot on the Costa Brava that the *Ten* had chosen to start training for their return to the Camp Nou, Bilardo had moved him: he had announced that he would be the captain of the national team. However, before he could put on the light-blue-and-white jersey and adjust the precious ribbon, Goikoetxea had destroyed his ankle and his dream.

'All those good things are going to come, you'll see,' I told him. Diego nodded, but I felt that he did it without conviction. I, on the other hand, had no doubts: providence would still illuminate his path.

One afternoon, Claudia greeted me and led me to a room where Diego was being checked by Oliva, who travelled a couple of times a week from Italy to monitor his bad ankle. Against the advice of the Barcelona doctors, Oliva had just removed the cast, fearful that the immobility of the joint would complicate the welding of the bones and the ankle would become rigid. This decision generated a controversy with the club's doctors, González Adrio and Bestit, who had warned that this was 'an inexcusable risk that could end the player's sporting career'. Time, we already know, would agree with the brilliant Argentine traumatologist.

At one point, Oliva, while moving Diego's left foot with his hands, commented aloud and without taking his eyes off the limb:

'Tonight, I'm going to Milan. I'll be back next week. Professor, listen to me: from tomorrow you make him walk, little by little. To climb a step carefully, to lower it, to do some crunches.'

I was stunned! The famous doctor was placing on me the responsibility of collaborating in the rehabilitation of the most important ankle in world football. Although I had ten years of experience in a rustic sport, which required comprehensive training – due to restricted budgets, the technical staffs were very limited and the physical trainer should be able to work also as a kinesiologist, a little as a psychologist, sometimes like a masseur – it was a gigantic challenge. It is often said that footballers are the same everywhere, but in Lincoln I have never seen one with a capacity even similar to Diego's. I couldn't miss the boat that would take me to the unique opportunity to work alongside the best player on the planet. Although I did it from friend to friend, ad honorem.

We began the recovery with simple exercises aimed at strengthening the affected area very slowly and with great care, since Diego was still moving with the help of crutches. I added some work so that he also started the rest of the body. Little by little, he began to show a rapid recuperation. So fast that, for his 23rd birthday, celebrated on 30 October, *Pelusa* gave himself the best of gifts: starting to walk without having to lean on crutches. Oliva himself, who made his umpteenth journey from Milan that day, was pleasantly surprised, very satisfied with the progress of his famous and beloved patient. González Adrio, once again, screamed blue murder: 'Certainly, Maradona moves his ankle well, but I think it is hasty to put his foot on the ground.'

Little by little, Diego went from walking to jogging, and from jogging to running. The garden of the house was small, so I proposed to him to continue the rehabilitation in a wide and flat space that I found on the Pedralbes hill, near the Carretera de las Aguas, where we could work without fear that he would put a foot in a divot. Anyway, he always trained protected by a bandage that covered the area that had been damaged. The first time we were alone in this fascinating place, which offers a privileged view of the whole of Barcelona, I asked him:

'Diego, to help you I need to know you.'

'Of course, *Profe*. That sounds fine to me'

'I need to know what type of workouts you feel best with, which ones do you consider to give you the best results.'

'I prefer intense but short jobs. I arrived at the World Cup with wet gunpowder because I had to do the same exercises as all the other players, which were very long and with a lot of effort.'

I understood immediately that his power management system did not work like those of the other footballers. Teaching and training are unique processes, which must be adjusted with their exercises to optimise the potential that a player has, which is individual and unrepeatable. This is what we have to care about: the optimisation of the athlete. Empower the player, develop his capacity so that he can better understand the game and thus be more effective.

The conversations with Diego were essential to achieve optimal preparation for each challenge that arose throughout his career. Listening is one of the best weapons available to human beings interested in helping their fellow men. It is the subject himself who must improve himself because only he knows in each action what he must do and the reasons for what happens. In that analysis appears the optimisation of his personal resources. That is the function of physical trainers in team sports: to seek self-structuring in our players. Get each one to be what he is capable of doing and what he is capable of being. More talent, better conditions. But we must focus on optimising each player and not building a footballer for the team model. It is not about adapting ourselves to the game but about creating situations that improve the player's ability. That is the commitment. And for that commitment, instead of focusing on the issues that have made sport change, we innovate them. How? Installing technical and tactical skills, in which this player has some competence. See what he is competent at. Help him to establish those tactical and technical skills at the highest level. You should not say, 'I have to adapt him to the competition.' No. You have to consider what impact the competition has on him.

There are players who train horribly and play prodigiously (or vice versa). What must be achieved is that all our footballers compete to the maximum of their possibilities, because that is the way to build their own differentiated optimisation. We must observe the impact of the competition environment. We have to make an effort so that the player knows issues related to the game, training and about himself, what he should do and what not to do. That he be able to evaluate himself, to work in cooperation, in mutual aid with his companions. What is the game, how does he conceive it. And not the other way around, as is usually understood for traditional pedagogy.

I am in favour of those teaching techniques that consider the student 'a flame to be lit, rather than a vessel to be filled'. By work and misfortune of some perverse psychic mechanism, many educators tend to develop behaviours impregnated with vanity and pride that prevent them from accepting truths that exceed their own, even more so if they come from their own students. Educating means 'leading out' and one of the greatest achievements of a teacher lies in encouraging his disciples not only to contradict him, based on reason and respect, but also to surpass him in knowledge. It is, no doubt, an unmistakable feature of higher spirits. The opposite of educating is to induce, that is 'to guide inwards', a way of teaching that is clearly coercive, since it limits the student to move within the cosmogony of his teacher, without being able to go beyond his orbit. However, I value as a treasure that saying that states 'there's a reason nature gave us two ears and one mouth'. One of the first lessons I received in this regard occurred shortly after starting my career as a physical trainer, at the Rivadavia club in Lincoln. I was in my second year when my friend Livio Biasussi, the team's central defender, invited me to take care of conditioning the players. On the campus there were about 30 footballers, all amateurs, who attended practice after complying with the hours of their very varied jobs. The training sessions were held on Tuesdays, Thursdays and Fridays, starting at 7.30pm, on the auxiliary court, under the guidance of the coach. Although my knowledge was meagre, the support of the boys and my growing enthusiasm created the foundations of an excellent relationship. The start of my first championship with them was approaching and almost everyone enjoyed an acceptable level of performance. 'Almost everyone' implies that there was one outside of that value. My concern was growing. I couldn't explain to myself how the most physically exuberant player in the group acted like a real wreck in every practice session. It took a few days until, finally, I decided to talk to him:

'How is it possible that you, with this muscular body, are always tired?'

'Do you know what happens, *Profe*? Work kills me. I always come to train very fatigued'

'Where do you work?'

'I am an employee of the municipal management of public works, I am in charge of the bulldozer.'

'Very good. How is that work?'

'I start at five in the morning and go out with the crew to where the foreman sends us. We fix roads, clean gutters, move dirt, build bridges and sewers.'

'What time do you finish?'

'At seven in the afternoon we arrived back, just in time to grab my sport bag and come to train.'

As I listened to his story, I was overcome by an annoying sensation, a mixture of helplessness and shame. There I discovered that it had taken me more than a month to do something that I should have solved the first day: listen to him!

'Let's do one thing: from tomorrow, as soon as you arrive, grab a ball, have fun for about 20 minutes, go back to the locker room, get massaged and go home. Agree?'

The season began and his level grew game by game. After a month, I was able to verify that the only player who did not train in my team … was the one who was better prepare physicallyd!'

Football is a team sport but the group is made up of individualities, each with their own physical, mental or emotional characteristics. I began to devise a work scheme that seemed to me the most appropriate for an athlete with Diego's characteristics, aware that the exaggerated attention to athletic preparation is one of the factors that has contributed the most to impoverishing the show and mortifying the technique – with great care, so that more muscles, more speed, more power and more workloads did not turn into less dribbling, less instinct, less fantasy. By lifting so much weight, the footballer can be crushed.

Diego received physical therapy at the club's facilities with great care, because when he underwent surgery to remove the prostheses used to fix the torn fibula, the doctors used pliers and, I don't know if by accident or lack of skill, they broke the nails and two pieces remained inside the bone. For this reason, Diego preferred massages from a masseur he had brought to Barcelona from Argentina: Miguel di Lorenzo, whom we all called *Galíndez* for his extraordinary physiognomic resemblance to the Argentine middleweight boxer Víctor Galíndez, who was world champion. They had met at Argentinos Juniors, where they became friends. When Diego was transferred to Spain, he asked *Galíndez* to accompany him, and he accepted, although his new job, on the other side of the Atlantic, meant a great family sacrifice because he was married and had two young children. Once installed in Barcelona, the masseur began to study physiotherapy at the express request of his new boss. Diego was always addicted to massages. He loved massages with creams and oils, relaxing and falling asleep. Every day *Galíndez* rubbed him for an hour, and each time *Pelusa* woke up fresh as a grape just plucked from his bunch.

I took care of the dynamic recovery. When he trained with me in the Pedralbes hills, I proposed to him very creative exercises, in order to motivate him, to ignite that spark that would later explode on the courts: dashes, dribbling, falling, getting up, jumping, somersaults. I designed work with a lot of reaction speed, including all the movements that a footballer of his characteristics, with a certain radius of action on the field, performs during the game: short accelerations forward and backward, to the sides, jumps, falls, roll forward or roll back, very quickly. They were explosive exercises of no more than ten seconds, with ten seconds of recovery. I was adjusting the intensity and the duration of the practice so that his body did not produce large amounts of lactate that could cause muscle injury.

Sometimes we used the ball, although the terrain was not the best: on that hill we had a flat space but not big enough. But, generally, I suggested activities without the ball although specific to football. No continuous or paced runs. That didn't work with Diego. He was a firecracker, he exploded at maximum speed, responding to different incentives that encouraged his power. He had to imitate the movements of a mouse, not a greyhound facing a 1,000-metre race. Likewise, when he trained in the gym, we worked each muscle group with sets of 15 reps. While he recovered, he did compensatory crunches and dorsal workout, stretching, and so on.

Little by little we forged a relationship of great affection and closeness, even tenderness. The talks, increasingly extensive and intense, helped me understand who this kid was, born in Villa Fiorito who, as he himself once said, had been kicked in the ass and had been sent to the top of success without guidance on how to function in his new habitat. While he pursued his main objective, to fight to improve the quality of life of his family, he allowed himself access to some luxuries unthinkable in his time in the poor town of Lomas de Zamora, and not a few whims. However, deep inside, he was still a humble and simple kid. He once told me that he had been invited to have lunch with King Juan Carlos de Borbón and Queen Sofía at the Palacio de la Zarzuela, in Madrid. Diego accepted. Upon reaching the dining room, the hosts offered him a seat in the central sector of a long rectangular table at whose head, in accordance with royal protocol, Juan Carlos and his wife were accommodated. Diego was overwhelmed by the pomp and pageantry of the room, richly decorated with paintings and sculptures by famous artists, tapestries woven with gold threads, and gigantic chandeliers with thousands of fine crystal beads. Even the attire of the chamberlains assigned to the service exuded opulence. When he came to his senses after so much dazzling brilliance, Diego noticed that he had in front of him a finely decorated plate and a battery of cutlery on each side, in addition to glasses of various formats. The meal began and Diego, being the guest of honour, received his plate before his hosts. He told me that, at that moment, he felt very uncomfortable because he did not know what piece of cutlery to take and was afraid that the king would be offended by his actions. No one had ever taught him how to act in such a formal context. He decided to wait for the waiters to serve the rest of the diners and imitate their movements. Queen Sofía, hardened in those kinds of situations that dozens of commoner guests had previously gone through, perceived Diego's indecision and, very astutely, made a slight noise to get his attention. When he looked at her, she took the first fork, the furthest from the plate, and took a bite with it. Diego, more relaxed, did the same. Then she wiped her mouth with her napkin and took a glass of wine, from which she took a light sip. Diego repeated the movements perfectly.

'You don't know how I suffered, *Fer*,' he confessed to me when the meal was a distant and uncomfortable memory. 'I ended up full of muscle cramps. I would have preferred to eat a chorizo sandwich!'

With the passing of the days and the talks, I recognised that within Diego there was a hyper-competitive spirit that sometimes emerged naturally, and other times it hid behind feelings such as anguish, fear or hesitation. Once, Cesar Menotti – a man with a gigantic experience from having shared episodes with exceptional athletes such as Pelé, Johan Cruyff, Mario Kempes, Franz Beckenbauer and Romario, to name just a small group – confided in me that among the many attributes that he considers essential for a footballer to deserve the nickname of *ace*, there are two that are non-negotiable: deep conceptual knowledge of the game and determination to try to improve each day. Diego, he explained to me, extremely combined these two properties, and he used an anecdote to clarify his thinking:

When Menotti arrived at FC Barcelona, Diego was already the most precious jewel of the Catalan treasure. The team also had an exceptional midfielder, Bernd Schuster, a notable German strategist with a sparkling game and an overwhelming personality. In them rested the dreams of the fans who, with justified optimism, in each game filled the seductive Camp Nou to capacity. One morning during a training session at the stadium, Menotti repeatedly congratulated Schuster on a series of plays resolved with one touch and with devastating force. After the activity, the coach went to his office to analyse the salient points of the practice together with his assistant, Rogelio Poncini. That's what they were doing when Diego peeked of out the door:

'Sorry, Cesar, can I come in?'

'Of course, boy. Something wrong?'

'No. I just wanted to tell you one thing.'

'Well, sit down.'

Diego sat down without reticence, and with calm firmness said:

'You know, Cesar, I'm sure that, sooner or later, what Bernardo does, I'm going to do.'

Menotti nodded and the *Ten*, while getting up from his chair to leave the office, finished:

'But what I do, he will never be able to do.'

'There I finished convincing myself,' Cesar concluded, 'that Diego was going to be a phenomenon, because his talent as a player was supported by that race that distinguishes real *aces*. He was determined to be the best and, to achieve it, he was willing to do anything. He knew all the players, he watched every game that was shown on television, he stayed after training sessions with the goalkeepers practising shots at goal, he loved talking about football, imagining plays … His love for the game was impressive. And, that day, he was jealous as a boy for the compliments I had given to Schuster. It was wonderful.'

When I began to recognise Diego's character, I considered that in order to extract his full potential in the face of relevant challenges, I first had to test how he would react to his own ego. I decided to experience what would happen one afternoon, after training, while we watched a match between France and Spain on television with some of his friends from Argentina. In the middle of the game, I noticed that the other boys always had negative concepts for the players. That Michel Platini was weak, that the Cantabrian Santillana (Carlos Alonso González) was a ghost, that the German Karl-Heinz Rummenigge – who was not performing that day but was also 'invited' to the discussion – could not even play card games. They were all lousy. Diego was silent. Faced with so much easy, empty and unfair criticism, I shot:

'Diego, do you consider yourself as the best of the good ones, or the least mediocre of donkeys?'

'Why?' he answered, confused.

'I hear here that everyone is horrible, and obviously it is easy to be the best of the bads, or at least it has no merit. On the other hand, I consider that Platini is an exceptional player, that Rummenigge is magnificent ... and that you are the best of all.'

Diego repositioned himself in his place, proud of my proposal.

'Did you listen, dumbs?' he yelled at his other guests, emboldened. I smiled. I had tested my hypothesis and loaded a revolver with some silver bullets ready to be used at the right time.

After a trip to Buenos Aires, where he continued with exercises and massage sessions at his villa in the town of Moreno and the family home of Villa Devoto, in the Argentine capital city, Diego returned to Barcelona hungry for the field. To satisfy his desire to put on Barça's No.10 again, we intensified our work on the Pedralbes hill, with the collaboration of his relatives. I used to make a circle of about ten metres in diameter with *Doña Tota*, Claudia, *Galíndez* and other participants, and Diego would place himself in the middle and had to start from the centre, at maximum acceleration, towards the name that I indicated, and return to the starting point also at full speed. There he jumped as if to head the ball and, when he was about to fall, I called him another name, and another, until he completed eight or nine seconds, which were followed by the same recovery period. We repeated this series many times, until Diego fell exhausted, generally after an hour and a quarter of vigorous work. I remember that the day I discharged him – because Diego did not have the official discharge from the doctors, but mine – we finished the job with great emotion. I specially reserved *Doña Tota* for the final dash.

'Last, *Doña Tota!*' I yelled.

Diego fell from the jump, ran to his mother and gave her a monumental hug.

'*Doña Tota*,' I announced with feigned solemnity, 'the boy is discharged to start playing.'

They all hugged each other and cried with joy. Diego swore to being his mother's favourite. He said that that special bond had been forged by being her fifth child and her first son, behind four women.

Diego returned to play for FC Barcelona on 8 January 1984, just 106 days after Goikoetxea's destructive blast. That day, the *culé* squad beat Sevilla 3-1, with two goals from their recovered star, plus an assist to Marcos Alonso Peña. A week later, he scored another double against Osasuna, at El Sadar.

Throughout that period, Diego continued to train his physique with me, two or three times a week. He loved what we did, he was happy. Me too, although I felt very exhausted because I still divided my time between preparing *Pelusa* and my work at the Barcelona Fairgrounds. With his team-mates and Menotti, Diego participated in football practices. As it is a team game, it is absolutely reasonable and understandable that there is a central core of the training of an unchangeable nature. There are many actions that can (and should) be exercised to perfect the technique and conceptual mastery of the game.

One night, around 11pm, the telephone of the apartment I shared with Carmen rang. We had moved into a small apartment on Calle Londres, near Plaça de Francesc Macià. I answered and it was Claudia, who said Diego wanted to speak with me ... personally. At that time the buses were not circulating, and I did not have money to pay for a taxi to Pedralbes. I suggested that if what he had to tell me was not urgent, we could talk about it the next afternoon, when we'd go to train. She consulted Diego and told me that there were no problems. The next day, when I arrived at the residence, I found the entrance gate open and *Galíndez* loading the items we used to work in the trunk of *Pelusa*'s Mercedes-Benz. Diego immediately appeared.

'Did you put everything, *Mono*?'

'Yes, Diego,' *Galíndez* answered.

'Well ... stay, I have to talk to the *Profe*.'

I was wondering what was going on. We got into the vehicle, *Pelu* at the wheel and me in the other front seat. We reached the hill where we did the exercises, we worked for about an hour and a quarter and returned to the car for the journey back home. Diego had not said a single word, except for the usual exclamations of an athlete when he reaches a point of pain or maximum demand during an exercise. I was really nervous. 'Is he angry with me for not going to his house last night?' I questioned myself. We started our return while chatting trivia about the team and its upcoming matches. Suddenly, in a corner, Diego stopped in front of a speed bump. Without looking at me, concentrating on whether a vehicle was approaching down the cross street, he finally got to the point:

'*Fer*, I want you to work with me as my personal fitness trainer.'

It took me three seconds to react. In fact, I was doing it … although in an informal way, without charging a single peseta. His proposal was to agree on a professional relationship with full-time dedication.

'Do you think it's OK, Diego? They are going to say that it is another one of your eccentricities,' I commented, finally.

'I don't care what the sons of bitches who always talk about me could say. I always thought about it, and I think now is the time, because until I fully overcome this injury I will need closer care.'

I was dying to say yes. I was without a formal job and the best player in the world was offering me to be his personal trainer. However, he was also thinking about him and whether that decision would have a negative impact when it was leaked to the Barcelona leaders and the press. Today, this proposal would be taken as a normal thing. The great players have a vast team of collaborators: physical trainers, nutritionists, masseurs, traumatologists, psychologists. But at that time, in 1984, no footballer had that kind of assistance.

'Look, we are going to do one thing: we are going to think for a few days on this. This is unprecedented, it does not exist!'

Diego nodded. I think he didn't like my indecision very much. We got to the house, we said goodbye and I had to make a superhuman effort throughout my trip to the apartment not to get off the bus, run to Pedralbes and tell Diego that everything was a joke and I accepted immediately. I matured the answer a little more, together with my wife.

A couple of days later, a very hot Sunday, I returned to the residence, although it was Diego's turn to rest for a game. I was attended by an Andalusian lady who did the housework.

'The boy is in the living room watching television,' she commented to me after opening the door. I passed by and found Diego alone, in a long armchair, sitting in a position that reminded me of the traditional image of the Buddha, with the remote control in one hand, frantically changing channels.

'What are you doing, *Die*, how are you going?'

'Everything fine, *Profe*. And you?'

'Look, I was thinking about the proposal you made me the other day.'

He turned off the television, which was very rare for him. I noticed him very, very interested, anxious as a boy on Christmas Eve.

'What did you think?' he said hurriedly, nervous.

'I say yes, let's start.'

His little face lit up. The wrapping paper had hidden the gift he wanted.

'Awesome! Please go to Jorge's office tomorrow.'

'For what?'

'To sign the contract.'

'No, no. What contract? I am not going to sign any contract with you. You told me that a lot of friends asked you for a hand and ended up suing you. This has to be a relationship of great trust, of great honesty, great loyalty. Contract, nothing. Gimme your hand and if one day you don't feel comfortable, you tell me and I leave without claiming anything, and I play with the cards from the same deck: if one day I don't feel comfortable, I'll leave and you can't claim either.'

Diego nodded and we shook hands. Thus was established the first private relationship of a professional footballer in the world with an exclusive physical trainer. I proposed to him to maintain the system that we had started, evaluating the efforts according to the bodily responses that he was giving me, always attentive to designing the exercises that best suited him and that made him feel better, while reinforcing the connection between us. He agreed. I also said to him that, having established the formal work relationship, I was interested in carrying out a battery of tests and controls on him to know exactly his physical capacity and to know the point that he could get to. He consented.

After analysing the evaluations that seemed most appropriate for him, and finding a place to carry them out, one afternoon I called Claudia:

'Tomorrow morning, early, I'm going to pick up Diego so that we can do some tests. Try to eat lightly, sleep well, and behave well tonight.'

The next day I arrived at Diego's house and we went to the Estadi Municipal Joan Serrahima, in Montjuic, the place where later the Olympic track was built for the 1992 Barcelona Games. The manager had opened the sport camp doors just for us. We got out of the car and headed to the athletic track, *Pelusa*, obedient and quiet. I explained to him that the first thing I wanted to do was a test consisting of running as far as possible in 12 minutes. I was going to count the remaining minutes for him to adjust his speed, because if he started too fast he would get tired, and if he started too slow he wouldn't get to meet the parameters that I estimate according to his physical condition. We warmed up well. I fitted him with a heart-rate monitor, something that did not exist in football at that time but was used in high-level athletic competitions and that I had bought especially. When Diego was ready, I set the timer and gave him the start signal. He began running at a medium, comfortable speed. I wrote an observation of his records in a notebook while I checked the time and shouted the remaining minutes – until I discovered that the guy always followed the same rhythm, without accelerating. I was worried: had he understood the methodology of the exercise? The ninth minute was up, and he continued without speeding up or slowing down the race; then eight, seven … Nothing! Diego was still trotting. God! Three, two, one – all the same, without even a final sprint. The time was up and I asked him to stop. I started to approach him, as he had finished next to our things and grabbed a bottle of energy drink. It was very hot. With one hand on his waist and the other on the container of liquid, he drank and shook his head, like a pendulum, from one side to the other, with gestures that were closer to annoyance than fatigue.

'Diego, is something wrong?'

He wasn't looking at me. He had fixed his eyes on a distant point.

'This is good for nothing!' he said.

I was perplexed. 'I've lost my job on the first day,' I thought. Hoping to overcome the situation, I opted to throw the entire athletic training theory at him.

'What do you mean, good for nothing? This was developed by Dr Kenneth Cooper of the University of …'

'It's useless!' he cut me off.

'But …'

'But nothing. How much was I supposed to do?'

'Well,' I said, 'a world-elite footballer who plays in your position, about 3,600 metres.'

'How far did I go?'

I looked at my notes.

'I measured 2,550 metres.'

He still didn't look at me.

'And you, how much do you do?'

I was 32 years old, I was quite trained.

'I don't know precisely, but at least 3,200 metres.'

He drank from his bottle, turned his head and looked me in the eyes, for the first time since the test ended.

'So on Sunday, you play!'

It was an unforgettable lesson. I definitely understood that Diego was an exceptional athlete, that theories and tests designed for other sportsmen did not work with him. My mission was to focus on diagramming a unique training session for a unique footballer. I kept the books that dealt with ostentatious theory and focused on designing works similar to those we had developed during his recovery, more adjusted to the different situations that Diego would face in games. The practices that Cesar Menotti led reached a high intensity, but they were basically conceptual. Footballers played a lot with one or two touches. Menotti had been enthralled with a reasoning of the writer Jorge Luis Borges: to write literature you need order and adventure. If you are orderly and have no adventure, you will not find success. And vice versa. Cesar applied it to football, to his football: the order was the team and Diego was the adventure, the one who could take the ball and do whatever he wanted. Obsessively making *Pelusa* participate in the 'hard' tactics and strategy meant conditioning his creativity, his magic. To complement our work with the sessions on the pitch, I concentrated the exercises on improving the speed of reaction, the height of the jumps, the power of his starts. Little by little, the work began to pay off.

One afternoon, Diego scored a double at Athletic Club, in San Mamés, for a 2-1 victory that he enjoyed as if he had won the Champions League. After his return, Barcelona won 12 games, drew three, lost two and were in third place in the table, just one point behind the champions, Athletic Club. They also reached the final of the Copa del Rey, which they lost against the Bilbao Lions, the absolute owners of that season, at the Santiago Bernabéu stadium. That clash remained in the black history of Spanish football for the savage fight that engulfed all the players after the final whistle. The winners mocked the Catalans and they responded with insults. The conflict remained on the verbal plane until one of the Basques had the magnificent idea of reminding Diego of Goikoetxea's 'caress'. The *Ten culé*, which that same day had received another dozen kicks, exploded: he became the Tasmanian Devil, distributing punches, knees and kicks everywhere. He also received several terrible blows and left the pitch with his soul appeased and his *Blaugrana* shirt destroyed.

Diego finished the season without official titles, but he won another league: that of overcoming the most important obstacle of his sports career. Faced with the ominous predictions that conjectured an early end, he fought tirelessly to return to the pitch in record time and in great shape.

Allow me to abuse Serrat's generosity and quote here another of his truths: blessed are those who are at the bottom of the well because, from that point forward, it is only possible to get better. Diego came out of the well in Barcelona and began his way to heaven from a new destination: Naples.

Chapter 4

Ho visto Maradona

(Translation: I've seen Maradona – a popular
stadium song in Naples)

IT STARTED out as a 'blind date', but it turned out to be love at first sight. At the end of the 1983/84 season, Diego wanted to leave Barcelona, tired of his constant discussions with the *Blaugrana* president, Josep Lluís Núñez. In addition, he had to see out a three-month ban for the battle at the Santiago Bernabéu in Madrid, and assimilate the arrival of a new coach to replace the resigning Cesar Menotti. With so many problems to process, his eyes turned to another peninsula. The clubs that could afford his transfer were in Italy's Serie A, the league which, at that time, was considered the most powerful and prestigious in the world, since in 1980 the possibility of hiring foreign footballers was rehabilitated. After Diego turned down a new *culé* contract with a blank space for his money but iron chains for his feet, Jorge Cyterszpiler designed the escape in secret. He made dozens of calls to managers and agents from all over Italy, although without much success. The news about Diego coming from Catalonia through the press – some invented, others exaggerated – had not pleased the owners of teams such as Juventus, Internazionale and AC Milan. The only institution that listened with lukewarm attention to Jorge's proposal was the Società Sportiva Calcio Napoli through its president, Corrado Ferlaino. The Neapolitan businessman, an engineer born in Naples although with Calabrian and Milanese blood, wanted to hire a star who would take his team off to reach conquests never achieved, although he feared that the rumours of whims and debaucheries were true ... or something worse. His indeterminacy left the door barely open, but Cyterszpiler swiftly stepped in. The shrewd manager invited a Neapolitan journalist to travel to interview Diego. He, in addition to declaring his interest in playing for the southern Italian team, posed for a photograph with a light-blue jersey. The image raised more dust than Vesuvius. Then, Cyterszpiler went to Naples for a key interview, but not with Ferlaino or any other club leader, but with a *tifoso* (note: *tifoso* (*tifosi* pl.) is a word for fan/fanatic in Italian football) of enormous prestige among the light-blue fans: Gennaro Montuori, better known as *Palummella*, leader of the Commando Ultra Curva B. The scene seemed to be copied from the movie *The Godfather*: Cyterszpiler visited *Palummella* on the day of his son's baptism. In the middle of the party, the Argentine called the host aside and told him that Diego wanted to play in Napoli. 'We need your support,' he explained to Montuori. Finally, upon learning that Núñez had rejected a preseason friendly match with Napoli, supposedly because Diego was injured, Cyterszpiler threw the apple of discord at Ferlaino: 'Maradona is not hurt. Núñez said it as an excuse because his relationship with Diego is very bad. Actually, Diego wants to go to another club.' Interested but hesitant at the same time, Ferlaino sent his right-hand man, Antonio Iuliano, to Barcelona to meet first with the agent and then with the members of the Barcelona board of directors. The engineer, who was still wandering between indecisions, defined himself when Montuori led a singular protest in front of his offices, in the Piazza dei Martiri: eight guys chained themselves to the columns of an old building and assured that they would stay there until Ferlaino paid for Diego's transfer. Another small group repeated the complaint at the gates of the old complex where the team was concentrated until 2004, in the Soccavo neighbourhood, and a third, more audacious, threw themselves on to the railways to stop the progress of an arriving convoy from Milan. Stimulated by so much passion, Ferlaino travelled to Barcelona and reached an agreement with his Catalan colleague; Napoli acquired Diego's signing in exchange for $10.5m. Never has a team paid so much for a footballer.

Claudia called me one afternoon to give me the great news:

'*Profe*, we are all going to the airport because Diego is going to sign the contract with Napoli there.'

I went to El Prat and there were the leaders of Barcelona and Napoli, along with Diego. Once all the legal papers were signed, we all went to Pedralbes's house to celebrate the transfer ... even though I thought I had lost my job. The celebration seemed excessive to me: the champagne not only ran through the glasses, but from so much celebrating in the style of Formula One, the water in the pool turned pink. I left, a little uncomfortable with so much superfluous exuberance. I never liked sparkling finery.

Never before has the president of a club been on the verge of dying of a heart attack after signing the biggest agreement of his life. A while after the negotiation closed,

Corrado went to his hotel bar to relax with a whisky on the rocks. After sitting down at the bar and ordering his drink, the bartender, who had noticed his foreign accent, asked him where he was from. 'Naples,' Ferlaino replied. The bartender finished filling the glass with scotch while he wore a caustic smile. 'Today we sold Maradona to the Napoli club for a lot of money,' he commented jokingly. 'We tricked them. Diego is fat and he did not fully recover from a fracture. At most, he will play a year, no more,' he said sarcastically. Ferlaino felt a burning in his chest. He did not know if it was the product of the alcohol or the comment of the foul-mouthed bartender.

I returned to Pedralbes the day after the great celebration, around two or three in the afternoon, in the midst of an overwhelming heat. I knocked on the door and the clerk informed me that they were 'all sleeping'. I left and returned the next afternoon, at the same time. 'They are all sleeping,' the woman repeated. 'Are they in summer hibernation?' I thought. I assumed they would have gotten up late and, with their schedules out of date, would have stayed up late again. On the third day, Diego and Claudia were together, sitting on lounge chairs in front of the pool, drinking maté. They looked very happy. After the usual greetings, Diego allayed my fears of unemployment.

'*Profe*, get ready because we're going to Napoli, and from there to Buenos Aires'

'Perfect, we continue,' I celebrated. Luckily my wife joined the adventure.

The presentation at the new club was exciting, unforgettable. Diego travelled to Naples on Wednesday, 4 July 1984 with Jorge Cyterszpiler and Guillermo Blanco, the press officer of Maradona Producciones, the company created to manage the image of the *Ten* and its advertising contracts. The trio travelled from the Roman airport of Fiumicino to their new destination aboard a van driven by a club leader. The small group had lunch with Ferlaino and some of his relatives in Capri, toured the San Paolo stadio in solitude and stayed at the Hotel Excelsior. The rest of the delegation – me included – arrived the next day. I remember that, from the airport, we were driven to the hotel and from there, with no more time than to leave our luggage, we all left in an electric caravan of vehicles of all kinds towards the Fuorigrotta neighbourhood, which the locals call Forerotta. The arrival at the San Paolo left me open-mouthed, and not only because the vast structure of the football arena was covered with travertine: almost 70,000 people had flooded the stands to know their new idol. Crazy! Seventy thousand souls who attended a stadium on a weekday afternoon and in the midst of unbearable heat, who paid a symbolic entrance fee – according to the press, the proceeds were later donated to an entity dedicated to charity work – to see Diego for just a couple of minutes. It also caught my attention that flags, t-shirts, pennants, balls and hundreds of different items with Diego's images had already been made. The profits from the sale of all these products remained in the pockets of the Camorra, a mafia organisation that operated in the city. The *Ten* did not receive a single lira.

Diego entered the field from the tunnel that connected the changing rooms with the grass, dressed in a Puma t-shirt, long sports pants and a blue-and-white *sciarpa*. He greeted the roaring crowd and, in the middle of the pitch, juggled the ball a couple of times and said just 12 carefully studied words:

'Buonasera, Napoletani. Io sono molto felice di essere con voi. Forza Napoli!'

The press conference that served as a formal presentation of the new Neapolitan star, held on a basketball court located below one of the stands, was packed with reporters of multiple nationalities, some from far away destinations such as Argentina or Japan. The question round started badly. A French journalist opened fire with an insidious approach: he asked Diego if he was aware that part of the money for his signing could have been contributed by the Camorra. He did not answer. Ferlaino took the microphone, shouted his disgust for what he considered an 'offensive question'.

'We have made many sacrifices, you cannot say this. We are honest and hardworking people,' replied the president of the southern team. Immediately afterwards, he expelled the Gallic reporter from the basketball court.

Calming the waters, Diego denied holding a grudge against Catalonia or his former club 'although I am very unhappy with some of the club's leaders'.

'I hope for tranquillity, the tranquillity that I did not have in Barcelona, and above all things, respect,' he added.

That same night we flew from Rome to Buenos Aires. Diego had planned to take a few days off, but I recommended that he rest his head but not his body. I warned him that the preseason of the Italian teams was very hard; they went to the mountains, they did terrible things:

'We are going to have to do a kind of pre-preseason because they are going to break you. You are going to arrive light and they are going to demand maximum effort.'

I am against the savagery of including massacres and endless climbs of dunes of loose sand, very steep, or to shaky ground hills, in the run-up to a demanding football competition. The most recognised experts in sports medicine agree that in both phases – ascent and descent –

the muscles, tendons and joints are seriously compromised when subjected to this type of excessive effort. On the rise, the quadriceps is impelled to push from an absolutely forced and unnatural position, which causes an overstretch in its fibres such that it ends up compromising the very integrity of the muscle, with the consequent risk to the tendons in their insertion phase. The knee joint goes from extreme flexion to maximum extension by a very violent upward thrust in its fight against gravity. All its structural elements are pushed to the very edge of the abyss. In this position of maximum extension, the entire posterior leg musculature reaches such a degree of stretch that the foot encounters a yielding support and the Achilles tendon must reach the end of its elastic possibilities to start the phase of recovery.

This series of brutal attacks compromises the immediate future of many players, who end up suffering the traumatic attacks of tendonitis, sprains, pubalgias or tears in a phase that is paradoxically called optimisation of the physique. This true lack of consideration for one of the most important preventive measures, such as respecting a gradual adaptation to effort, is required at the very beginning of the preseason and the risk of injury then increases considerably, as the players return to the field activity after a pleasant vacation period. It is essential to evade this type of bestiality to avoid an undesirable balance of multiple traumas of varying severity. The physical trainer who works with footballers must commit to carrying out a preparation based on rational efforts, similar to those that the game proposes. And the ridiculous habit of running around the court? It can be understandable on rainy days if you do not want to spoil the floor, or in some other case of urgent need, but never as a routine. If what is intended is the increase of specific energy systems, why not travel that distance at the determined pace, respecting the action-pause times within the field and using all the actions and modes of running that are imitative of the game? In this way, the footballer will be able to train all the required muscle groups, and the inevitable and risky imbalances that occur when running in one direction will be prevented. These variabilities are aggravated if, on top of that, they are carried out over long distances in which an improper stride length for the game and extremely harmful to the fibres involved is perpetuated. Why denaturalise the intrinsic vivacity of the game, through such monotonous, mechanised and predictable races? The same occurs with the use and abuse of sleds. Wouldn't it be preferable, for example, to indicate one-on-one opposition movements, in which the players must fight to get hold of the ball that a third guy is carrying, using all kinds of movements during the action time, pauses and repetitions that the coach chooses? Why run only linearly, as in the past, without applying a single variant? Honestly, there are things that make me feel embarrassed for others. How can you have so much callousness and lack of common sense, not just to use them but to even imagine so much nonsense? Personally, I still believe that the best way to train to coach footballers is related to three essential elements:

1) Having played since childhood, because the experience collected in the form of their own experiences is non-transferable, regardless of having transcended or not as a professional.
2) The possibility of learning from those who know the most, since in general the best students are the product of the best teachers.

3) The degree of vocation and sensitivity necessary to see what is seen and what is heard.

We cannot expect a footballer to improve elements of the game by running through the forest; not even going to the mountains to do alpine skiing. He is not perfecting anything in football, not even endurance to play. Nothing. We have to understand the game in its entirety and from there seek the dynamic interactivity between the elements that constitute the systems of the human being that is going to participate in that global situation. If we go running in the forest every day, we will be specialists in the forest. If we go to do weights every day, we will be weightlifters. In this way of structuring training, we have the possibility of choosing exercises that provide that dynamic interactivity that the athletic exercises of individual sports do not have, which are based on other types of experiences. If we want to enhance the potential of our footballers, we must fundamentally think about training them through exercises taken from the game.

Attentive to all these concepts, and trying to balance my ideas so as not to overwhelm Diego, but to stimulate him to draw his own conclusions through his possibilities, we stayed for about eight or nine days in the villa he had bought in Moreno, west of the city of Buenos Aires, which had good facilities for our work, such as a football field with lighting. Assisted by *Galíndez*, *Lalo* and Hugo, we did a good preparation that allowed him to start the preseason with the right foot ... or the left, in his case.

We went back to Italy but not to Naples: the club leaders picked us up at the Rome airport and from there they took us directly to a small and quiet Tuscan town, of barely 5,000 inhabitants, called Castel del Piano, the place chosen to train the team. Well, not so quiet in those days, because many Neapolitan fans – some chronicles, somewhat exaggerated, claim that about 10,000 – came from the south to see the training of their new idol. The light-blue tide filled the local hotel capacity and also that of the neighbouring towns. Some people rented rooms in family homes and others camped with sleeping bags under the pines in Piazza della Rimembranza. One morning, a bar owner discovered a *tifoso* resting on the floor between two pool tables. Mayor Francesco Forti decided to leave the access gate to the Stadio Comunale open so that visitors who had not found a standard shelter could use its bathrooms.

Just as Diego had been warned by me, Rino Marchesi, his first coach at Napoli, decided to carry out basic physical preparation at Monte Amiata: every morning, he would take his players to a spot where he forced them up and down covered hills of chestnut trees. Diego fulfilled his whims, although with some concessions, since in his contract he had clearly established that he would work on his physique together with his personal trainer. For example, one day Marchesi ordered the football players to perform the Cooper Test – the same one that Diego had found useless when he did it in Montjuic – hours before playing a friendly match.

'Don't do that!' I ordered him. I was afraid that he would suffer a muscle injury before starting the championship.

Every night, after dinner at the Grand Hotel Impero, where the team was staying, Diego used to go for a walk with Claudia and her little dog *Popi* – usually surrounded by affectionate but courteous fans – to a nearby ice-cream parlour that prepared an exquisite dessert called *affogato*, made with cream, chocolate, hazelnuts from nearby forests, black cherries, and a blend of two liqueurs.

Diego's first game with the Napoli jersey was played on 2 August 1984 against an amateur squad, Neania Castel del Piano. The sky-blue team won 13-1 and the Villa Fiorito-born footballer scored four goals, one of them through a picturesque scissor kick, despite the sticky marking of a boy named Corrado Corsini, who worked as a baker. Every goal of the *Ten* was celebrated with euphoria by the multitude of visiting fans who flooded the small cement area of the Stadio Comunale and also the short hills that surrounded the field, used as natural stalls.

After the preseason, Diego returned to Naples very worried. Despite the fact that the club had also incorporated his compatriot Daniel Bertoni, world champion with Argentina in 1978 who arrived from Fiorentina – at that time, the Italian Federazione Giuoco Calcio only allowed teams to hire a maximum of two foreign footballers – and Salvatore Bagni, ex-Inter, the team was quite weak. He believed that he had arrived at a powerful institution, but the truth was that Napoli had been fighting for several seasons to avoid relegation: in the 1983/84 championship they had been saved by one point, and by two in the previous year.

The season started badly. Napoli lost as a visitor 3-1 in their debut against Hellas Verona, a squad that would become champions with the valuable contribution of the Danish Preben Elkjær Larsen and the German Hans-Peter Briegel. Then they drew 1-1 with Sampdoria at San Paolo (Diego scored his first official goal with the light-blue jersey) and fell to Torino 3-0. One point out of six possible, since in those years each victory was still awarded with two points.

Cesar Menotti, who had travelled to Naples to watch the second game, asked me during the match:

'How much do Diego's team-mates pay to play for this team?'

Napoli was condemned to battle from the middle of the table towards the bottom, and not for the title, without a doubt. But I was confident that the *Ten* had a lot of magic to offer. One morning, I picked Diego up at his new address, a spacious apartment located in a condominium on Via Scipione Capece 3/1, in the Posillipo neighbourhood – for the first few weeks he had occupied, together with Claudia, a suite on the eighth floor of the Royal Hotel. He trained with great enthusiasm in a gym called Contourella, which was on the edge of the sea, with a spectacular view of the gulf. The owner was the American Eddie Cheever, a Formula One driver. As in Barcelona, we continued to condition his body based on power work. I had noticed that Marchesi abused the 100m runs around the pitch. 'You start and stop, start and stop,' I told Diego, 'because that is what you are going to do during the game.'

Adapting to Italian football was not easy. Marchesi, like most of his colleagues in those years, adhered to a tactical line that, more or less, was based on throwing the ball up, as far as possible, for the strikers to invent something. A philosophy in which the good Marchesi was wrapped in his own spider web, since it threatened against the possibilities of creating the best footballer on earth. It was difficult, even for Diego, to organise anything while the ball, whipped mercilessly, came and went four or five metres high, propelled by goalkeepers and defenders, monotonous and submissive to the point of exasperation. Openly, the guys gritted their teeth and kicked the ball hard anywhere. Seeing that style of play made my eyes hurt. One afternoon, while we were returning from the gym, I said to Diego:

'On Sunday, I won't go to San Paolo.'

'Why?'

'Italian football bores me a lot. The worst thing is that the only player who amused me is an idiot: he passes the ball to his team-mates and they give it to the rivals.'

'What do you want me to do?' he questioned.

'The best way to be supportive of the team,' I explained to him, 'is to be as selfish as possible. You have to do like in Argentinos Juniors: dribble everyone and give the ball to a partner, as you did with Carlos Álvarez, do you remember?'

'Yes …'

'Álvarez scored 25 goals in a championship thanks to you. When you left Argentinos, his luck finished. He did not reach the net again.'

I used to point these kinds of things out to him to cheer him up. It was not bad: on Sunday, Napoli thrashed Como 3-0.

Also, I would mark tactical questions for him that seemed wrong to me. For example, it had caught my attention that, every time Napoli had a corner kick against their goal, Diego went down to the area and stood next to the first post.

'Why when you have a corner against your goal are you in charge of covering the first post?'

'Because the manager sends me.'

'Ah, because the manager sends you. And if in the next game he asks you to sit on the crossbar in the corner kicks against you, do you do it?'

Diego hesitated.

'Listen to me: you are Maradona, who is the manager? If you stay at the first post, even the rival goalkeeper goes up to head. But, if you stay in the attack, they are going to leave three men, at least, to mark you. Do you understand?'

Of course, my words had a single purpose: to motivate Diego. In fact, I had a very cordial relationship with Marchesi. I never had a problem with him, or with any other coach, in all the years that I worked with the *Ten*.

Two days before the last game before the winter break, Napoli was in 12th place, close to the clubs that occupied the relegation zone (at that time, three of the 16 teams went down). The team had lost three games in a row, against Internazionale, Roma and Juventus, and had to face Udinese at the San Paolo, a tough rival in which the talented Brazilians Zico and Edinho played. A couple of days before that meeting, I said to Diego:

'Napoli bought you because of how you played. As you are doing now, they are going to kick your ass and send you back to Argentina. Naples is a very beautiful city and we can stay for many years.'

He looked at me surprised and did not answer, although his eyes revealed that they were waiting for my explanation for that consideration, completely justified by the statistics: he had only scored three goals in 13.

'In the games,' I continued, 'you do not receive more than 14, 15 balls. Why don't your team-mates give it to you?'

He continued in silence, simply because he did not know the answer. Neither did I, but I did have advice.

'Go in and have fun, because if you are not having fun, it means that you are playing badly, and thus you do not amuse anyone!'

The night before the match, the team stayed at a hotel in the Castellammare di Stabia area and Diego transmitted my question to Italo Allodi, the club's general manager. Allodi, a brilliant guy, immediately called a meeting with the entire squad, Diego included. Surrounded by all the players, he asked them the reasons why they did not give the ball to the *Ten*. One of them, Salvatore Bagni, replied:

'What happens, Mister, is that Diego is always marked.'

Allodi, who knew a lot about football and had already held similar positions in important clubs such as Internazionale, Juventus or Fiorentina, replied:

'If we are going to wait for Maradona to be alone on a football field ...'

'Boys,' Diego interrupted him enthusiastically, 'throw me the ball! Give it to me and I'll see what I can do with it later.'

The following day, amid a storm that had flooded several sectors of the pitch, Napoli won 4-3 with two goals from the *Ten*.

When we started back home, surrounded by the euphoria of the fans, a relief contained for days exploded. Diego, at the wheel of his car, turned his head towards me and with his face lit up with happiness, he warned me:

'Remain calm, *Ciego* (blind), we are going to stay in Napoli for many years.'

He called me that because I'm short-sighted. I am very myopic, since I was a child. When I played football at Lincoln kids' tournaments, the coach put plasters on my temples to keep my glasses from falling off. Yes, I used to compete with thick spectacles on! I was never bothered by that nickname from Diego because he pronounced it with affection, without malice. I know how to recognise the difference because, during my childhood, I suffered from disgusting bullying: some classmates called me *Anteojito y Antifaz* (*Eyeglass and Mask*, characters from a famous children's magazine that existed from 1964 to 2000, but was really popular during the 1970s and 1980s). Several times I ended up punching those who made fun of me because of my thick glasses.

In the remaining 16 games, Napoli lost just one – 2-1 against Milan at the Giuseppe Meazza stadium – and accumulated more points than Serie A champions Hellas Verona, although the light-blue team barely ranked eighth in the table. Diego? He scored nine more times, forming together with Daniel Bertoni the highest-scoring foreign duo with 25 goals (one more than the French Michel Platini and the Polish Zbigniew Boniek, from Juventus) and he was chosen by the sports press as the best player of the season.

In May of that year, Diego taught a masterclass on love to the national team. In a period in which there were no 'FIFA dates' that would release players from their professional club commitments to join their national teams, whether in official tournaments or friendly matches, Diego decided to put on the *Albiceleste* shirt again. His last performance had taken place almost three years earlier, a defeat against Brazil at the 1982 World Cup in Spain. Hepatitis and fracture had prevented him from performing in the first commitments of the team led by Carlos Bilardo, the coach appointed by the Argentine Football Association to replace Cesar Menotti. Likewise, the preseason with Napoli denied Diego the possibility of participating in a tour of the Argentine squad in Colombia, Switzerland, Belgium and Germany.

Bilardo had made two friendlies at River Plate's stadium, on 9 and 14 May 1985, against Paraguay and Chile, and Diego decided to be 'present' at the Monumental. To do this, he asked Ferlaino for permission to travel to his country, but the president denied it, arguing that he needed his top star in the last three games of the season, all complicated, against Juventus at San Paolo, Udinese in the north and Fiorentina again at home. How was the issue resolved? Diego assured Ferlaino that he would not miss any of the commitments with Napoli.

'You don't worry: I'm going to play both games with Argentina and all three with the club.'

'But, Diego, are you going to travel 50,000km in less than two weeks to participate in two unimportant friendlies?' asked the Neapolitan president.

'For me they are important,' he answered, 'and I don't care about the distance. If I have to go to the moon to play for the Argentine national team, I will do it!'

On Sunday, 5 May, Diego played against *Juve* at San Paolo. The match ended without goals and, after the final whistle, several Neapolitan journalists discovered the presence in the stadium of the owner of the Turin team, the businessman and aristocrat Giovanni Agnelli. The chroniclers surrounded the owner of the Fiat industrial group as he left the official box to ask him some questions about the game. Agnelli, a very elegant and charismatic man, accepted and answered each query with natural courtesy. The impromptu press conference came to an end when one of the reporters tried to humiliate the businessman, perhaps shielded by the mass of journalists who accompanied him:

'Why did Maradona sign with Napoli and not with Juve?'

Without losing his poise, Agnelli looked at the journalist and replied:

'Guys, I must tell you the truth: because we are not rich enough to have him.' He saluted, turned to continue his walk toward the stadium exit, took a couple of steps, and stopped. He turned his face towards the chroniclers and finished:

'But not so poor as to need him.'

With his subtle wit, Agnelli gave a notable lecture on public relations.

After the always tense duel with Juventus, Diego travelled that same afternoon by car to Rome and there he took a flight to Buenos Aires. On Thursday, 9 May, he scored the Argentine goal in the tie against Paraguay (1-1) and the next day he returned to Italy: after landing in Fiumicino, he boarded another plane, to Udine, where he joined his team-mates who were already preparing in a hotel for the duel with the Friulani squad. On Sunday, Diego scored a *doppietta* (two goals, in Italian) to seal another draw, this time 2-2. He returned to Buenos Aires, via Rome, and on Wednesday he scored a goal for Argentina, beating Chile 2-0. He rested another day and travelled the last 12,000 kilometres to Naples: on Sunday 19 May, he led the team that beat Fiorentina by 1-0 in the last match of the Serie A season. Incredible! Diego strictly respected the promise he had made to Ferlaino, but fundamentally with his love for the shirt of his country – an unconditional passion that excited him to commit anything crazy, such as the enormous sacrifice that that marathon of trips meant. A feat he would repeat years later, although from Seville.

Surprised by his excellent performance and knowing that aboard a plane one does not get enough rest, even in the best of seats, I asked him how he managed to regain strength to perform fully in so many matches in a row. He confided to me that, although he had tickets for first class, as soon as the plane reached its cruise level, he would take his pillow, some blankets and go to the back, to the cheapest area, where he would look for a deserted row to lie down and sleep ... on the floor! Thus, he rested the entire flight and arrived fresh at his destination.

For me, that was Diego's best year in Italy. But, as the team was eighth, his work was overshadowed. As of the arrival of his magnificent goals, the sales of annual tickets began a vertiginous rise that reached to cover 86 per cent of the 77,000 seats of the San Paolo stadium. The commercialisation of t-shirts and merchandising also skyrocketed, which strengthened the economy of the institution. With that injection of money, the club was able to fortify the team in some key positions. It was essential to invigorate it with players of good quality and experience in the league, because Diego could play at a high level but with the squad from that first cycle there was no way to become champions. For the 1985/86 season, Ferlaino hired goalkeeper Claudio Garella, recently champion with Hellas Verona; defender Alessandro Renica, after an excellent performance at Sampdoria, who had finished fourth in the table in the previous tournament; and Bruno Giordano, who had scored 86 goals with the Lazio jersey. Diego and Bertoni continued to be the two foreign footballers.

During the first years in Naples, Diego's life was very monotonous: from home to training and from training to home. People used to crowd in front of the balcony of his apartment and, shouting, they demanded his presence to take a photo, ask for an autograph or simply express their affection for him. Diego enjoyed the displays of passion, but he also needed some peace to rest. I didn't like seeing him locked up. I suggested that he go to the gym every day, even if he hardly did any work of relaxation, mobility, flexibility, so that he could interact with other people in a quiet environment where he could converse without harassment, and thus also begin to learn the language. If he stayed locked up all day, he was never going to get it. But he learned it, of course, and before me! His head was working at incredible speed!

For his second Italian season, Rino Marchesi was replaced by Ottavio Bianchi, an *allenatore* (coach, in Italian) who had played several seasons in the sky-blue jersey in the 1960s. There was also a very important change within the team: Diego became the captain. The transfer of the tape created a very tender situation. The *Ten* wanted to empower himself as team leader, but at the same time he did not dare to express his desire to Giuseppe Bruscolotti, the central defender who had been captain for several seasons. What did he do? He asked another of the defence players for help: Pierpaolo Marino. He accepted, although he was afraid that Bruscolotti would be angry with him. One night, at the hotel where the team had stayed for the preseason, Marino made an effort and faced his team-mate with the greatest possible tact.

'Beppe, what do you think about the possibility of giving the *fascia* [armband] to Maradona, to be the captain?'

The answer not only surprised Marino, it brought him great relief:

'I was just thinking about it and I wanted to offer it myself to represent us as of this season. The armband will stimulate him.'

After a while, Marino brought Diego with Beppe, who in a simple ceremony made the delivery of the emblematic official ribbon with moving words. The anointing as a brand-new *capitano* brought the *Ten* to tears. He was like that: he was moved by questions that for many people may be simple or of little importance, but that he found stimulating and really meaningful. Like when Patricio Herandez gave him the number 10 jersey before the World Cup in Spain. For the 1978 World Cup in Argentina, coach Cesar Menotti had decided that the numbers on the official list should be defined in alphabetical order. Thus, it drew the attention of the footballing planet that goalkeeper Ubaldo Fillol caught the ball with the number 5 jersey, or that midfielder Osvaldo Ardiles performed with 1, a figure generally reserved for goalkeepers. Before the 1982 World Cup in Spain, Menotti decided to repeat the alphabetical classification of his boys. In this way, Diego got the 12. Dissatisfied with his number, he asked Jorge Cyterszpiler to intercede with Menotti to grant him an exception and assign him the 10 that, by chance, had been assigned to Patricio Hernandez, coincidentally the roommate of the kid from Villa Fiorito. Menotti replied that he was not opposed to changing the numeral order of the list, but only if Patricio accepted. The next day, while they were drinking maté in their room, Diego, shyly, told Hernandez that he had always worn the 10 and that he would also like to do it at the Iberian World Cup. Before the former Argentinos Juniors star formalised his request, Patricio told him, 'No problem, it's yours.'

Happy, Diego opened the drawer of his nightstand, took out a gold watch decorated with precious stones that a sponsor had given him and wanted to gift it to Hernandez, but he did not accept it: he explained that he had agreed because he considered him his friend and because, in addition, he had earned the right to wear the prestigious 10 jersey on the field. That was Diego: generous, detached, with simple values that put friendship and affection before luxury.

I started to work more closely with the team's new physical trainer, Ernesto Milano. Depending on the exercises and efforts scheduled for each day, I would tell Diego to do them, or I would adapt them to him in the most convenient way so that the long, high-intensity routines would not burn him out. His body was not predisposed for certain risks, he needed something else. Even today the mistake is made of training everyone in the same way when each of the footballers has his characteristics, not only physically but also emotionally. Between us, we kept talking a lot so that I could get to know him inside and out, and not just from a physical and physiological point of view: I needed to be aware of his insecurities, his fears, his relationships, his anxiety, his dreams, his moments of sadness. The dialogue was essential to get to know him in depth. He was still a little unsure about his ankle injury: he told me that there were things that he could not do as before, that it worried him. As a result of the fracture, the operation and the welding of the broken bones, the ankle had been left with a rather obvious impossibility in terms of mobility. Diego had first turned to the kinesiologist Aldo Divinsky, whom he had known in his time with Argentinos Juniors. He travelled to Buenos Aires and worked with him twice a day, with massages and different movements to try to break some adhesions, but practically nothing was achieved.

'Diego, you are a Ferrari, you need a Ferrari mechanic,' I said.

'What do you mean?'

'That you have to look for the best ankle joint specialist in the world.'

'And where is he?'

'I don't know, we'll have to look it up. But if you keep doing the same, you will not achieve what you want.'

Through the Argentine Football Association, the most prestigious ankle traumatologist in the world was detected in the United States: he was the head of the medical services of the National Football League, the sport in which the most brutal injuries occur. Diego travelled with Dr Raúl Madero, a former Estudiantes de La Plata footballer who had been summoned by Carlos Bilardo to the National Team's coaching staff. The American traumatologist reviewed Diego, analysed his studies and X-rays and assured him that there was nothing to do: the ankle had been welded in a way and he had to get used to playing with that limitation.

'Complaining is useless,' he explained to me upon his return from the United States.

But Diego was not satisfied with the specialist's diagnosis. He knew himself better than anyone, and he perceived that there were things to do … and many! As the radius of action of his ankle was not going to improve, he began to practise a new way of supporting his foot, moving his leg, turning his hips more, getting closer to the ball. Together, we began to design very specific workouts to modify the entire kinetic chain of movement to achieve the same effectiveness as before … and he did it! He retrained his ankle and achieved the same effectiveness, or more. Of course, this exceptional improvement did not happen overnight, or without a formidable effort. Diego must have sweated a lot. In addition to performing exercises that allowed him to achieve greater joint flexibility, he had to start from scratch with the ball. We got a pitch where we put a rickety barrier in front of the goal. He kicked several times and the ball always went to hell. So, I suggested that we move on to a plan B: just as he had overcome the stage of the cast, first stepping on crutches, then walking, later jogging and finally running, he had to do the same with the ball: go step by step.

He resumed his romance little by little, putting the ball on the bottom line, at the apex with the small area. From there to the first post of the goal there are five and a half metres. He started with a string of soft shots, with a lot of spin: the balls entered placidly. Little by little, as he gained confidence, he continued with stronger shots, until he reached the stage of ferocious kicks. Diego hit it with his soul, challenging himself. The ball opened up and into the goal with great power, like a cannonball coming out of his foot, spinning rapidly in the air and embedding itself in the net at the second post. Gaining so much control at a very close range made it easier for him to hit the angle later over a longer range. He also stayed after the training of the whole team, with a goalkeeper, to hit to them from all sides. He drove them crazy. This is how his best goal, to me, was created, the 'impossible goal', as it was baptised in Italy for its complexity and difficulty: the one that was scored against Juventus on 3 November 1985 for a historic 1-0 victory at the San Paolo. The game took place under a persistent rain that had left the pitch wet and unstable. Halfway through the second half, referee Giancarlo Redini ordered an indirect free kick inside the visiting area. Diego adjusted the ball. Goalkeeper Stefano Tacconi set up a barrier with six tall players – the shortest was Michel Platini, who was around 1.8m tall – that was at a distance of five metres, and the goal was about six metres behind the black-and-white wall. Diego asked his team-mate Eraldo Pecci to touch the ball softly backwards as soon as the referee whistled. But Pecci, suspicious, albeit with some reason, refused. The ball not only had to pass over the heads of the Turinese players, but also come down immediately, and there was not enough space for that unreasonable trip. While the crowd roared for a new Maradonian miracle, the No.10 and the No.8 became involved in an unusual discussion.

'Pass it to me,' Diego demanded.

'No, the wall is very close.'

'Touch it, I tell you.'

'It's not possible ...'

'Touch it, son of a bitch!'

Pecci finally obeyed, bowed down by his captain's insult. Diego took a step towards the ball and caressed it, docile, a little with his prodigious left foot, a little with his supernatural recovered ankle. The ball rose like a soap bubble. It overcame the wall and sneaked into the left corner of Tacconi's goal. The goalkeeper flew uselessly towards an unreachable target. Nobody knows how, but Diego scored a goal of a complexity bordering on the impossible, which has no logical explanation. But it was written: it had to happen that way. Despite the injury and reduced mobility, he, thanks to his effort and talent, achieved more than an astonishing regeneration: he managed to overcome. There is no setback that stops a genius.

In his first season in Naples, Diego and I came to a conclusion: while in Spain the more rustic defenders resorted to kicking to stop their rivals, in Italy the back players were better trained, more agile and, moreover, played with the ball. Therefore, it was essential to strengthen his power, but increase speed. When we went to some remote and quiet natural place, I would draw him a square ten metres on a side and he had to move inside, starting from the centre, according to what I yelled at him: sprints at maximum speed, jumps with the knee to the chest, push-ups, abdominal, running backwards or to the side, roll back and forth, without going beyond the limits of that space. They were short jobs of eight to ten seconds, with the same payback period. Sometimes we did it with a ball, but always on fire, with very high intensity and short duration. When I noticed that his agitation was high, or he himself noticed that he was going into oxygen debt, we stopped so as not to produce so much acidosis. The objective was to manage the power of his body in time and space: when you play football you have to push, pull, drag. Strength and agility are the key for the body to be able to balance, move forward, and kick or head. To that purpose, we also did five-second maximum-speed jobs, but never linear: starting, braking, jumping, falling, back and forth, five seconds of walking to recover, and again. Five by five, adding and adding, until relaxing with a lot of joint mobility, anterior and posterior, generally on the floor. We ended with some sit-ups and stretching and, after five or six minutes of recovery, we started again. We did that according to what he had done in the morning: if he played a lot of football and the field had been heavy, in the afternoon at the gym we did leg relaxation and did exercises to strengthen the muscles of the upper body, or a bit of boxing (shadow, pads, bag) that also served to fortify arms and shoulders. Boxing offered another advantage: the possibility for him to abstract himself from everything and unload his head. We played loud music with a lot of percussion, sometimes the soundtracks of Rocky movies, and I used to screw with him to motivate him.

'Did they give you the armband of captain of Argentina? To you, coward, who is not capable of doing one more series?' I provoked him to incite his soul when he relaxed or exclaimed that he was not giving more.

It was a way of helping him: sometimes, to excite him, I had to insult him, and he also insulted me looking for extra strength to complete an exercise. Going beyond the limit of pain allows overcoming, although that causes a lot of suffering. He loved to dress up as a boxer, with gloves and a headgear. He would stand in front of the sandbag and, seconds before starting the succession of blows, I told him that inside the sack were those who envied him, those who criticised him with bad temper, Ferlaino ...

'Did you understand? Are you sure you understand? Then bust them, tear them to pieces. Let's go!'

Diego unloaded a gale of punches, kicks, elbows, with a power that made the bag rock everywhere. When he was exhausted, I would send him to the floor to relax for a few minutes ... and again, to hit the bag. He was an animal! His arms looked like two cannons firing rubber balls.

It is said that man is a product of his environment, and Diego expressed it like no one else. Once, a Napoli colleague, Pietro Puzone, asked him to participate in a match for the benefit of a boy from Acerra – a town located a few kilometres north of Naples – who had to have an urgent palate operation and did not have the economic means. He accepted, but the club leaders found out and asked him not to, because they knew the stadio comunale where the game would take place – a dirt field that had been turned into a quagmire because of a heavy rain the night before – and they feared that their star would be injured. Diego didn't care. He loved helping everyone ... and also playing in the mud. For him, a muddy pitch was better than Wembley. It represented returning to the sources, to Villa Fiorito. Play ball and not football. The taste for the simple, for the authentic. We went to Acerra and Diego enjoyed that muddy and slippery terrain, from which everything came out brown and dripping. But the most important thing was that he raised the money to pay for the boy's operation.

We returned to Naples by a narrow and winding road. Diego's car led a caravan that included the vehicles of other boys who had participated in the benefit match. In a curve to the left, we saw that an automobile that was travelling a few metres in front of us, in the same direction, lost control and rolled over. Diego braked and got out to help the injured: three boys who had escaped from their car with bruises and cuts caused by the blow. But, as soon as they saw who was standing next to them, they recovered immediately!

'Diego, Mamma mia! Cosa ci fai qui? [Diego, my Mother! What are you doing here?],' the kids shouted. They were so happy that they forgot about the bumps and pains, and asked their idol to pose with them for a photograph. Diego had miraculously cured them.

Speaking of miracles, shortly before the start of the 1985/86 Serie A season, Diego showed up at the headquarters of a laboratory to take the clinical examinations required by the Italian federation of all footballers. One of those studies consisted of a blood test. The nurse who was in charge of taking the sample purposely extracted more fluid than that required for the examination, placed it in a small tube, took it to the altar of the Duomo (Cathedral) di Napoli and placed it next to the urn that, according to tradition, contains the solidified blood of Saint Gennaro, the patron of the city. For 400 years, every 19 September, the date on which Gennaro died, beheaded by the Roman pagans, hundreds of faithful flock to the cathedral to attend the 'miracle of liquefaction': the solidified blood turns liquid and reddish. Apparently, during the other 364 days of the year, the most devout pray to another saint. One who has been dead since November 2020.

Diego's second season in Italy closed with an outstanding third-place finish for Napoli in Serie A, which qualified the southern squad for the UEFA Cup. In addition to the goal against Juventus, the team that won the *Scudetto* that season, Diego scored another ten goals in the league, one against AC Milan for a resounding victory at the San Siro. His name was also recorded on the scoreboard in a thrilling win over champions Hellas Verona, 5-0 at the San Paolo. The successes of the powerful teams from the north strengthened the love of the *tifosi* for their beloved captain. Napoli had lived 84 years in a shadow of frustration. But, thanks to Diego, the sun of hope had begun to appear on the horizon, and to warm the slope of Vesuvius with its rays.

Chapter 5

México lindo y querido

'Beautiful and Beloved Mexico' –
traditional mexican song

MR MANUEL Ballarino, an esteemed teacher I had in
high school, explained in a class that digestion does not start
in the mouth, but in the saucepan. Depending on how food
is prepared, whether cooked or raw, our body will process
it more or less easily. Paraphrasing that educator, I must
say that Diego's success in the 1986 World Cup in Mexico
began to take shape months before his debut against South
Korea, and even the arrival of the Argentine team to Aztec
soil to stay at the facilities of local club America.

The first obstacle Diego faced on his way to lifting
the World Cup occurred in the Venezuelan city of San
Cristóbal, where Argentina played its first qualifying match,
on 26 May 1985. As in Naples, I accompanied Diego as his
personal trainning coach. After the last practice, the day
before the duel against the *vinotinto* ('red wine') squad, the
team returned to the El Tama hotel. In the lobby, Diego
graciously agreed to sign autographs and and pose for photos
with a group of boys. While the footballer was signing the

papers that the children handed him, a man appeared, possibly unbalanced or with an altered mental state, and kicked him in the back of his right knee, in the popliteal hollow, which caused a parameniscal injury. After the attack, the guy ran out of the building and no one stopped him. There was a group of Venezuelan policemen, supposedly posted to take care of the visiting players, who were more surprised by the episode than we were. Diego spent the whole night on ice and painkillers, and the morning of the game he couldn't flex his leg. Before leaving for the Pueblo Nuevo stadium, doctor Raúl Madero extracted a complete syringe of synovial fluid with blood so that he could play. And he did fantastically well: even on one leg, he scored two goals!

After the inaugural victory, 3-2, the team flew to Colombia for their second match, another 3-1 triumph at *El Campin*, the largest Bogota stadium. That day, Diego achieved something amazing: he transformed insults into applause. How did he do it? In the middle of the match, he went to take a corner kick. As he approached the stands, a spectator cussed him and threw an orange at him. Instead of getting angry and responding to the aggression, Diego stepped on the fruit, lifted it off the ground and began to play keepy-uppy as if it were a small ball. *Tick, tock*, foot, knee, five, six, seven ... Pure talent! I did not count the touches, but someone counted 18, another 21. But, beyond the number, Diego, with his enormous quality, won the ovation of the entire audience, including the one who had tried to hit him with the orange.

When the Argentine national team returned to Buenos Aires to face the rematches of the games that had opened the *Albiceleste*'s way to Mexico, Diego's knee worsened. He was in so much pain that a meeting was arranged with Madero, the SSC Napoli doctor, Emilio Acampora, and the renowned Rubén Oliva, the orthopaedic surgeon in whom Diego fully trusted. Acampora and Oliva travelled especially from Italy. The three experts reviewed Diego in the Club Recreativo Ezeiza, the sport campus of the Trade Employees Union, where the national team used to train at that time – the complex that the Argentine Football Association owns in that same Buenos Aires town had not yet been inaugurated. After the examination, Madero and Acampora thought that the damaged knee should be operated on; Oliva, on the other hand, declared, 'You are not going to operate and you are going to play, without problems.'

Diego accepted the recommendation of the traumatologist who had saved his ankle after the cruel onslaught of Andoni Goikoetxea. He did not have surgery, he played against Venezuela, scored another goal and never stepped into an operating room in the rest of his sports career.

In addition to that blow that had affected his knee, Diego had to endure another bitter episode: the iron marking that Luis Reyna subjected him to in the match between Peru and Argentina played in Lima on 23 June 1985. Reyna stuck like a stamp behind the back of the *Albiceleste* star, and used grabs, blows and other illicit manoeuvres to nullify the magic of his famous rival. The referee? A luxury spectator who let the Peruvian boy act at will. The regulations at that time were not helping much either. Today, after several updates, they protect those who want to create. Years later, Reyna admitted in an interview with the Argentine newspaper *Clarín* that he was not very happy about his performance in that qualifying round. 'I didn't like that at all,' he said. 'I don't feel identified with what I did that day. It was ugly, unpleasant. I always liked to play good, make beautiful moves. I do not understand how Maradona could tolerate it. I was very irritating with him. I would have thrown a punch [if I were him]. I clarify that I had no bad intention. I was not aggressive nor did I speak to him during the match. Yes, instead, it was sticky marking. It all happened because the manager of that Peruvian team, Roberto Challe, told me that, if I cancelled Maradona, Peru would have won 90 per cent of the match. I always tell the young players not to do what I did with Maradona. There are other ways to mark an excellent footballer.'

Peru won 1-0, with a goal from Juan Carlos Oblitas. In Buenos Aires, the match ended 2-2 thanks to a monumental play by Daniel Passarella that Ricardo Gareca pushed into the net with ten minutes remaining. Argentina, thanks to the four victories against Venezuela and Colombia, qualified directly for the World Cup. Peru went on to a play-off, in which they were eliminated by Chile. The irony of fate was Gareca, the scorer of the goal that took away the direct passage to Mexico from the Inca squad, would be the technical director of the *rojiblanco* team that returned to a World Cup after 36 years, for Russia 2018.

After the qualifying round and with the ticket to the World Cup in Mexico confirmed, I started looking for information related to the preparation of elite athletes for competitions held at altitude. During the first phase of the World Cup, Argentina had to play two games, against South Korea and Bulgaria, in the Federal District located about 2,200m above sea level, and another against Italy in Puebla, a city in the highlands, central Mexico, located at 2,000m. In addition to the geographical location, I was concerned about the environmental condition of the capital, since it was considered the most polluted city in the world. I was afraid that the cocktail of altitude, smog and intense heat (the World Cup was played in summer and most of the games had been scheduled to start at noon, so that television broadcasts in Europe would capture a larger audience) and the lower partial pressure of oxygen would severely affect Diego's performance on the pitch, but also fundamentally his health.

Towards the end of February 1986, a report reached me about the group that, two years earlier, had helped the cyclist Francesco Moser break the record for the one-hour race in Mexico City. The Italian beat, twice in four days, the mark that the Belgian Eddy Merckx had achieved in 1972. The team had purposely chosen that scenario because, at a greater distance above sea level, the resistance of the air against the advance is lower, a condition that the regulations did not contemplate at the time when the marks were approved, and that was later vetoed. Among the people who had collaborated with Moser, a physiologist trained at the State University of Milan named Enrico Arcelli, who had worked with several athletes and was a professor at the Faculty of Exercise Sciences of the University of the Lombard capital, stood out. I proposed to Diego that we contacted Arcelli so that he could provide us with as much information as possible about the environment where he had to compete in June.

'Look, one of the peculiarities is that you have to learn to breathe differently,' I warned him.

'How?'

'With constant gasps, because although the percentage of oxygen in the air is the same as everywhere, 21 per cent, the body has to make a greater effort to capture it because there is less environmental pressure.'

'Go ahead! See if we can see that doctor,' he finally accepted.

Arcelli lived and worked in Milan, so I arranged an appointment with him at the Grand Hotel Brun in that city, where Napoli had to stay for a match against AC Milan to be played on 13 April. Arcelli arrived with two collaborators and the five of us sat down at a table in the hotel bar. Coffee in between, I explained the reason for the meeting, and immediately I began to ask him questions, many, one after another. Diego practically did not open his mouth. Arcelli answered all my requests with punctilious professionalism. We were talking for about an hour. When the meeting ended, we thanked him for all the help that knowing him would give us. The guy was delighted to have met the famous footballer, and took advantage of the meeting to take a picture with him and ask for several autographs. Diego responded with great kindness and complied with every request. The physiologist departed and, when he had already left the hotel, Diego looked me in the eye and said:

'*Ciego*, don't ask him so many questions. If not, the doctor will think you don't know anything.'

'But, son of a bitch! If I don't ask, how the hell do I help you? I asked 500 questions, but I should have asked a thousand! What do you think, that the altitude thing is a joke? These guys are specialists, and if I want to help you I need them to give me as much information as possible.'

There I reflected that, surely, Diego would have dared to ask many questions ... but Maradona, no! How was he going to have the luxury of showing a weakness, of showing ignorance on a subject?

In that talk, Arcelli gave us the name of an eminence in sports medicine that would be essential for Diego's career: Antonio Dal Monte. This man had more titles than Juan Manuel Fangio, Michael Schumacher and Lewis Hamilton combined: he was a doctor in Space Medicine, Scientific Director and chief authority of the Department of Physiology and Biomechanics of the Italian National Olympic Committee, and head of the Aerodynamics Research Services of the Ferrari Formula One team. He was also a world-famous inventor: he had designed the lenticular wheel for racing bikes, which had no spokes but a single solid structure that reduced air resistance. Dal Monte had his research laboratory in a beautiful neighbourhood in Rome called Acqua Acetosa, which is surrounded by two large green spaces: Villa Ada Savoia and Villa Glori. I arranged an interview for a Monday afternoon and we travelled to the Eternal City from Naples in Diego's car. When we saw the complex where Dal Monte's laboratory was situated, we almost fainted; that place had numerous rooms equipped with advanced infrastructure to evaluate athletes of any discipline and develop the most modern and efficient training and recovery programmes – also, a park with different adapted stations, such as a small and ultra-sophisticated swimming pool to study the technique of highly competitive swimmers, an athletics track, a tennis court and a football field. The facilities included a wind tunnel that was used by the Ferrari cars that, that year, were driven by Michele Alboreto, Stefan Johansson and René Arnoux. We also admired a device, similar to a large table, which made it possible to scale the tracks that would host all the Formula One Grand Prix, with its straights, curves and the entry and exit area of the pit stop. Through a computer, the replicas were used to display on a screen all the information related to turning angles, braking and acceleration zones, the influence of the wind and a thousand other factors that were analysed and processed to produce a report that was handed over to the team leaders, and these were then show to the drivers. We were dazzled, it looked like a NASA laboratory, the agency in charge of the United States space program. Diego also loved to meet other elite and world-famous athletes in that place, such as the sprinter Stefano Tilli, Italian record holder of the 100m sprint and world runner-up in 1983 in the 4 x 100 relay, who trained there with his Jamaican girlfriend Merlene Ottey, who had won medals at the 1984 Los Angeles Olympics and would achieve more at Seoul 1988 and Barcelona 1992.

We met with Dal Monte and the first thing I explained to him was that I wanted to understand Diego on the inside, to find out how his energy reporting systems worked. I knew they had to be similar to those of any player, but I was interested in knowing his biotype as deeply as possible to prepare him for Mexico with the greatest possible precision. I also clarified to Dal Monte that Diego had suffered an atrocious injury to his left ankle and that I considered it necessary to reinforce that area which had been brutally beaten. The expert was not only interested in the proposed challenge, but he did it in a generous, almost paternal way. We started going to the clinic every Monday morning, after the football games. If Napoli played at home, the next day we would leave very early by car to Rome; if the team played as a visitor in the capital or the northern cities, we would stay on Sunday night in a Roman hotel. Dal Monte worked with Diego along with a group of collaborators from his crew, including Marcello Faina, who had collaborated with his teacher in the production and writing of several technical books.

A week after I told Dal Monte that the ankle that had endured a fracture needed to be strengthened, the ingenious doctor had designed and built a weight-added device for Diego to work specifically on that joint. I was amazed by the talent of Dal Monte, that he showed that the professional titles that overflowed his CV were not simple diplomats framed and hung on the wall of his office to impress his patients. Every Monday, Diego would climb onto the 50cm-high iron structure, set his right foot on one side and put his left in a kind of metal shoe, with straps, attached to a shaft to add weight. He first walked on a treadmill, then he jogged, later he ran with that ingenious device attached to his foot that allowed him to greatly improve his radius of action reduced by the injury and the operation performed in Barcelona. Then, with the same device, Diego executed external rotation exercises, tilting the ankle outward, and also internal, anterior and posterior translation, with circular movements to the left and to the right. Few know that this device travelled to Mexico so that Diego could continue exercising his left ankle during the process of adapting to the height, and also between the games of the world championship.

Another accessory that captivated us was a last-generation treadmill, with a computer loaded with thousands of programs for different needs and a huge structure. I think even an elephant could have climbed on it. Dal Monte put electrodes on him, everywhere, the lights flickered and Diego enjoyed so much technology at his disposal. He started by walking, then jogged smoothly, later accelerated and reached a very demanding pace. The doctor made him work in front of a mirror because, in his opinion, looking at himself during exercise not only motivates the athlete, but also adds depth, an illusion of spaciousness. Based on that experience, we put mirrors in the gym at Posillipo's house and in all areas where we train together. Of course, I also incorporated them in all the venues where I worked.

Dal Monte was the one who also recommended us to use a very interesting technique to treat the back pain that constantly affected Diego: using staples to hold the ankles and leave the body hanging for a while, upside down. Thus, gravity releases pressure on the lumbar vertebrae.

A fundamental piece of information that we obtained in this process was that, when the specialists noticed that Diego's pulsations showed great effort, or he increased his oxygen consumption a lot, they made him slow down to preserve him from possible risks. I kept this in mind throughout my entire career with him. Training aimed at optimising power and speed must be very precise and careful to avoid the proliferation of injuries in the athlete.

During the tests, Diego sweated like a goat, but he loved that his body dripped like a waterfall, seeing all those cables stuck to his anatomy. Being surrounded by machines and computers and rubbing shoulders with the elite of high-performance sports fuelled his already burning enthusiasm for a new World Cup.

Dal Monte taught him to breathe gasping for air in smaller quantities but with a greater number of puffs; he subjected it to balance tests with suitable devices to vary the speed, angle or resistance through counterweights. We were all speechless when Diego was subjected to complicated movements that flipped him through the air to test the control of his body in time and space: the fantastic guy always fell standing, like a cat. One of those exercises was reproduced in a traced way when Diego scored his second goal against Belgium during the World Cup semi-final, at the Azteca stadium: he passed between Stéphane Demol and Patrick Vervoort, eluded Eric Gerets and fired at the goal of Jean-Marie Pfaff. After kicking the ball into the net, Gerets hit him with a thud that would have brought down the Empire State Building, but Diego did not fall. He spun in the air, like a top, landed with his right foot and, regaining verticality, ran to the corner flag to celebrate. He offset the thrust with the weight of his arms, shoulders and hips, the strength and endurance of his muscles, exceptional agility, and the formidable motivation that drove him.

Another characteristic of the *Ten* that strongly attracted Dal Monte's attention, even above his physical dexterity, was his peripheral vision.

'Your friend would have been an exceptional warplane test pilot,' he explained to me one day, at the end of a neurological study. 'His field of vision and the way he perceives details are exceptional. Very few human beings have these powers.'

This analysis also detected that Diego had a faster reaction to the stimulus, even than the best sprinters, the 100m and 200m runners. The order of the brain and the consequent response of the muscle, which are measured in thousandths of a second, had exceptional characteristics.

In addition to his knowledge, his initiative and creativity to design new artefacts, what surprised us the most about Dal Monte was his personality. Every Monday, when we finished the analysis and tests, he invited us to have lunch at his house in Piazza dell'Oro, located a few metres from the Tiber river and with Castel Sant'Angelo as a majestic background. We ate with his wife and his children, all educated, humble, loving, charming people.

During one of those meals, I asked Dal Monte if the coaching staff of the Italian team, led by Enzo Bearzot, had required his services to prepare the team for Mexico, given his reputation and his well-known and important contribution to the Azzurro Olympic Committee. He replied that no, no one had called him. 'The shoemaker's son always goes barefoot,' I thought at the time. Having such a famous guy in his own land, neither Bearzot nor his collaborators thought of consulting this wise man in the field of physiology and, fundamentally, the preparation of athletes to compete at altitude. Perhaps the draws against Bulgaria and Argentina, the tight victory over South Korea and the elimination at the hands of France in the round of 16, explain the poor showing of the defending champions from four years earlier in Spain.

Thanks to the knowledge and advice of Dal Monte, with Diego we reinforced the preparation of his body for the World Cup, which at the same time improved his performance at Napoli, which, as I said in the previous chapter, finished in third place in the table.

During the practices with the team, Diego graduated his efforts to avoid the risks of a psychophysical saturation, so common in these circumstances. The Napoli coaching staff led by Ottavio Bianchi was aware and there were no problems in agreeing on the planning. Except for Thursdays, when football was played in the afternoon at the San Paolo stadium, training sessions were held in the morning in Soccavo. After lunch and a restorative nap, with Diego we had a personalised session at the Virgilio Club. It consisted of demands of very high intensity and short duration, since the controls carried out in Rome had determined that their energy reporting systems needed quite long recovery periods to express themselves at the highest level. Diego agreed. He had already warned me that long-term jobs (continuous career or long passes) left him very sore and were too boring. Normally we spent a good amount of time doing exercises aimed at increasing his joint mobility, combined with others to optimise his muscular elasticity. Most of the practices were based on imitative actions of the game, and among the preferred variants were fiery tennis matches and boxing sessions in the gym that we had set up in the garage of his house. This type of training, which Diego loved, was ideal for achieving high-speed and intense movements aimed at enhancing his muscles, based on a sparkling dynamic that required almost the limit of his neuromuscular coordination possibilities.

I do not know if it was a coincidence or consequence, but since our work with Dal Monte began, Napoli played eight games, of which they won six (the last four, in a row), drew one and lost the remaining, both away from home, against Juventus and Udinese, respectively.

One afternoon when we finished training, I was touched by his vigour and passion.

'I don't know how Argentina is going to do, but the Mexican World Cup was made for you.'

'Why do you say that?'

'Because the lower partial pressure of oxygen, the very high temperature that there will be and the impressive smog will not allow the persecutory marking that you suffered in Spain. And you, unlike the others, are going to arrive very well prepared to face all those conditions. It's going to be your World Cup, remember this.'

'You think?'

'I don't think so, I'm sure. It is going to be your World Cup ... or Platini's. It depends on you, on what you decide.'

I ignited him because Platini was the star of the *Vecchia Signora*, Napoli's worst enemy. I always mentioned Michel because I knew that disturbed him a lot. In addition, a few months before Mexico, France had won a friendly against Argentina in Paris, 2-0, without Platini, but with Diego on the defeated side. I did it on purpose, without knowing if Argentina and France would meet in the World Cup, something that in the end did not happen:

'While you are fooling around, the French guy is thinking of a thousand ways to humiliate you on the field.'

Diego needed that kind of provocation. Sometimes, to motivate him, an order was not enough: he also needed to have his head shaken. I prepared it from the physical point of view, but also from the psychological, the emotional. One gram of brain tissue weighed more than the 76kg in Diego's body. If the mind wanted, the body would be able, for sure.

One afternoon when I arrived at his house to go to train at the Virgiliano club, which belonged to Gianni Improta, a former Napoli footballer, I noticed Diego a little unmotivated, perhaps down. We got into the car and, as soon as he turned it on, my light bulb went on.

'Wait a bit, I forgot something.'

'What?'

'Nothing, something I want for training.'

I got out of the vehicle, went into the house and asked Claudia to get me an Argentine shirt and one of the captain's armbands that he used with the national team. I put everything in a bag and went back to the car.

'What did you go looking for?' he asked me, curious.

'You'll see ...'

'No, come on, tell me, *Blind*. What do you have there?'

'A surprise.'

'What surprise?'

'Don't break my balls! If I tell you, it will stop being a surprise. Drive, come on, we're going to be late.'

We got to the club locker room and Diego began to undress. He took off his sneakers, long pants and t-shirt, and when he was about to put on the jersey he had in his bag, I opened the bag and threw the light-blue-and-white one at him.

'Put that on.'

When he did, I went over and put the captain's armband on his right arm. He smiled but didn't say anything. He enjoyed the detail.

We started to work. At one point, noticing that he was having a hard time completing a series, I yelled at him:

'Are you wearing the Argentine shirt to do this shit, mother fucker? Chickens cannot dress in light blue and white ...'

My God! He was transformed into a hungry, caged lion. He ran, jumped, thrashed furiously, as if his tail had caught fire. He finished the exercise and, while he recovered, I went to his ear and said slowly, although there was no one around us, 'When you wear this shirt, you have to kill. With those colours on the chest, there is no tiredness or pain. You understand me?'

He nodded, although I could read the '*Blind*, son of a bitch' that had formed in his head. Afterwards, we ended up hugging, as always, but he needed that aggressiveness to burn off the irritation inside him, which I had discovered when I went to look for him. I couldn't tell him 'Come on, *Dieguito*, one more round trip,' because in the World Cup they weren't going to treat him delicately, precisely. In Spain 1982, the Italian Claudio Gentile had annulled him with grabs, elbows and other caresses. That couldn't happen again. He had to be prepared because the Briegel German tank or the giant English were not going to receive him on the field with affection.

The Argentine team arrived at the Benito Juárez International Airport in Mexico City on Monday, 5 May 1986, after a tour that had not awakened a shred of hope for the great sports tournament. No way. Although they had beaten Israel 7-2 in Tel Aviv, with two goals from Diego, four days earlier they had lost in Oslo to Norway, a very weak team that had not qualified for the World Cup for half a century.

Loyal to his style, coach Carlos Bilardo had told his players to pack a suit and a white sheet in their suitcases – the suit, in case they won the championship; the sheet, to make a tunic because, if they were eliminated in the first round, they would have to go into exile in Arabia.

With the exception of the local team, which was already in their country, Argentina was the first foreign squad to arrive in Aztec territory to begin their preparation and adaptation for the big event. Bilardo and the president of the Argentine Football Association, Julio Grondona, had managed to get the team to stay at Club América's training camp, which was called 'El Nido del Águila' (The Eagle Nest) and is located south of the Federal District, on the grounds of an old hacienda, Santa Úrsula Coapa. The complex had a large structure where the coaching staff, their collaborators and most of the footballers stayed. They assigned me a room that I shared with Miguel di Lorenzo – who no longer worked with us but for the national team – and Salvatore Carmando, the Napoli masseur who had travelled especially to treat Diego, and Roberto Mariani, a Bilardo collaborator. The coach gladly accepted my presence on the spot and Carmando's because he wanted his top star and team captain to be in the best possible shape. Diego shared his room with Pedro Pasculli, who had been his team-mate in Argentinos Juniors FC and at that time was playing for the Italian club Lecce.

Since I mentioned Diego's first professional club, he met again in El Nido del Águila with Miguel Ángel *Zurdo* (Lefty) López, who had been his coach in Argentinos Juniors and at that time was working as manager of Club América. In addition, he advised Bilardo, with whom he had played at Estudiantes de La Plata in the mid-1960s. During one of our training sessions, Diego told me that in 1980, the day before a game against Boca at the Vélez Sarsfield stadium, *Zurdo* López had approached him at the table where the players were having lunch and had thrown him a newspaper containing an interview with the *Xeneize* goalkeeper, Hugo Gatti.

'Look at what Gatti says about you: that report says that you are a chubby,' López incited him.

Diego read the article and was furious.

'How is he going to say this to you? How disrespectful! Do you know what to do?' asked the coach, throwing more wood on the fire.

'What?'

'Score two goals, so that he learns to shut his mouth.'

'I'm not going to score two, I'm going to score him four,' he assured, dominated by the anger.

He fulfilled his promise: the next day, Argentinos won 5-3 with four goals from the 'chubby' one.

Diego arrived in Mexico like a well-tuned violin. He had managed to stabilise his weight at 76kg long before the World Cup. His physical condition was optimal from the feet to the neck, and little by little he managed to acclimate to the Aztec high habitat. The place chosen as the training camp was ideal for the footballers – although they baptised it as 'Alcatraz', the famous American penitentiary located on a small island in the San Francisco Bay. They could perform the necessary exercises to adapt to the altitude, enjoy many hours of rest and sleep, a good diet and a relaxed, calm atmosphere. Bilardo, who had already rehearsed acclimatisation to the altitude with a group of players – although without Diego – in Tilcara, a town in the province of Jujuy located about 3,000m above sea level, also organised several training sessions at the same time were set as the games, so that the boys would also get used to the torrid heat of the Mexican summer.

Diego trained with the team on the field, where Bilardo ordered his tactics and strategies. As in Naples, I worried about choosing what work to do so as not to overload his muscles. The Italian season had been very demanding and I couldn't allow him to overtrain and reach the World Cup with wet gunpowder, as had happened in Spain four years before. I also set out to motivate him, to help him free his mind from understandable hesitations, from the fears that stage fright can generate. One night, I decided it was time to adjust the last nut on that incredible 1.68m-tall football machine. I got to Diego's room and found him on his bed, reading a magazine, lying on his back and with his legs bent. I said hello and only Pasculli answered, who was entertaining himself by watching television. The *Ten* continued, engrossed in reading. He didn't answer me. I took advantage of his concentration to give Pedro a knowing wink, making him understand that I needed his collaboration.

'How are you, *Profe*?'

'How are you, Pedrito?'

'Well, and you?'

'The truth? I am perfect. Today was a great day, Pedro!'

'Why? What happened?'

'Today I realised that all these guys who came to be World Cup stars are in fact a bunch of cowards!'

'Nooooo! Really?'

'Believe me! In one of the newspapers, I read that Zico declared that he prefers a great performance from Brazil rather than his personal brilliance. Platini said more or less the same; Rummenigge, the identical music ...'

I made a deep, brief, deliberate silence. And I added:

'And one I know ...'

I could not finish the sentence. Directly alluded to and beside himself, Diego, apparently concentrating on reading, flipped the magazine over and shouted at me:

'But what do you think, fucking *Blind*, that this is as easy as you think?'

With a very calm voice and looking into his eyes, I replied:

'Easy? Very easy I would say! God gives bread to those who have no teeth. If I had your conditions, you'd see!'

He wanted to interrupt but I, pretending to be angry, raised my tone and concluded:

'Convince yourself once and for all, pig head! If not, what the hell did we do everything we did for? If you decide, you win the World Cup alone. Understand it!'

I did not say 'pig head' in a derogatory sense: that is what tremendously noble guys with well-defined principles are called in Argentina. Diego knew that I always spoke to him from affection and protection.

I took two steps back, opened the door, and went to my room. As I walked down the corridor, I heard the loud insults that Diego dedicated to me resounding, combined with Pedrito's laughter.

The next day the press was authorised to enter the Club América campus and a cloud of journalists from all over the world invaded the place to talk with the boys. As always, Diego was the favourite prey of the reporters, among whom Bobby Charlton stood out, the unforgettable England midfielder and world champion in 1966. The *Albiceleste* captain stood before the cameras and microphones with excellent humour. He answered all the questions with wit and determination. That night I stopped by his room and saw him excitedly playing cards with other guys, so I said hello and left. The next morning I got up for an early breakfast. At the bar, Jorge Valdano and the delegation's cook, Julio Onieva, chatted animatedly. Scattered on a round table, the just-arrived newspapers were waiting. I started flipping through them until one headline made a huge impact on me. The title that headed a photograph of Diego with a huge smile announced: 'Maradona opens the fire: "I will be the star of the World Cup."' I experienced infinite pleasure. 'Now we are ready,' I decreed. Today, when the outcome of the tournament is already known and recognised, I must say that what followed was, for me, a fantastic experience that should be titled 'Chronicle of an Announced Victory'.

But, logically, no one could predict anything before the opening whistle against South Korea, at the Olympic

Stadium in Mexico City; nor when that game ended, because the Koreans gave Diego so many kicks that I thought he was out of the World Cup in the first match. The most egregious blow came from Jung-Moo Huh: within four minutes of the first half, Diego eluded two rivals, and Jung-Moo, whom he should rename Kung-Fu, landed a terrifying kick in the knee. The Korean launched himself directly to destroy his opponent, without any intention of reaching the ball – if you don't believe me, you can relive it thanks to YouTube. He would have deserved to go straight to jail, but Spanish referee Victoriano Sánchez Arminio didn't even show him a yellow card. This is how FIFA cared for the skilled: with matches played at high altitude, during the midday of a hellish summer, without repressing criminal violence? Meanwhile, João Havelange, the guy who presided over FIFA at the time, filled his mouth with words like 'show', 'sport' or 'fair play'. Pure blah-blah.

I don't know how Diego recovered from that and another dozen blows, but in that match he provided three assists for Argentina to win 3-0: two to Jorge Valdano and one to Oscar Ruggeri. The *Ten* seemed a beast as hungry as he was insatiable. The physical preparation and internal fire had made him an unstoppable bulldozer, who also threw rays of genius, like the goal that he scored against Italy. Frankly, I can't find how to describe what he invented in Puebla. Valdano played a ball that seemed complicated and he turned it into a poem: flying into the rivals' area, closely marked by the experienced defender Gaetano Scirea, Diego jumped over the corner of the small area and, in the air, as if suspended, he managed to get his left boot to caress the ball so that it passed away from goalkeeper Giovanni Galli. It seemed that the ball was going out, but no: it stung and twisted its course towards the net. How did he do it? No one could explain it. Not even he found a coherent justification. What I did notice is that in that action, which was resolved in a second or two, Diego used his privileged peripheral vision that Dal Monte had told me about, because only in this way can it be explained that at that moment the guy knew exactly where the ball, Scirea, Galli and the soda vendor who was passing by the stand were. Years later, when the goalkeeper went from Milan to Napoli, I asked him about that goal. He explained to me that he believed that Diego, from that angle and with the ball floating, would hit a powerful shot to the first post. Galli stiffened to hold the shot, which he anticipated going violently to his right, but when the ball took off towards the far post, he tried to turn and jumped to his left, but he couldn't. The only thing he did manage was to see the ball passing gently towards the bottom of his goal.

Diego told me many times that his best game in Mexico was the match against Uruguay. In that South American derby, the crossbar and the Italian referee Luigi Agnolin prevented him from establishing himself as the top scorer of the tournament. The referee unfairly annulled a goal scored by the Argentine captain in the second half, which would have allowed him to finish his World Cup with six goals, a record reached by top scorer Gary Lineker, from England, Argentina's rival in the quarter-finals. That was probably the most important game in Diego's life. From that 2-1, with a goal signed with his hand and another after a colossal slalom, he reached his throne in the pantheon of great myths, for his art and for the context in which he expressed it: that duel posed one of the greatest socio-political connotations in the history of football. Possibly bigger than the 1966 World Cup Final between England and Germany, two of the nations with a leading role in World War II. That game played in London happened 20 years after the end of the conflict, while the one that took place in the Azteca stadium hardly happened four years after the Malvinas War. If Argentina had not lifted the World Cup, perhaps things would have been more attenuated, but there is no way to measure that.

Against England, Diego perpetuated himself as a unique artist, endowed with inexplicable conditions for playing football and, especially, for tricking. First, with the 'Hand of God'. When I found out how his first goal had been made, because I was placed behind the goal and from there I did not see what he had hit the ball with – well, he always called me 'Blind' for a reason – I told him:

'The cheating is a mess, in sport as in life.'

'Don't tell me that, *Blind*, I stole them their wallet.'

'What a wallet! If Lineker had done it and England won by that goal, we would enter the war again, not for Las Malvinas but for the game.'

I am sure that if he had acted like the German Miroslav Klose – who playing for Lazio against Napoli asked the referee to cancel his goal because he had scored it with his hand – after a while he would have scored another, in addition to his famous 'Goal of the Century', of course. He had me by his side so that I could help him improve. Diego did not have to be an example of anything, but he was also a symbol for millions of boys in the world who must know that cheating is wrong. Sometime later, I read that, in the United Kingdom, the gambling agencies decided to return money to those who had bet on a draw between Argentina and England: beyond the official result of the match, the guys judged that Diego's first goal, scored thanks to the 'Hand of God', hadn't been legitimate.

The truth is that Diego was also used to cheating because, perhaps, without that help, many times he would not eat. He had practised that first goal against the English since he was a little boy: he went to the Fiorito train station, where there was a stand for the sale of fruit. He had studied that the train arrived, stopped on the platform, the doors opened, passengers got off and on, the doors closed after 30 seconds and the formation resumed its march. Diego was walking along the platform and, when the convoy stopped and the doors opened, he had already chosen the apple or the banana or the orange. He would slap his hand, get into a car through one door and get out of another. When the stallholder reacted, Diego was already a couple of blocks from the station enjoying his snack.

In the second goal against England, the one that encouraged the famous pundit Víctor Hugo Morales to describe him as a 'cosmic kite', Diego also made use of a trick. From the moment he took the ball that Héctor Enrique passed him to the finish, he took 12 seconds to run 55 metres. I have no doubt that, in a race over the same distance on a running track, Diego would have lagged behind the five Englishmen he left behind. But he surpassed them all thanks to his mischief. Deception makes the weak strong; and the slow fast. It is the most important resource in football: pretending to do something and invent something else. The main quality of a player is not being fast. It has been demonstrated by the Jamaican Usain Bolt, who tried several times to become a professional footballer and never reached the high level. Nor is it strength: Arnold Schwarzenegger could not have played football. Nor is it jumping: Cuban Javier Sotomayor does not know how to head a ball. The most important resource is knowing how to play, which is equivalent to a sum of physical and brain aspects, because the essential thing is to be quick of mind, strong of mind, agile of mind to be precise with the ball and solve complex situations in milliseconds.

By the way, I didn't see that goal well from my position either. In part because of my unprivileged view, but mainly because, as Diego approached Peter Shilton's goal, the photographers began to stand up to capture every moment of the masterpiece, and several of them, very tall, stood between the *Ten* and me. I was only able to enjoy the fantastic work of art when we returned to the campus. Someone asked Diego what he felt when he finished that prodigious play:

'That I was falling between two Englishmen, but raising a country.'

Like Leonardo da Vinci or Michelangelo, he was not born to be explained but admired. Like a lot of things – how do you measure love? How do you measure friendship? How do you measure the beauty of a landscape? From his achievements against more powerful countries or clubs, fighting from the supposedly weaker side, he became an argument of hope and joy for hundreds of millions of people, especially those who have the least. Diego was, ultimately, one of them. The most beautiful thing about him, what I value the most, is his commitment to his class status. He not only respected his origin: he was always proud of it.

When the passionate final against Germany came to an end, I advanced on to the pitch with hundreds of fans. I took a few steps and, when I reached the centre circle, I met Diego, who was surrounded by dozens of happy people.

My bones still ache from the tight, excited hug we gave each other! In that moment, Diego granted me the most precious gift that I could have imagined. With a broken voice and tears in his eyes, he whispered in my ear:

'Thanks for everything, *Fer!*'

A while later, after the awards ceremony and the lap of honour, the players, the coaching staff and the leaders of the Argentine Football Association improvised a party inside the dressing room, although brief, because we all had to return to the sports complex of Club América to pack our bags and split to the airport to take the flight that was going to take us to Buenos Aires. The boys had incorporated a very curious habit to attract good luck: when we returned from defeating Uruguay in Puebla, for the round of 16, one of the players noticed that no one had put their things away or packed their luggage, even though a fall against the South American rivals would have meant elimination from the tournament. From that day on, no one packed their bags before any of the matches, not even the final, despite the fact that, that same night, we all had to board a plane to Ezeiza Airport no matter how the match ended.

Having finished the concise celebration, everyone began to go to the bus except Diego and I, who were left alone in the shower area. Since he'd arrived from the field of play, he hadn't taken a second away from the cup to protect it while everyone else took pictures with it. Finally, he undressed, turned on the tap, and asked me to hold the trophy for him while he bathed. I was blown away by that little golden sculpture! As I looked at it and listened to the patter of the water, I remembered all the sacrifice Diego had made to win it. The hours and hours invested in improving the plasticity of his magical fractured ankle in Spain, and all the effort to physically prepare for a tremendous challenge, amid the heat, the altitude, the smog, the rivals.

Diego finished bathing and began to dry himself off. He laughed, seeing me hypnotised with the cup.

'So, *Blind*, do you like it?' he asked me, amused.

'Yes, but it has already passed.'

'What are you saying? How has it "already happened"?'

'Now you have to win the *Scudetto.*'

'Go on, *Blind*, don't break my balls: let me enjoy this!'

'I'll let you enjoy it, but just for a while. You achieved an objective, the one you longed for the most in life, but you still have many more laps of honour to do.'

He looked at me seriously, and after a few seconds he smiled. His eyes lit up, anticipating the battles looming on his horizon.

The flight back to Argentina and especially the arrival at Ezeiza Airport were unforgettable. When the plane began its approach manoeuvre to the head of the runway, all the passengers were dazzled by the spectacle that came through the windows: a massive and frenzied multicoloured anthill had approached to pay tribute to its sporting heroes. I remembered that when that same group left for Mexico, no one went to the terminal to say goodbye and wish good luck, except a few relatives. But, well, success is like that.

We got off the plane and, when we were crossing the airport hall full of people, Diego came towards me to tell me that we had to leave immediately, since we would go by bus to the Government House where President Raul Alfonsin was waiting, for the official congratulations.

'*Blind*, we're going to the Pink House. The President is waiting for us.'

'No, what Pink House? I do not go.'

I did not want to meet the national officials, including Alfonsin himself, who a few months earlier had pressured Julio Grondona to remove Bilardo, fearful that the team would fail. Those guys who wanted to kick him out, they ended up hugging and kissing with the coach. Also, I believed that the natural place to celebrate should have been a football field, and not the seat of the political power.

'No, stop fucking with me. I'm going to have maté with your mom and your old man at your house, I'll wait for you there.'

Together with *Doña Tota* and Don Diego, we followed the images of the Plaza de Mayo shown on television. The delegation arrived at the Government House, was received by the then-president Raul Alfonsin and, after the formal greetings, all the players and the coaching staff went out to the famous balcony of the *Casa Rosada* (Pink House) and celebrated the title with the thousands of fans who packed the traditional square. 'Alfonsin,' Diego would recall later, 'gave us the balcony. It was something very important and he understood it. He gave us the possibility of being next to people, he behaved very well.'

Several hours later, Diego appeared at the house on José Luis Cantilo Street, in the Villa Devoto neighbourhood, with Claudia, her siblings, and other people. We ate something and, after a while, I told him that I had to go to Lincoln, to see my wife and my family.

'Take a car,' he ordered me.

'What?'

'Take a car. Which one do you want, the Mercedes?'

The guy was showing his heart of gold again.

'No, *Die*. I appreciate it, but I came by bus, and I want to go back by bus.'

'Well, whatever you want, but I'll take you to the bus terminal.'

We got into the Mercedes-Benz and in a few minutes we reached the platform where passengers are dropped off by taxis or vehicles of friends or family. We said goodbye and I got out of the car. Diego rolled down the window and gave me one last greeting, affectionate as always. As I was walking towards the platform to board my bus, I came across two guys who were walking in the opposite direction, I guess they were newcomers after a long trip from a distant city of the country.

'Hey, it seems to me that the one driving the car that left was Maradona?' said one of them.

'You're crazy!,' replied his friend. 'What the fuck is Diego going to be doing around here?'

Chapter 6

'O sole mio

(Famous Italian song)

WHEN DIEGO returned to Naples loaded with glory and relaxed after a vacation with Claudia in Polynesia, the *tifosi* were torn between two feelings: on the one hand, hope, for the arrival of their messiah with a golden star on his chest; on the other, distrust, caused by the fear that the Mexican conquest would have appeased his hunger for titles. Neither group imagined what the 1986/87 season would bring them!

In our first meeting, I repeated to him what we had talked about in the Azteca stadium dressing room: the world title should not cloud his career. In Mexico, Diego had reached the top of the Himalayas, but that success had a precedent in the history of the Argentine team, because the light-blue-and-white national squad had made that lap of honour in the 1978 edition. However, nobody, absolutely nobody, had achieved leading Napoli to the Olympus in Serie A, a place that until then was inaccessible for the peninsular clubs located south of Rome since the birth of the professional league in 1929, nor during the amateur era, from the first championship, in 1898. The only 'different' team that had achieved a *Scudetto* had been the islander Cagliari, in the 1969/70 tournament.

The campaign began with a curious distaste. Diego, who enjoyed certain privileges granted by the president of the club, Corrado Ferlaino, decided to travel to the preseason in his own car: a black Ferrari Testarossa that he had just bought to celebrate the title he won in Mexico. Eager to test it, he decided to drive his brand-new vehicle to travel the 800km that separate Naples from the town of Lodrone, in the northern province of Trento, very close to the border with Switzerland, a place chosen by coach Ottavio Bianchi to prepare his team to face the demanding sports calendar. I got into the luxurious car and sat in the passenger seat. Diego got behind the wheel and we drove off. Within minutes, he was dominating the Ferrari like a professional driver. He accelerated on the straights, took turns with great skill. When we passed Bologna, Diego pressed the accelerator to the bottom and the vehicle flew up to 180km per hour. Within a minute we had a Polizia Stradale car behind us, chasing us with sirens howling and lights flashing. Diego pulled up to the side of the road and a uniformed agent approached to ask for the driver's registration and vehicle documentation. After checking identification and papers, the policeman informed him that he had exceeded the speed limit – Diego and I already knew it, without a doubt – and that he should seize the Ferrari. There the privileges ended. In addition, for the agent the situation had become very profitable: stopping a guy like Maradona, the best footballer in the world, was a pearl on his résumé. After a while a tow truck arrived with the back ready to load cars. In a few minutes, the driver put the Ferrari on the truck with the help of chains pulled by an engine. When the young man finished his work, with great dexterity, the policeman told us that we should go in the patrol car to the local station to pay the fine. Diego refused.

'I'm not getting into a police car,' he assured him with a tone loaded with annoyance.

'Well, there is another alternative: you can travel in the cab of the tow truck,' said the uniformed man, with a half-smile. He seemed to be enjoying the unusual situation that fate had brought him.

We climbed into the truck. Diego sat down in the seat in the centre, next to the driver, and I stayed on the side of the window. We left for the police station and the *Ten* would not stop bitching and cursing. 'You made progress, huh?' I joked. 'In half an hour you went from driving a Ferrari to being a co-driver on a tow truck.' He wanted to kill me!

'Can you imagine your friends watching you travel in this truck? What an embarrassment!'

He had a tremendous rage. We arrived at the police station, he paid the fine, they returned his car and we continued the trip. We arrived quite late at our destination, the Hotel Castel Lodron. Diego went to sleep immediately, without even saying 'good night' to me.

The next morning his mood had changed. I found him chatting animatedly with the owners of the lodge, Ferruccio and Gianluca Luzzani, to whom he had given watches. Diego became close friends with Ferruccio: several nights he went to his house in Ponte Caffaro to play billiards, and Claudia and Dalma, who was a baby at that time, stayed there the following year. Although Napoli stayed there for the last time in 1988, every summer dozens of Neapolitans make a pilgrimage there to fulfil a very unique wish: to spend a night in Diego's room in Castel Lodron.

The village of Lodrone, near the exquisite Lago di Garda, was an ideal place to prepare the team. The decision to move the preseason to that town was the work of coach Ottavio Bianchi, who was born in Brescia, a city located a few kilometres away. In that quiet and relaxed place, with just a handful of fans arriving from Naples, a team began to be forged that would remain in the history of Calcio. The training sessions were held at the Stadio Grilli, which was a couple of kilometres away but already in another town called Storo. It caught my attention that, after the enormous effort made in Mexico and the holidays in Polynesia, Diego was in excellent condition to face the preseason. He worked with a very high rhythm and, when Bianchi ended the afternoon football session, he would spend more than an hour practising free kicks. Afterwards, he would spend a long time satisfying the demand of the local boys, who asked him for autographs and photos. The stay closed with a friendly match against a local team, Unione Sportiva Benacense, at the Quercia stadium in the town of Rovereto.

For the 1986/87 season, the team was reinforced with the arrivals of Andrea Carnevale, from Udinese, and Fernando de Napoli, a former Avellino player. Meanwhile, the club got rid of Daniel Bertoni, who went to Udinese as part of the deal for Carnevale. In this way, Diego was the only foreign footballer in the squad.

The Serie A campaign got off to a successful start, with a win against Brescia as a visitor, 1-0. The goal? No, it was not a goal, but a great goal by Diego, very similar, almost traced, to the second that he had scored against Belgium a few months earlier at the Azteca stadium. 'Fortune is with Maradona,' he brightly commented to a television journalist. The aura that surrounded the victorious Diego prompted the reporter to compare him, once again, with the Brazilian Pelé. 'Maradona is Maradona. Pelé is the greatest. I'm just a normal footballer,' replied the *Ten* while he wielded a mischievous smile.

Despite the successful start, Diego's happiness would last very little. Six days later, on Saturday, 20 September 1986 in the afternoon, I returned home after the last training session prior to the match with Udinese, scheduled for the following day at the San Paolo. Around 2.30 in the afternoon, I received a telephone call from an Argentine guy named Carlos D'Aquila, who has played basketball for several Italian teams and had settled in Naples. He told me that he was in his apartment with a lawyer, Enrico Tuccillo, who represented a young woman named Cristiana Sinagra. Tuccillo wanted to speak with Diego because that night the RAI Campania newscast was going to present a report on the birth of a boy at the Sanatrix clinic.

'The lawyer tells me that if Diego agrees to declare himself the father of the child, he is going to prevent the broadcast from getting out.'

'Well, Carlos, this is something that exceeds me. Wait, I'll call Soccavo, because Diego is staying there. I'll talk to him and I will call you back.'

I knew Cristiana because she was a friend of *Turco* (Hugo) Maradona's girlfriend, Delia, and she had also given my wife Italian language classes.

I cut off and immediately called to the Napoli pre-game meeting place. The team was staying there for the match the next day, for the second fixture of the season. Fernando di Napoli, one of the new team-mates of the *Ten*, picked up the phone. I explained to him that I urgently needed to speak to *il capitano* and he offered to look for him, because he was in his room. Diego arrived in a good mood when he took the phone. With no alternative, I broke his good humour into a thousand pieces.

'What's up, *Blind*?'

I conveyed to him what D'Aquila had told me and suggested that we go to talk to Tuccillo.

'No, no, no, leave me alone!'

'No way. I'll take a taxi and pick you up. Wait for me at the gate of the complex.'

I went out and got a taxi. We went to Soccavo and, upon arrival, Diego was waiting for me alone. That afternoon, strangely, there was not a single Napoli fan at the entrance. He got into the vehicle and we left for Carlos D'Aquila's house, which was in the Posillipo neighbourhood, the same one where the Maradona family lived. The driver of the car couldn't believe who was sitting in his vehicle, and he spent the whole trip talking about the games he had seen, the goals he had screamed for ... but I barely answered, in monosyllables. Diego, on the other hand, did not open his mouth throughout the trip: grief had silenced him. To make matters worse, a day before, the *Corriere dello Sport* newspaper had published on its cover that Claudia was pregnant.

We arrived to D'Aquila's, got out of the taxi and went up to the apartment. Carlos and his wife welcomed us and we sat in armchairs in front of the lawyer. Tuccillo, heavy and bombastic, gave a lecture on talkativeness without content.

'I know that you are a champion in football as in life. Here is at stake the future of a baby who is obviously not guilty of anything. If you sign a document for me acknowledging paternity, I will prevent the RAI from issuing the note it recorded at the clinic.'

Diego followed his verbose statement with his head down, as if so many words were crushing his understanding. At one point, fed up with so much speech and sorry for what he was going through, I interrupted him. I couldn't control myself.

'Excuse me, lawyer, how are you so sure that Diego is the father of the child? How do you know that Cristiana was only with Diego?'

Tuccillo looked at me in surprise, as did D'Aquila. Diego, on the other hand, raised his head. His face had recovered a little colour and freshness.

'What are you saying?' the lawyer murmured, after several seconds of uncertainty. His sharp tongue had been nicked.

'How do you know that Cristiana was only with Diego?' I repeated.

The troubled lawyer did not know what to say. To this day, I still believe that he expected the *Ten*'s collapse and that he would offer him to strike a deal right there for a ton of money. I screwed up the advocate's strategy.

'But … but …' Tuccillo stammered, puzzled.

'But nothing. I ask you for the third time: how do you know that Cristiana was only with Diego, that he,' I pointed to Diego, 'is the father of the baby?'

The lawyer, almost on the verge of a heart attack, tried a ridiculous move. He cut off his conference with me and addressed Diego, whom he believed was still dejected.

'Mr Maradona,' he said, trying to compose himself from his hesitations, 'are you the father of the child?'

Diego looked at me before answering. He noticed my fiery and bloodshot eyes. There was no need for me to make a gesture. He understood everything instantly.

'Not in any way! And I'm not going to sign anything!'

Tuccillo's shoulders slumped. His lower lip trembled. His face turned red and a vein in his neck throbbed, as if he were about to burst.

'Very good,' he said, feigning sudden composure. 'So there is nothing more to talk about.'

We retired from D'Aquila's house. As we returned to Soccavo, Diego left his renewed spirit and plunged into a darkness that predicted a very black night.

'You already knew it?' I asked him without further details and in Spanish, so that the taxi driver, who pretended to be distracted but tried to guess what the Neapolitan star was doing inside his car on a Saturday at that time, wouldn't find out what was happening. Diego nodded.

'Before going to Mexico?'

He nodded again. At that moment I understood that the *Ten* had achieved the greatest individual performance in the history of the World Cup despite having the Sword of Damocles hanging by a very thin thread over his head, threatening to destroy his career, his world, his life as he knew it until that moment. Diego achieved an incredible power of abstraction during the Mexico World Cup that allowed him not to deviate from his great goal. He never stopped surprising me.

'What do I do now, *Blind*?' he asked me, dismayed.

'What are you doing now? We go urgently to your house. You have to prepare Claudia for the mess that is coming.'

Diego got off at his home and I continued to my apartment, from where I called the president of Napoli, Corrado Ferlaino, to update him on what was about to happen. He replied that he was immediately going to go to Diego's house with Coach Bianchi to restrain him.

Shortly after six in the afternoon, the RAI released a report recorded inside room 509 of the Sanatrix clinic, in which a journalist interviewed Cristiana, who was resting on a bed with a baby.

'You have given your son a very famous name. Why?'

'Because his father is a Napoli footballer.'

'Diego Armando Maradona?' the reporter insisted, with forced drama.

'Yes.'

A few days later, we met with Diego's lawyers, Giovanni Verde and Vicenzo Siniscalchi, who were devising a strategy to face a paternity lawsuit filed by Tuccillo in the city courts. Siniscalchi proposed to advance on the scenario that I had proposed at D'Aquila's house, although with greater cruelty. Verde refused:

'There is a boy involved,' he said.

The story has a known ending: the *Ten* denied being the father of Diego Maradona Sinagra, Justice ruled that he was the boy's legitimate dad and, some 29 years later, he finally recognised Junior as his legitimate descendant. But this story has one more twist, which could become the epitome of the best soap opera.

A few days later, a Neapolitan friend of mine, Alessandra, told me that she had been to Cristiana's father's hairdresser salon. When he learned that she knew me, Alfredo Sinagra asked her to ask me if I agreed to have a meeting with him.

'Perfect. But as long as he is at my house, and if he comes alone.'

Two or three days later, Alfredo Sinagra arrived at my apartment on Vía Manzoni.

I believed that the man was offended by what I had implied to Tuccillo. Instead, he surprised me with a cordial greeting.

'I just want to tell you that I fully understand what you suggested to the lawyer,' he said. 'I know that you know that it is an absolute lie, but I understand that you did it to defend your friend. That proves very well of the concept you have of friendship.'

He said goodbye with a handshake and we never saw each other again.

While the paternity case exploded in all the Italian media, Napoli ended the year with a remarkable succession of matches without losing: 13 in Serie A (six draws and seven victories, one of them highly celebrated, against Juventus in Turin, 3-1) and five in the Coppa Italia, all triumphs. Diego scored eight goals that helped consolidate leadership on both fronts. The only setback was recorded in the UEFA Cup: against Toulouse, Napoli won 1-0 at the San Paolo, fell by the same score in France and were eliminated on penalties. Diego missed the last one, which meant the defeat against a team that had two Argentines: Alberto Márcico and Alberto Tarantini.

Meanwhile, the *Ten* was training hard. The power work allowed him to discharge the negative energy that he absorbed in other areas. He had to fight against Michel Platini's Juventus, Silvio Berlusconi's Milan, Giovanni Trapattoni's Inter and especially in opposition to the northern press.

The year 1987 began with a loss to Fiorentina, but then the team got a fantastic series of five consecutive wins that allowed them to consolidate their leadership and not let go until the end. Diego destroyed any uncertainty regarding his motivation to conquest the *Scudetto* after winning the World Cup. He was at such an extraordinary level that only he occupied the two slots allowed for foreign players. He trained in parks, on the street, in the garage of his house, sometimes at night. He had one goal stuck in his head: to win the league title with Napoli, and he solved it masterfully, in a big way.

On 2 April, Diego got a new title: that of dad. The birth of Dalma Nerea made him very nervous. First, because he and Claudia had decided that the baby would be born in Buenos Aires. She travelled to Argentina and he stayed in Naples: he could not abandon the team in the final stretch of the tournament and with the *Scudetto* at hand. Second, because Dalma's arrival occurred one day before the date scheduled by Claudia's obstetrician. When he learned that his wife was about to be hospitalised to go into labour, Diego turned into a nervous wreck, called the Clínica del Sol in Buenos Aires from his home in Posillipo and stayed on the line – cell phones would only become popular a decade later – biting his nails until his mother *Doña Tota* announced that the baby had been born without complications and that both she and her mother were in perfect condition. The news did not calm the restlessness of the *Ten*, but rather the opposite: excited and eager to meet Dalma, Diego wanted to go to Rome to take the first flight to the Argentine capital city. I managed to control him. I explained to him that everything had turned out well, that waiting a couple more days would not change the life of the baby, but a stumble at Empoli could demoralise the team only five games from the desired title. Diego understood and calmed down. Well, more or less: his performance against Empoli, on Sunday, 5 at the Carlo Castellani stadium, was very weak. He had his mind on something else, logically. Luckily, the match ended goalless and Napoli were able to salvage a valuable point that brought them a little closer to winning the championship.

After that match, Diego travelled by car to Florence, took a plane to the Roman airport of Fiumicino and, mounted on another aircraft, flew to meet his daughter.

The following Saturday, Diego returned in time to focus for a very difficult duel, against Hellas Verona at the Marcantonio Bentegodi Coliseum in the city located in Veneto. However, Napoli again wandered the pitch and their rival crushed them mercilessly, 3-0. The defeat lit internal warning lights ... and external. Several newspapers published opinion columns of so-called 'specialists' who predicted a fall to pieces of the team. One journalist even had the courage to call the players *cretini* (idiots). At the foot of Vesuvius, the atmosphere had become rarefied, especially since the next rival was none other than AC Milan – with Fabio Capello's debut as coach – albeit at San Paolo. That week I decided to work in depth with Diego, but more from the mental than from the physical. Although I noticed that he was much calmer for having met Dalma and for knowing that both the baby and Claudia were very well cared for and looked after in the house they had bought in Villa Devoto, I injected his spirits with very spicy phrases while he demanded of himself intensely with power exercises.

'What do you want Dalma to eat, caviar or shit?' I yelled at him, and he killed himself to complete each series.

'Do you want Dalma to suffer the ridicule of her companions because her father is a chicken who lost the *scudetto* in the last game?' I was spurring him on. He would go crazy, he would vent fury up to his ears.

One afternoon I proposed to him to make a little bag in the garage of his house. He pulled on his gloves, eager to ease the tension that ran through his veins. I took the stopwatch and, before shouting 'now', I told him that inside the bag was

the journalist who had called him an idiot. My God! Poor
bag! He gave it so many punches and kicks that if the guy
had really been there, he would have died in three seconds.
My mental work had a prodigious effect: the following
Sunday, Napoli defeated Milan and Diego scored a goal, one
of the best of his career. Bruno Giordano played a precise
and precious pass to the back of sweeper Franco Baresi and
the *Ten*, from a legal position, without committing offside,
beat the defensive line and his personal follower, Filippo
Galli, killed the ball without letting it sting, made another
touch of a juggler to overcome with a dribble the approach of
goalkeeper Giulio Nuciari – Giovanni Galli did not play and
that day escaped being the victim of another brilliant piece
of art of his greatest executioner – and finished with a flush
left-foot shot that could not be covered either by Filippo by
the closing by Paolo Maldini. 'We put our hearts in, and our
hearts win,' Diego celebrated. 'This is the strength of the
dressing room, a dressing room that responds to those who
cover us with accusations, criticism and doubts.' A journalist
asked him what had changed in him since Dalma's birth:
'I am a father, that is the only change. I am still the same
footballer as before.'

That day, Napoli consolidated their leadership, which
they extended to three points ahead of Inter and four points
over Juventus a week later, drawing against Como on the
shores of the famous lake of the same name. The great
consecration finally came on 10 May 1987, a date before
the end of the contest, through a draw against Fiorentina
at the San Paolo and a fall of Inter in Bergamo, against
Atalanta. 'It is the most important triumph of my life,'
Diego declared to the press. 'I did not get the World Cup
in my land and this victory has been in front of a people who

esteem me,' he explained before the microphones. I did not agree, nor am I now, and I think, deep down, neither did he. Those were not studied words but an outlet, the product of having swallowed many unpleasant things since his return from Mexico.

Napoli accumulated 42 points in just 30 games, at a time that still rewarded victories with two points. They finished undefeated at San Paolo, and took three points ahead of second, which was Juventus. Frankly, I have never seen a celebration even similar to the one that was unleashed in Naples. The delirium engulfed the city completely, which ignited in such a way that it even aroused the envy of Vesuvius. Half a million people took to the streets and overflowed the historic centre with light-blue colour and joy. The horns of cars, motorcycles and scooters – called there *motorini* – sounded for several days, without ceasing. At last the poor south had brought the rich north to its knees. A pizzeria invited everyone for a slice of its new creation: the *Scudetto* pizza, which brought together the colours of the Italian flag with the format of the badge that would be embroidered on the Napoli jersey during the following season. On Monday, the banks did not open; cinemas either. There were no classes and no Justice courts. The Neapolitans enjoyed a spontaneous holiday.

The conquest of Serie A did not appease the hunger for glory of Diego and his team-mates: less than a month later, Napoli destroyed Atalanta in the Coppa Italia Final, 3-0 at San Paolo and 0-1 in Bergamo, and grabbed a second title that season.

Diego returned to his country confident of obtaining an award that was missing from his glass cabinet: the Copa América. Carlos Bilardo put together a team with many of the stars who had been crowned in Mexico, plus rising figures like Claudio Caniggia. In addition, Argentina was the host country. But Uruguay, also with a mix of veterans and young talents, spoiled the party: they defeated the white-and-light-blue squad 1-0 in the semi, beat Chile by the same score in the final and took a lap of honour.

Diego quickly passed the bad taste of the continental tournament. After the South American championship, I took the opportunity to go to Lincoln to visit my relatives. It won't have been more than two days when my home phone rang. The *Ten*, again!

'Hey, listen to me, what do you think if instead of going directly from Buenos Aires to Italy, we spent a week in Cuba?'

The first thing that occurred to me was that dark clouds were coming from the Neapolitan horizon.

'I don't know, Diego, don't you think …'

'I have an invitation from Fidel,' he interrupted me. 'He wants to meet me.'

'When do we go?'

So it was, I could not resist. Not every day is the opportunity to visit an admired country and meet with the legendary leader of the Cuban Revolution, Commander Fidel Castro Ruz.

I flew to Cuba with Diego, Claudia, Dalma, *Doña Tota* and three or four other people, among them the journalist Carlos Bonelli, who had managed the trip with a contact he had in the government of that Caribbean country. We landed in Havana, where an official delegation was waiting for us and took us to Varadero, a seaside resort that is about two hours by car from the capital of the country. There we stayed in a beautiful residence, in the middle of a dazzling seascape.

The days went by, splendid, but from Fidel Castro ... no news! The day before our return to Buenos Aires, when we were almost all convinced that we would only fulfil half of the dream, a government emissary came to the house and announced:

'Mr Maradona, in an hour we must leave for Havana. The Commander awaits you.'

They transported us to a house in Havana. We got there at noon and around seven in the afternoon they called us to tell us that at nine we had to be at the House of the Revolution for our interview with Fidel. Before going, I put eye drops in my eyes to see everything as best I could see and I uncovered my ears to hear everything, because I didn't want to miss a word.

We waited a long time – as they explained to us, the president had to attend to a series of off-schedule commitments that delayed the meeting – until, shortly before midnight, the imposing figure of Fidel received us adorned by a warm smile. Diego almost disappeared fleetingly as he was surrounded by Castro's long limbs as the two clasped in a moving embrace. For more than five hours, we were captivated by the overwhelming personality of the Cuban leader, full of enthusiasm and fine sense of humour. His boundless curiosity led him to ask if there was an infallible formula for shooting penalties.

'Tell me, how do you shoot penalties?'

'I take two metres of running, and I only raise my head when I support my right foot and I have my left foot ready to hit the ball. There I choose the post.'

'But what do you say? Do you shoot without looking at the ball?'

'Yes. Before kicking, I look at the goalkeeper,' Diego confessed. The Cuban president took a notebook, wrote down the formula, and replied:

'Tomorrow I will try it,' which unleashed the laughter of all those present.

During the historic meeting, which was accompanied by delicious oysters – produced in artificial hatcheries built to avoid contamination – and refreshing beers, Castro had proven to be a scholar on various topics, from seafood and child nutrition, to sports training.

'But you're not also a journalist?' he asked me.

'No, I'm Diego's personal trainer.'

'Hey, buddy, you're playing a trick on me. Why then have you made me talk so much about speed, endurance and other things?'

'Because I wanted to learn,' I replied. Fidel looked at me and smiled, while he nodded slightly.

Diego asked him if he had ever thought of cutting his beard.

'Just once, *chico*, just once. But luckily I realised what a mistake I was going to make, mate. My beard is already a symbol for many. Tell me, do you like Naples?'

'I don't know … it seems like a joke but after three years of being there, I still don't know the city.'

'Hey, mate, how is that?'

'I can't go out, Commander. Neapolitans are like that, only they understand it. I have to change the phone number every fortnight because we can't sleep because of the calls. I do not know, I am to them like a demigod. They compare me to Saint Gennaro. I tell you this in all humility.'

'I know, boy, I know. And what are you going to do with all this?'

'Put up with it. What else is left for me? They are like that, incredible.' After 3.30 in the morning, an assistant approached and gave us a wide range of gifts. Diego returned the courtesy with a shirt of the Argentine national team to which he wrote a beautiful dedication and stamped his signature. For my part, I gave Fidel two cassettes of the live recital that Horacio Guarany had recently performed in a packed Luna Park stadium, in Buenos Aires.

I had brought four books on the history of the Revolution for Fidel to autograph for me so that I could give them to some Argentine friends. The Commander not only agreed to sign them with pleasure, but he asked me who the recipients of these gifts were, in order to add a dedication.

'Who is this for?' he consulted as he opened one of the copies.

'For Cesar,' I answered.

'And who is Cesar?'

'Cesar Menotti, the coach.'

'I know him perfectly,' he interrupted. 'World champion in 1978. And this one for whom?'

'For Cain.'

'The relations between his family and the Catholic Church would not go very well when they chose his name. Who is this Cain?'

'He is a Veterinary Doctor from the city where I was born, Lincoln.'

'Lincoln … The only Yankee I would have chosen to play on my team,' he added, amused. 'Did you say Veterinary Doctor?'

'Yes, a specialist in animal genetics, an eminence worldwide in regard to ovum transplantation by surgical method in bovines. He was the first in Latin America to open a specialised clinic on the subject.'

'When was that?'

'I don't remember exactly. I think 1978, Commander.'

'Tomorrow [he ordered his secretary] you are looking for me in the file for the date we opened our clinic in Santiago. Because as you know [he turned to me again], there are two procedures for the transfer of eggs: a surgical transplant and a non-surgical one, in which local anaesthesia is used. And what is the difference? Well, the surgical guarantees a higher percentage of efficiency in terms of the number of conceptions, but it requires a lot of time and work to carry them out. On the other hand, the non-surgical one is simpler, but it is not as effective, in addition there are another series of …'

We could not believe the vastness of this man's knowledge. I was fascinated by his culture and his eloquence. Shortly before sunrise, Fidel began his farewell by thanking us for having accepted his invitation. At that moment, while the commander greeted *Doña Tota*, Diego whispered in my ear:

'May I ask him for his cap?'

'Yes, *Die*, of course. What is the problem?'

'Commander, excuse me, can I have it?' the *Ten* consulted as he pointed to the cap. Fidel, without hesitation, took it off and handed it to his illustrious guest, but before giving it to him he stopped and folded his arm.

'Wait, I'll sign it first, because, if not, it could be from anyone.'

He pulled a pen from a pocket of his military jacket and initialled the visor.

'Now, yes.'

Excited, Diego took the gift from him and put it on his head.

'I won't take this off anymore. I am going to go everywhere and I'll leave it in the squad hotel until the moment I enter the field. I won't wear it to play because it is illegal. If not ...'

The impending sunrise marked the end of a radiant night. When the farewell was completed and when we were on board the vehicle that would take us to the house, Fidel came running, and with a worried gesture, to the window where Diego was standing.

'So, before kicking the penalty, I have to look at the goalkeeper, right?'

Napoli successfully started the 1987/88 Serie A season. Diego kept the inner fire that drove him to fight each game in pursuit of victory active. In addition, Corrado Ferlaino had the lucidity to fill the second place destined for foreign footballers and to hire a great striker: the Brazilian Antônio de Oliveira, known by the nickname of Careca. With Diego, Careca and Bruno Giordano, Napoli put together a fearsome offensive trident that started the league in an overwhelming way: they won the first five games. The only bitter drink in that first segment of the season was experienced in the European Cup, against Real Madrid. The coach of the *Merengue*, the Dutchman Leo Beenhakker, arranged for defender Miguel Porlán Noguera, popularly known as Chendo, to mark Diego tightly. With the Neapolitan *Ten* annulled by the tenacious pressure of Chendo and the complicity of the passive Romanian referee Ioan Igna, Real Madrid won 2-0 in an empty Santiago Bernabéu: UEFA had sanctioned the Spanish club for violent incidents the previous year in a match against Bayern Munich. Only 70 people were allowed into the stands, and one of them was Ferruccio Luzzani, the owner of the Hotel Castel Lodron,

Diego's special guest. In the return leg, an early goal by Giovanni Francini, at nine minutes, enlightened the light-blue hope, but a goal from Emilio Butragueño, in the last play of the first half, put an end to the dream of the Neapolitans to win the biggest continental trophy.

Back at the local level, Napoli remained firm – they had nine victories and three draws in the first 12 matches – but in the 13th the alarms sounded: AC Milan, who had replaced Englishmen Ray Wilkins and Mark Hateley with the Dutch Ruud Gullit and Marco van Basten, and also had hired a very intelligent coach named Arrigo Sacchi – who had never played as a professional footballer and had even been a shoe salesman before becoming a coach – crushed Napoli at home 4-1.

At the beginning of November, Diego took advantage of a Sunday without Serie A to intervene in two very curious games. The first, on the 11th, took place in the city of Jedda, in Saudi Arabia. Diego accepted an invitation from a sheikh, Khalid bin Abdullah, to perform in a friendly with the Al-Ahli club shirt, against Brondby of Denmark. For performing in that one game, the *Ten* collected 250,000 American dollars and also received expensive gifts, such as a diamond-decorated scimitar and a solid-gold shield and medal. In that match, which served as a double celebration for the club's 50 years and the sheikh's 37, Diego scored two goals for a 5-2 victory.

Four days later, Diego flew to the Spanish city of Granada to fulfil a dream that had haunted him since he was a child: to play an 'official' game with his two brothers, Raul and Hugo. The meeting was organised at the Los Cármenes stadium of the Andalusian team – where *Lalo* was playing – to celebrate the club's promotion from Second B to Second, against the Swedish club Malmö FF, and also to raise part of the money for the travel costs of the footballer (and former tennis player) with a famous surname: Raul had come to the Iberian Peninsula from Boca Juniors. Diego and Hugo – at that time a forward for the Italian team Ascoli – did not charge a single peseta to accompany their middle brother. Granada won 3-2 thanks to a goal from Diego and another from *Lalo*.

Back in Italy, and after the stumble at the Giuseppe Meazza stadium, Napoli scored seven consecutive wins, but Milan were not far behind. After matchday 20, Napoli had 35 points; Milan, 30. With just ten games to go and five points ahead, when two were still awarded for a win, the league title seemed close at hand. One morning, during a training session, a journalist from *La Gazzetta dello Sport*, Rosario Pastore, told me very happily, 'The second *Scudetto* is coming.'

However, it didn't seem so clear to me. The heat had come on a bit early that year, with temperatures higher than usual, and coach Ottavio Bianchi was demanding too much from the boys in practice, which I found to be devastating.

'If the coach doesn't loosen the intensity of the training sessions, this team is going to fall apart,' I mused.

Unfortunately, my prediction came true: over the next seven games, the Neapolitan team won two, drew three and lost two. They reached matchday 28 with 42 points, the same amount they had collected to become champions the previous season, and there were still three games left – the first against Milan, who had come dangerously close, to within only one point, after four wins and three draws.

At that time, Diego showed me, with a gesture that was as transparent as it was coherent, that he had a good memory and that he would never betray his lineage. In 1982, while the media in Argentina debated the European fate of the Boca Juniors star, the aristocratic and millionaire María Amalia Lacroze de Fortabat, fed up and with obvious signs of irrepressible obfuscation, complained to a camera of a major television channel:

'With all the things that happen in the country, it is a shame to give so much importance to the sale of a simple football player.'

Diego learned of the prejudiced comment of the wealthy businesswoman – who, curiously, in those years was actively acting as a patron of a football club in her city, Loma Negra (founded by the homonymous cement company so that its employees could have fun playing sports in their free time), who had qualified for the national tournament – but preferred not to comment, despite harassment from the sports press. Six years later, when the silhouette of the *Albiceleste* champion shone majestically against Vesuvius, a young man appeared at the condominium on Via Scipione Capece 3/1 to announce to the *Ten* that he had a personal message from the famous owner of the cement company. Curiously, since he never agreed to receive strangers in his house, Diego accepted with pleasure (at least that was the state of mind that betrayed his wide smile) to listen to the message of the guy, whose hand he warmly shook.

'The lady wants to invite you for a ride around the gulf on her yacht, which is anchored on the island of Capri. It would be an honour for her.'

Diego crossed his arms, looked fixedly at his interlocutor in the eyes and replied very slowly, as if savouring each word with pleasant relish:

'Tell Mrs Fortabat that I am still a simple football player, the same one who left Argentina a few years ago, and that if it is an honour for her to be with me, for me it is no honour to be with her.'

In a split second, his wild smile had turned into a grim and spiteful gesture. And he finished with a blunt dart:

'Ah! Please, tell the lady that she can put her yacht into her ...'

Before saying goodbye, Diego regained his calm, gave the envoy an autographed shirt and very graciously agreed to take a couple of photos with him.

On 1 May 1988, San Paolo was the scene of an extraordinary match. Antonio Pietro Paolo Virdis opened the scoring for the visiting squad, and Diego equalised with a goal from a free kick in the last moment of the first half. In addition, the Neapolitans were left without legs and the Milanese took advantage: Virdis, again, and Van Basten, in a meteoric counterattack commanded by Gullit, finished off the task. Careca scored shortly from the end, but the draw never came. Discouraged by the *Rossoneri*'s forcefulness, Bianchi's boys deflated and also lost the last two games of the tournament, against Fiorentina and Sampdoria. Diego was the top scorer in the championship with 15 goals, a prize that in no way compensated for the lost *Scudetto*.

Diego's life in Naples continued to be difficult, as he himself had posed to Fidel Castro during our visit to Cuba. Once we tried to go to dinner at a restaurant in the Mergellina neighbourhood, but at a traffic light someone identified him and so many people gathered that it was impossible to continue to our destination. Another day, we managed to enter a jewellery store because he wanted to buy a watch. We were only able to escape the business when the *carabinieri* arrived and organised a kind of corridor for us to go inside our car. The *tifosi* surrounded the vehicle to ask Diego for an autograph or to take a photo with him, and as we started, the car was followed by a swarm of motorcycles and scooters to the place we were supposed to go. That was not how you could live with peace of mind!

After the 1987/88 league ended, Diego accepted the offer of a Japanese company to record a series of television commercials for a coffee that was sold in a can, to be taken cold, called Nova. The Japanese company had decided that the filming sessions would take place in the Colourado Canyon in the United States. However, when there were a few days left to travel, Diego changed his mind:

'I am not going to the United States. We'll do it in Argentina or we don't do it.'

Pelusa was willing to reject the contract, which was for a lot of money, if it was not done in the country he wanted. The businessmen asked for three days to answer, after which they replied that they accepted the footballer's position because they had found another scenario that perfectly fulfilled the idea they had approved for the commercial: the Talampaya National Park, in the Argentine province of La Rioja. We travelled with Diego and his brothers *Lalo* and Hugo, who would also act in the advertisements, and we settled in a hotel in the capital of the northern province. During the filming, the three Maradonas, dressed in a light-blue shirt, a little darker than Napoli, played little games and ran, passing the ball over the reddish and stony ground of the splendid place, which has nothing to envy in the famous tourist place of Arizona. Diego finished off each commercial by drinking the iced coffee straight from a can. Each of the three or four days that these advertisements lasted, Diego travelled to the set by helicopter, while the rest of the group did so by bus.

One night, the governor of La Rioja, Carlos Menem, invited us to dinner at the Government House. They all attended ... except me. I preferred to go to the casino, rather than share the evening with that politician who seemed very unpleasant to me.

For the 1988/89 season, the president of Napoli made several signings aimed at strengthening the team in the search for more trophies. Midfielder Massimo Crippa and defender Giancarlo Corradini arrived from Torino, and Hellas Verona sold goalkeeper Giuliano Giuliani, who replaced Claudio Garella, sold to Udinese. But the main addition was the Brazilian Ricardo Rogério de Brito, who was known as Alemão because of his blond hair. This player arrived at the club thanks to the opening of the quota of foreign footballers, which was extended to three per squad. Likewise, Serie A increased its number of teams, from 16 to 18. Well reinforced, the Neapolitan team had a very good first half of the season, with 12 wins, three draws and two losses. They were only one point behind the leaders, Internazionale de Milan, who had drawn one more game and lost one fewer.

After Napoli drew goalless with AC Milan at Giuseppe Meazza, an unusual incident took place: Diego took advantage of the trip to the capital of Lombardy to visit a clothing store – if I remember correctly, from the Versace brand. The game ended and he went from the stadium to the city centre. I went with the club's sports director, Luciano Moggi, to the airport, where the team was supposed to board a regular flight. We waited for the *capitano* until the last second and, as he did not arrive on time, we left without him. How did Diego return to Naples? When he arrived at the airport, very late, there were no commercial flights left to leave and the place was about to close. The hall was almost empty. Suddenly, a boy approached Diego to ask for an autograph. He, although he had been stranded by his delay, was in excellent humour: he took the paper and the pen from the boy's hands and stamped his signature. Then he handed them back to him and patted his head. The kid walked away, happy. While Diego was debating what to do to return to Naples, he was approached by a very elegant gentleman, impeccably dressed. The man introduced himself as the father of the boy who had asked for his autograph and thanked him for the gesture he had made with his son.

'What are you doing here at this time?' he asked.

'I came to take a flight but I was late and the plane left without me.'

'Are you travelling to Naples?'

'Yes.'

'Do you want to get to Naples tonight?'

'Yes, but there are no more flights ...'

'Wait a moment please.'

The man walked away to make a phone call and returned to Diego.

'If you want, I'll take you. I'm going south on a private plane. I can drop you off in Naples and then I will continue my journey.'

Diego accepted and returned that same night to his house. He is the first person I've known to hitchhike on a plane.

During the second half of the season, Napoli were losing valuable points, while in Europe they advanced in the UEFA Cup: PAOK of Greece, Lokomotiv Leipzig of East Germany and Girondins Bordeaux of France were their first victims. In the quarter-finals, Diego's team lost 2-0 to Juventus at the Stadio Comunale in Turin. But, in the rematch at the San Paolo, the *Ten* and his cronies gave a festival of football and courage and won 3-0.

In the first match of the semi-final, the Neapolitan squad prevailed with great authority over Bayern Munich, with a goal from Andrea Carnevale and another from Antonio Careca. A few days later, and before the return game at the Olimpic Stadium in the Bavarian capital, we met for dinner at Diego's house with him and the Brazilian forward, with whom we had formed a deep friendship. Over dinner, Diego and Careca started speculating about the match in Germany.

'It's a difficult game,' Antonio said at one point.

I got involved, because I disagreed with them and also to lift their spirits:

'Sorry, what is the difficult game?'

'The rematch with Bayern.'

'You are crazy! Any serious team that goes two goals ahead and is going to play away cannot lose. And in your case, it is practically impossible. Napoli is already in the final!'

'No, *Fer*, it's not so easy.'

'That's not easy? Look, Antonio: at some point, the Germans are going to open up, because they have to score two goals to draw level. You, with your speed and his left foot,' I pointed to Diego, 'you're going to have a picnic. A piece of cake! Remember well what I am telling you!'

'Do you think so?'

'I repeat: Napoli is in the final.'

On 19 April 1989, Napoli eliminated Bayern Munich and fulfilled my prediction. They drew 2-2 and Careca scored both goals for the Italian team, both from a counterattack and after two assists from Diego. Exactly as I had said.

A month later, Napoli established themselves as brilliant UEFA Cup champions after beating Stuttgart 5-4 on aggregate: 2-1 in Naples and 3-3 at the Neckarstadion. The Maradona–Careca tandem performed so well in this contest that between the four semi-final and final matches, the Brazilian got five goals, all after assists from Diego. In those four games, Napoli scored another four goals: one by Andrea Carnevale and the other by Ciro Ferrara, both after a pass from the *Ten*, who also got another. Impressive! Diego was involved in eight of the nine Neapolitan goals in those decisive matches.

There is a very interesting fact that I do not want to miss: before the start of the game at the Olympic Stadium in Munich, Diego warmed up as usual, jumping, shaking all the muscles, playing with the ball, with his boots untied. As in almost all football scenarios in the world, during the minutes before the kick-off, music usually plays through the loudspeakers. That day, one of the songs was 'Live is life', performed by the Austrian band Opus, and Diego took advantage of the rhythm to get ready for the match. This series of pre-competitive exercises was not seen on television, but a Dutch journalist, Frank Raes, recorded the movements of the *Ten* to the beat of the music and used those images – which the fans also savoured that day on the giant screen of the Bavarian coliseum – to a documentary that went around the world. Today, in almost all football stadiums, 'Live is life' sounds before the games. Thanks to Raes ... but mainly to Diego.

Warming up should be a personal act. When I worked with Cesar Menotti at the Italian club Sampdoria, I had the opportunity to see a very curious aspect of professional footballers. Before the start of the first session, Cesar gathered the squad in the central area of the field and, after a brief introductory talk, he left me in charge of the group. I looked at the players and passed them a very simple warm-up instruction:

'You have ten minutes, each player should do whatever comes to mind,' I said.

The players, surprised as I had anticipated, looked at each other and immediately directed their gaze in an almost inquisitive way to the defender Moreno Mannini, historic captain of the Genoese club, who with visible perplexity walked down the centre line towards the side of the pitch. Once there, Mannini began to trot gently to one of the corners, counterclockwise, followed by his companions in a long line, two at a time. When they reached the opposite half, I called them all to midfield and asked:

'Moreno, how many games have you played as a professional?'

'Close to 400, *Profe*.'

'And you, Siniša?' I consulted Serbian defender Siniša Mihajlović.

'About 300, more or less.'

'You, Jürgen?' I continued with the German Jürgen Klinsmann.

'It must be around 500.'

'Very good. And tell me, please: do any of you remember having gone around the pitch in some of those games?'

'How? I don't understand,' Mannini intervened, giving voice to the general confusion.

'Of course, I'm asking if you remember having to go around the pitch in the middle of one of the hundreds of games that each of you has played.'

The Neapolitan Vincenzo Montella, a faithful exponent of the slyness that characterises southern Italian footballers, intervened with an astute phrase:

'Obviously not.'

'So why do you do things in training that you never did or will never do during the game? Why is everyone doing the same thing that Moreno wants to do? Can anyone think of anything different?'

The boys looked at me disconcerted.

'Let's start again! But from now on, I want everyone to do something you normally do in matches, with absolute freedom, for ten minutes.'

It caught my attention to see the enormous difficulty that most footballers had to imagine any of the infinite possible variants to start the warm-up for training. Always accustomed to respecting instructions, the freedom that I invited them to enjoy worked, paradoxically, like an invisible net that imprisoned them.

It does not take a great intellectual effort to understand how harmful it can be to try to impose changes in habits so opposed to the models usually used. This type of aggression to the customary patterns provokes in its victims an understandable and spontaneous rejection, due to the insecurity that it generates. It is advisable, at the beginning, that a physical trainer adapts himself to 25 or 30 players, rather than all these to just one person. Common sense, patience and good manners are, in my opinion, the appropriate weapons that experience and intelligence put at our service, since convincing is better than imposing.

The continental title was achieved on 17 May, one day after the birth of Gianinna Dinorah, Diego's second daughter, in a clinic in Buenos Aires, like her sister Dalma. Of course, the *Ten* dedicated the title obtained to the newcomer.

The UEFA Cup was celebrated with a rain of goals (4-1) that flooded the San Paolo when the light-blue team received Torino for the 29th matchday of Serie A. However, the *Scudetto* was far away: only five games away from the end, Inter had 50 points, while the southern squad, second in the standings, had 43. The two teams met in Milan the following Sunday: Napoli took the lead with another goal from Careca, but Inter got two goals and, with that vibrant victory, made a lap of honour at Giuseppe Meazza four games before the end of the league season.

The 1989/90 season began with a change of command in the team – Alberto Bigon replaced Ottavio Bianchi – and with a conflict between Diego and President Ferlaino, based on the interest of a French club, Olympique de Marseille, to acquire the *Ten*'s services. The owner of the Provençal team, Bernard Tapie, had become obsessed with incorporating Diego, to the point of offering him a contract that exceeded, and by far, the salary that Napoli paid him, in addition to proposing to him to live in a villa facing the Mediterranean Sea. The offer was made by the team's coach, Michel Hidalgo – France's manager in Mexico 1986 – who met Diego at Posillipo's house a few days before the end of the 1988/89 season. Tapie also started a negotiation with the Italian club, but Ferlaino refused to let his top star leave and flatly rejected the proposal. Diego, very angry, went on vacation with Claudia and the girls to Argentina.

In Buenos Aires, the *Ten* agreed to participate in a meeting named the 'Solidarity Game', called by Argentine President Carlos Saúl Menem, who had assumed his mandate a few days earlier. The match pitted a team of local figures against an Argentine squad led by Carlos Bilardo, made up of many of the players who would travel to defend the title at the 1990 World Cup in Italy – Nery Pumpido, Ricardo Giusti, Néstor Fabbri, Julio Olarticoechea, José Basualdo, Claudio Caniggia and Diego – and Menem himself, who was 59 years old at the time, as a starter with jersey number 5 and the captain's armband on his left arm! Diego had invited me to go to the Velez stadium to witness that parody set up to praise that despicable guy – his opponents, more like accomplices, did not mark him all night and gave him as much space as possible for him to show off with a pair of successful passes – but I refused to be a spectator of that charade.

I took the opportunity to take a bus and go to Lincoln for a few days to see my family and friends. After the holidays, I returned to Naples, but Diego left for a few days to Esquina, the town of Corrientes where his father was born, to fish and hunt with a group of friends. Bigon started the preseason with almost all of his footballers, except his best player. Italian newspapers, especially northern ones, feasted on the story – also the Argentine magazine *El Gráfico*, through its correspondent in Italy, Bruno Passarelli. This guy wrote several articles with a lot of bad blood. In one, he emphasised that, while waiting for the *Ten* to return, I had gone to Capri for a weekend to sunbathe. What did he want me to do? How could I train Diego with me in Naples and him in Argentina? In addition, I had not gone to Bali, but to a place located just about two hours by boat from the Neapolitan port. I was very angry with the attitude of Passarelli, a journalist whom I myself had once invited to Diego's house for an interview. He had arrived with his son, for whom Claudia very kindly prepared chocolate milk and a sandwich. But later, as Diego was angry with the directors of the magazine, Passarelli decided to play for the bosses.

Finally, the *capitano* arrived. Bearded, somewhat misaligned, downcast, unmotivated. The first day we met, he told me that he didn't want to play for Napoli anymore, that he couldn't stand Ferlaino, that he needed a change of air. I had to face, once again, the double responsibility of preparing him physically and mentally. There was less than a year left before the World Cup in Italy and he had the possibility of ratifying his football status and being a leader in the largest football arena.

'Diego, next year the World Cup will be played. You are in an ideal moment: you are not young or old, you are an expert. No one can guide the national team better than you.'

The phrase clicked inside his head, and he quickly traded sloppiness for motivation. I started to design the work to get the machine ready. Since Serie A had already started, with a Napoli side that had climbed to the top thanks to three victories and a draw, the first thing that occurred to me was to carry out a brief preseason in Soccavo, in full view of journalists, to stop the commenting nonsense. For the opening session, I telephoned Gennaro Montuori, the well-known *tifoso* nicknamed *Palummella*. I warned him that at four in the afternoon we would go to train with Diego and I asked him to come to the sports centre with some fans, to deny that the fans were angry with his greatest idol. When we arrived with Diego at Soccavo, there were about 70 supporters who cheered to the *Ten* with great affection, in front of about 20 or 30 journalists who had also attended the appointment. I remember that we closed that first training session with a penalty shoot-out between Diego and me, 'face to face', in one of the goals of the auxiliary pitch where the team practised. We began to kick and catch, alternately.

The first eight were sent to the net, all of them. Four of his and four of mine. I always shoot to the same side, to the left of him, instead of hitting across the ball, and I made fun of him every time I converted. He too, of course, made fun of me. He was more relaxed and his desire to return to San Paolo began to show. Diego kicked his last penalty and the ball hit the crossbar and went out. It was my turn for the tenth: if I converted, I'd won. Before running towards the ball, I thought, 'If I win, over in front of the press and many fans, he will feel bad.' But I immediately reconsidered: it was just a simple game, and I probably wouldn't have another chance to beat the best player in the world. I shot to the left of him again, and he flung to the right again. Goal. With my victory accomplished, I began to walk towards the locker room. Their screams for revenge must still be echoing through Soccavo:

'*Blind*, son of a bitch, give me revenge!'

'What do you think, this is the end of the world? I'm not giving you a damn about revenge.'

He bitched at me three days in a row!

On Sunday, 17 September, Diego came out through the tunnel of the San Paolo stadium wearing a different shirt: number 16. With a leisurely step, wearing only socks and his ankle boots linked by the laces and hanging from his left shoulder, he walked towards the substitutes' bench greeting the public, the ball boys and other acquaintances who welcomed him on the grass with a huge smile. The first half of that match, against Fiorentina, was a monologue by a young star: Roberto Baggio. He put in a wonderful performance, scoring two goals and driving the entire Neapolitan defence crazy. At half-time, Diego told Bigon that he wanted to come on. The coach approved the suggestion and sent him on to replace Massimo Mauro. The first ball that touched the No.16 was a penalty, which was saved by the Tuscan goalkeeper Marco Landucci. History seemed decided, but the gears were quickly adjusted and the local team showed that they were in for great things when they turned the score to win a thrilling 3-1.

'I'm very happy because we managed to turn it around,' Diego commented to a journalist at the end of the meeting. He also reserved a few words to formulate a healthy self-criticism. 'I was walking and my companions were flying at a thousand kilometres an hour. I hope to be back in shape as soon as possible.'

And he was. In the following five matches, Diego scored one goal per game.

On 7 November 1989, Diego and Claudia were married in Buenos Aires. The religious wedding was held at the Basilica of the *Santísimo Sacramento* (Blessed Sacrament) and the party at Luna Park stadium, which was lavishly decorated for the occasion. Diego, Claudia, their daughters and their parents occupied a seat of honour on a box raised 1.5m above the ground, from where they could observe the more than 100 tables where their 1,200 guests were located, many of them having arrived especially from Italy on a charter flight, like the Napoli footballers or Dr Antonio Dal Monte.

I did not attend the 'bachelor party' held the night before the wedding, but some of its participants did tell me that the issue was very spicy. And it was dramatic for goalkeeper Giuliano Giuliani: there, as Giuliani himself confessed, he contracted the HIV virus. The Italian newspaper *Corriere della Sera* published that, shortly before he died in the Sant'Orsola hospital in Bologna, in November 1996, the goalkeeper declared to his ex-wife, a very beautiful woman named Raffaella Del Rosario, who was a television presenter, that he had contracted the disease on that 'crazy night' in Buenos Aires, in which he had had 'unprotected sex'.

Back in Serie A, Napoli and Milan reached the penultimate round of the season neck and neck, with 47 points. That day, the southern team beat Bologna 4-2 at the Renato Dall'Ara, and the *Rossoneri* fell at the Marc'Antonio Bentegodi stadium, the home of Hellas Verona. The second Neapolitan *Scudetto* crystallised a week later at the San Paolo, with a 1-0 win over Lazio. Despite not having been present in the first four and a half games, Diego established himself as Napoli's *capocannoniere* (top scorer), with 16 goals.

The luxury yacht of Corrado Ferlaino finished off the great celebration, to which strange faces of politicians and other characters of obscure profession crept in. I toasted Diego's success, and the World Cup that was approaching radiantly to invite him to a new adventure.

Chapter 7

Un'estate italiana

*('An Italian summer' – official song of the
Italy 1990 World Cup)*

IF IN Mexico Diego was crowned the most valuable player at
the World Cup, in Italy he established himself as a hero who
put passion before pain. I have never seen a greater example of
courage, commitment and self-love on a pitch than the one he
demonstrated during the Italian World Cup. Diego irrigated
Italian football fields despite the conjunction of two injuries
that, even separated, would have ruled out the bravest. He
played the seven games – three in the first round and four in
the second, from the eighth to the final – in totality, with two
extra times – one in the quarter-finals, another in the semi
– without leaving the pitch for a single second, despite the
big toe of his left foot being shattered, and that his left ankle
had swelled so much from a blow that, more than a joint, it
looked like a grapefruit. But let's go in stages because, as had
happened for the Mexican Cup, Diego began to experience
the 1990 World Cup long before the opening match.

About three months before the kick-off of the universal
contest, we returned to the teacher Antonio Dal Monte's

institute to carry out another general check-up prior to the great challenge. Also joining us were Claudio Caniggia, Sergio Batista and Oscar Ruggeri, who had some injuries, and Jorge Valdano, who had retired in 1987, affected by hepatitis, but was trying to play his third World Cup after Carlos Bilardo proposed to him to join the Argentine national team. Bilardo made the offer to him during Diego's wedding party at Luna Park. Later, when the 'European' group was returning on the charter flight, I introduced Jorge to Dr Dal Monte. Valdano had planned to arrive in Naples and take another plane to Madrid, but he agreed with Dal Monte that he would call him to make an appointment and get his studies done at his clinic. Jorge worked hard, made a great effort, but in the end Bilardo decided to leave him out of the Italian tournament. Disenchanted, Valdano once said, 'I swam across the ocean and drowned on the shore.'

A few days after he left the team to compete in Italy, we were drinking maté with Diego and he told me:

'I also want to quit'

'Why?'

'I feel sorry for the brutal effort made by Jorge.'

'Well, *Die*, it was one of the risks I was taking. He made an amazing recovery, yes, but Bilardo's decision is also within the rules of the game.'

Diego understood, although he was hurt for his friend. Not only because of everything Valdano represented for the group, but because, when he found out about Bilardo's offer, the *Ten* had ended up convincing him that he could play the World Cup.

After the examinations, Dal Monte determined that Diego was very well, although he showed in his body the weight of a season that had been hard: in addition to having fought until the end of the Serie A that awarded his second *Scudetto*, Napoli advanced to the semi-finals of the Coppa Italia (in which they were eliminated by AC Milan) and in the UEFA Cup he added three rounds, until falling to Werder Bremen of Germany in the round of 16. Dal Monte, who kept his flame as a researcher and inventor alive, offered us a bicycle ergometer with a very high-definition technology, designed to evaluate the physical condition of high-performance athletes. As always, Diego was fascinated by the device and his dashboard full of lights, buttons, knobs and connections for cables that I attached to him with small suction cups in different parts of his body. We bought and installed it first in the Neapolitan house, and then in one of the gymnasiums of the training camp chosen by Carlos Bilardo: the Fulvio Bernardini sports centre of the Associazione Sportiva Roma located in the Trigoria area, in the southern portion of the Eternal City. There, some 40km from the famous Colosseum and the old Forum, we also installed a very modern treadmill, in front of which I placed a mirror, following the advice of our guru from Acqua Acetosa. Dal Monte also recommended to Diego the services of a masseuse who worked on his back and his waist every day, where he used to feel pain. Likewise, he followed a special diet prepared for him by a Catalan nutritionist named Henri Chenot, designed for him to arrive at the World Cup at his ideal weight: 76kg. We had met Chenot at the Hotel Palace Merano, a detoxification, energy regeneration and Spa centre located on the outskirts of Bolzano, in the Italian Tyrol, where Diego stayed a couple of times with Claudia and me to regain strength and take a break from the exhausting Serie A.

To shore up his state of mind, I insisted that, at 29, he could compensate with experience and his inexhaustible winning character for any eventuality that impaired his physical display. I was not wrong. One week before the World Cup, Bilardo organised a practice match against a youth team from AS Roma club. In one play, a boy tried to take the ball from Diego and accidentally kicked the tip of his boot. Diego fell in pain and, when we checked him, we discovered that the blow had ripped the nail of the big toe of his left foot. From there, he entered a situation of anguish because, after so much sacrifice made a week before the World Cup, in a friendly against young boys he had to suffer a very untimely injury that had put his participation in the World Cup at risk. But, once again, based on a lot of self-esteem and the talent of Dr Dal Monte, Diego was reborn. Dal Monte made him a carbon splint that had to be adhered to the injured toe before each training session or games. The prosthesis solved one problem, but created another, because Diego, when putting on the cast, suffered a horrifying stabbing pang, so much so that the team doctor, Raúl Madero, had to inject him with an anaesthetic before each match. He played all seven matches of the tournament with his toe anaesthetised!

On 7 June 1990, a few hours before the light-blue-and-white team faced Cameroon at the opening of the World Cup in Italy, the players and the coaching staff visited the Giuseppe Meazza stadium to carry out the usual reconnaissance of the field. Diego and I began to practise penalties in one of the goals. We were kicking and, through one of the entrances to the field, behind the opposite goal, a group of people appeared, led by Argentine President Carlos Menem.

'Wow, shit!' I yelled to the *Ten*, loud enough for him to hear me, but not for the troupe approaching us from the side of the pitch. Diego continued, without giving much importance to the presence of the president that he himself had met in La Rioja during the filming of a series of commercials for a Japanese drink.

I had read a very funny note from *Humour* magazine that listed a series of unfortunate events that coincided with situations involving the former governor of La Rioja, whom many called *g* precisely so as not to attract misfortunes: the article mentioned that, during the electoral campaign of the presidential elections of 1989, two trucks with people who had greeted him during a ceremony fell apart, and that on that same tour a plane belonging to the delegation had crashed. The next day, Menem visited the two survivors … who died three days later. During that campaign, his personal doctor also had an accident and died. On the day he was sworn in as president, his son Carlitos suffered a collision on his motorcycle. The list was quite long and some of the adversities were hilarious. 'Please, tell him do not travel [to Italy for the first game],' claimed the publication. But he travelled. I don't believe in witches, but I admit that that afternoon, when I saw him, I was one of the many present who, almost without realising it, prayed to God. It had occurred to Menem to give Diego an official passport and to appoint him ad honorem advisor to the government 'for sports matters and dissemination of the Argentine image abroad' – a demagogic stupid thing whose sole objective was to take advantage of the popularity of the best footballer in the world. When *Méndez* needed to let go of his hand and plunge him into a barrel of shit to cover up the corruption reports that exploded in the press, he did it without blushing. But that Milanese afternoon, an advisor to the Argentine president approached Diego to ask him to accompany him to one of the stadium halls where the official ceremony would take place to receive the distinction from the president.

'Will you accompany me, *Blind*?'

'No, don't fuck with me! I'm staying here, you go!' I replied. As had happened in La Rioja, I preferred to stay away from that despicable man.

Diego was very happy with the designation, which he celebrated with his parents. But I have no doubts: what happened the next day in that same stadium had a lot to do with the presence of *Méndez* in the official box. Not only because Argentina, the world champion, lost to Cameroon – a team with just one World Cup antecedent, Spain 1982, in which they had not progressed past the first phase – 1-0. Diego also received two terrible impacts: a murderous blow to the chest from his personal marker, Víctor N'Dip, and a devastating kick to the left ankle, which had been fractured by Andoni Goikoetxea during his time in Barcelona. As if all that were not enough, during that same game a ball hit him in the ear and blew a diamond ring that Claudia had given to him. The jewel, valued at some thousand dollars, could not be recovered.

A while later, when facing the microphones of the press, Diego unloaded some of his anger with a shrapnel of irony: 'The only pleasure was to discover that, thanks to me, the Italians of Milan stopped being racists: today, for the first time, they supported the Africans.'

One thing I remember, and with pride, happened during the opening game warm-up. The pre-competitive exercises were not done on the grass of the Milanese stadium – at that time the opening ceremony of the World Cup was taking place – but in a covered gym located under one of the stands, with the two teams distributed in two rectangles marked on the floor, separated by just five metres. While the African boys were warming up, Diego appeared, his laces untied, as always. He started playing games, passing the ball from one side to the other, as he usually did in Naples, and the rivals stopped running and stretching their muscles to see him. They were shocked! The Cameroon physical trainer had to give several screams to wake them up from that magnificent hypnosis. Later, when all the players headed towards the changing rooms to put on their official jerseys, they all wanted to take pictures with the light-blue-and-white captain. Photos that later were 'thanked' with strong kicks.

Back in Trigoria, Diego's room looked like the Snowman's cave: we put ice bags on his ankle, on one knee, on his chest where N'Dip had left his studs tattooed. The Argentine captain was a pack of ground beef! I thought that he was not going to be able to continue, but by dint of infiltrations, of courage, of rebelling against everything, he returned to the fields, game by game. I saw him as a wounded animal that prefers to die fighting than to surrender meekly to its hunters.

The joint injury worsened in the match against Romania, the third and last of the initial phase. The defender Iosif Rotariu delivered a brutal puncture to his left ankle which, due to his successive blows, inflated like a balloon. It seemed that Diego had a tennis ball or an orange tucked under his skin at the level of the joint, which the next day dawned black, like the eight ball in a pool game. Between the big toenail problem and the swollen ankle, no boot fit. Diego had to ask the people from the Puma company to make him a special shoe for the next match, against Brazil. Nothing less than against Brazil, a classic rival by neighbourhood, which Argentina had never been able to beat in a World Cup – they had faced each other in 1974, 1978 and 1982, with a balance of one draw and two victories in favour of the yellow-and-green jersey. Diego, on the other hand, had to face two of his Napoli cronies: Antonio Careca and Ricardo Alemão de Brito.

After a couple of Italian newspapers published the days before the South American duel that Diego's ankle was a pure lie, I recommended that he appear before the journalists in flip-flops, so that everyone could see and record the condition of the joint. I did not do it to open the umbrella in case of a possible defeat – which the general press predicted as the most logical result, because the *Albiceleste* team played very badly, with many of the footballers at the limit of their possibilities, and their rival had won the three games from the group stage – but to raise awareness in the referees and to assume a more protective behaviour of the talented players.

Before leaving Trigoria to face Brazil at the Stadio delle Alpi in Turin, the wealthy city of Juventus, Diego was asked by an Argentine journalist if the light-blue-and-white squad had a chance to overtake their classic rival. He replied with a smile:

'In football there are miracles.'

Upon arriving at the Turin hotel, Bilardo noticed that a wedding party was taking place in one of the rooms. The coach remembered that one of his Italian grandmothers had once told him that brides usually convey good luck, so he sent all the players to greet the newlywed. Fortunately, her husband and the rest of the attendees took on the Argentine invasion with humour and good vibes.

On the morning of the game, Diego could barely step on his affected foot. He would take a step and see stars. When he got to the locker room, he asked Dr Madero to extract some of the coagulated blood that was piercing his ankle. After several unsuccessful attempts, the doctor finally stuck the needle in while Diego bit a towel to endure the pain. The joint was in misery, but Diego, anyway, was Diego. With unrivalled self-esteem and bravery, he created the play that defined the fight. He took the ball inside the central circle, on the Argentine side, eluded his Neapolitan team-mate Alemão, surpassed Dunga in speed and, surrounded by Mauro Galvão and Ricardo Rocha, drew a perfect pass, with a right touch, which enabled Claudio Caniggia. *El Pájaro* (The Bird) dodged goalkeeper Cláudio Taffarel and scored the only goal of the game.

The final result, it must be said, does not reflect at all what happened that day on the field. Brazil were much superior and did not win due to the perfect work of goalkeeper Sergio Goycochea and the help of the posts, who denied the *Verdeamarelos* a goal three times. For me, that match was one of the greatest sporting injustices that I had the opportunity to witness.

Much has been said about a serious complaint made by the Brazilian left-back Cláudio Branco Leal: in a stoppage of the game, *Galíndez* – who also acted as a water man for the Argentine team – entered the field and distributed canteens with crystalline liquid to his compatriots, but he reserved one with an adulterated mixture, which he handed over to rivals. Branco drank and, according to him, began to feel bad. I admit that, during the game, I noticed that he was not well. Sometime later, I heard what *Galíndez* and Diego himself said in television interviews.

The way of understanding football is also a way of understanding life. You cannot dissociate the coach from the man. Cesar Menotti was a guy who made a flag out of ethics. And Carlos Bilardo could use any means to win. This assessment of ethics is what I call 'diametrically opposed', because if you had to put what they put in the bottle to Branco in the World Cup in order to get the result, Menotti would have taken the canteen and drank all its content himself. On the other hand, I think that Bilardo was generally a very weak guy, who needed as much of the triumph as the timorous ones need so much of the power. Confident men and women are not interested in power; perhaps they exercise it without knowing it, but they do not seek it as an end in itself. Bilardo did not care about the forms in his obsession to win, and Menotti put the forms before the triumph, and it seems great to me because it is a learning for life. Cheating is filth in sports and in any field. As I said in the chapter dedicated to the World Cup in Mexico, Diego's hand was crap. Football is a wonderful excuse to be happy, but it is also a powerful weapon in favour of the formation or deformation of young people and, faced with this dilemma, you have to choose which way you are going to take to advance throughout your life.

I admit that many of my attitudes that I have do not correspond to the classic model of fitness coach or 'football man', and are taken as bizarre. For me, winning is not the most important thing. Much less, the only thing that matters. It was always like this for me. Almost 40 years ago, during the second leg of the semi-final of the Western League Tournament between the team with whom I worked, Rivadavia from Lincoln, and Matienzo from the city of Alberdi, I starred in a distinctive situation of my way of seeing the situations. With just three minutes to go until the game ended, we tied without goals and, with that result, we qualified for the final. The referee whistled a corner kick in favour of Rivadavia and our players invaded the rival area, putting aside any hint of caution and ignoring the energetic indications sent from the bench by the coach, Juan Torres. The pass arrived, pumped and open, and a defender rejected the ball, which reached a short and fast forward, who began a vertiginous race down the right wing, desperately pursued by his marker. Upon reaching the height of the large area, and at full speed, the attacker took out a formidable large pass with an inward spin, which Matienzo's centre-forward connected with a volley as wild as it was spectacular. The ball was shot with annihilating power, and after bursting the base of the crossbar, it was stinging inside the goal. The sublime beauty of the play and its exquisite definition made me jump on the bench and, with clenched fists, shout for the goal. Better said, the great goal. Torres, open-mouthed, grabbed me by the shirt and yelled at me:

'*Profe*, have you gone crazy? How are you going to celebrate their goal?'

Still excited by such an aesthetic display, I replied:

'What do I care whose goal it was? It was a great goal, and that's enough for me!'

I never understood how the mechanism develops by which some people deprive themselves of the pleasant emotions that beauty (in any of its forms) instinctively unleashes in our spirit.

The perversity that a misunderstood sense of belonging causes in the present, gives rise to behaviours impregnated with a retrograde and nefarious fanaticism, which equates those who suffer it with the remote barbarian tribes of the Stone Age. There are countless games won by teams whose coaching staff I was part of, of which I don't remember anything at all. However, that match against Matienzo, which not only ended in defeat but also left us out of a final that we believed was safe, remains a precious and indelible memory in my mind, thanks to that fantastic play.

The game with Brazil also left a very funny story: the morning of the match, I went down to the hotel lobby to relax a bit and found Carlos Bilardo's brother, who was with two other people. They had gone to look for the tickets to go to the stadium, but Carlos was sleeping and they were worried because they feared they would not arrive on time for the game, since the field was quite far away. I offered to go to the coach's room, but they replied that they were afraid that my intervention would break his routine and, him being a very superstitious man, he would get very nervous. I went to his room anyway and knocked on the door:

'Who's there?' I heard Bilardo say from inside.

'It's Fernando, Carlos.'

'Come in, what happened?'

He was lying on the bed, his legs bent, his hands crossed. I explained to him what was happening with his relatives and his tickets. So he gave me the envelope and I left. After the game, when I got on the bus, I went up to Carlos and said:

'Listen to me: don't come to me now with your strange rituals, because I will not be part of them!'

I cut him off before it occurred to him to ask me to wake him up every game morning, to take the envelope to his brother.

'Wake up by yourself!' I warned him. He was laughing, but I think it was only because he was intoxicated with euphoria.

When we returned to Trigoria, Diego was exultant. He was very moved by the reception that his daughters gave him, singing court songs about the Argentine team. Despite an annoying swollen ankle, smeared with anti-inflammatory creams and bandaged, the Argentine captain walked around the complex with a huge smile and wearing the shirt of the Italian team that his Napoli mate Ciro Ferrara had given him. He had promised both the defender and Nando di Napoli and Andrea Carnevale that he would wear it on the happiest day of his stay at the AS Roma sport centre, and he fulfilled it. In fact, he approached a group of photographers from the press to take photos of him dressed like this, so that the message would reach the hotel where the local squad was staying.

Unlike what happened in Mexico, where the Argentine team imposed its hierarchy from the beginning to end, and was only down on the scoreboard for a little while of the first phase duel with Italy, in the 1990 World Cup each game seemed like an effort electrocardiogram. The clash with Yugoslavia, played in the city of Florence for the quarter-finals, was a martyrdom. Argentina suffered a lot in the 90 minutes, in extra time and on penalties. On top of that, Diego missed his shot from 12 yards, saved by goalkeeper Tomislav Ivković and celebrated in the stands by the Tuscan spectators. At that moment, far from having any hint of optimism, I thought it was all over. We started going down together with Julio Grondona and another Argentine Football Association (AFA) leader, and an Italian cameraman who was around says 'Forza Yugoslavia'('Come on, Yugoslavia!') and I answered *va fanculo* (fuck you). It came out of my soul. But *Goyco* saved the next penalty and the three of us returned to our seats to see how Argentina finally prevailed in a frenzied tiebreaker.

That result of the shoot-out had two very curious stories behind it. The first happened the day before the meeting with Yugoslavia. Carlos Bilardo organised a 'penalty shoot-out championship' to practise shooting, in case the game ended level after 90 minutes and the half an hour extra time. After 18 rounds, Diego and Pedro Troglio reached the final without missing a single shot. Troglio hit his 19th shot and *Ten* missed his, so the former River and Gimnasia player won the competition. Curiously, the moment of truth came and the two most effective players failed: Diego's shot was stopped by Tomislav Ivković and Pedro's one hit a post.

The second peculiar circumstance began on 27 October 1989, when Napoli and Sporting Lisbon also had to resort to shots from 12 yards to decide a series that had ended goalless after two games, one at the San Paolo and the other in the Portuguese capital, for the first round of the UEFA Cup. The tiebreaker began and, after four shots per team, Napoli were ahead by three to two. It was Diego's turn: if he converted, the Italian club would go on to the next phase. The *Ten* took the ball and, when he was about to place it on the spot, the goalkeeper of the Lusitanian team, the Yugoslav Ivković, grabbed him by the arm and proposed to bet $100, convinced that he would save the Argentinian's shot. Diego accepted, but had to pay at the end of the match, because Ivković guessed the direction of his shot, on his left post. That blunder, at least, did not cost the Neapolitan captain because the Italian squad finally prevailed over the Portuguese one thanks to a mistake by Fernando Gomes. About ten months after that unusual bet, Diego and Ivković were again face to face separated by 12 steps, although without money in between. The Argentine, who remembered what happened in Naples, fired at the other post, the goalkeeper's right. The Yugoslav, who also had a good memory, guessed that his rival would change the fate of his shot, and stopped it again. The Tuscan spectators celebrated as if Ivković had been the Italian *portiere della Nazionale* (goalkeeper of the local national squad). But fate would have it that, in both cases, the glory was not complete for the Yugoslav goalkeeper, because his team fell in both series.

The semi-final against Italy began long before the opening whistle of French referee Michel Vautrot. Fate wanted that transcendental encounter between the host team and the defending champion to take place in no other than Naples city, Diego's kingdom, and at the San Paolo, his castle. In any other scenario, the South American squad would have been received in the worst way. But, at the foot of Vesuvius, things turned out very differently, because hearts were dyed blue and satisfied with titles thanks to the incomparable Diego. To further heat the atmosphere – or cool it down, depending on how you look at it – the *Ten* spent the days leading up to the game shouting into every microphone to fans from all over the peninsular country: 'Ask the Neapolitans to be Italian for one night, while the other 364 days they call them *terroni* [a derogatory term for the southern citizens dedicated to working the land],' and to beg their beloved *tifosi* 'to remember that, for the rest of the Italians, you are not part of Italy'. His clever move was magnificent: nobody dared to whistle the Argentine anthem, or to throw the first stone. It was like the public wanted to do something but couldn't. Likewise, many Neapolitans would surely have wanted to encourage Diego, but they also wanted to do so for Italy. There was something in the air that I don't really know what it was about, that didn't allow them to show themselves to one side or the other. I think if Italy won, they would have been sad for Diego. It was a very difficult dual feeling to resolve. A small group just hung a flag with a tepid legend: 'Maradona: Napoli ti ama ma l'Italia è la nostra patria' ('Naples loves you, but Italy is our homeland'). The Argentine team stayed at the Hotel Paradiso, which was packed with fans from Argentina. When we travelled from the pre-game meeting to the San Paolo, I sat in the last seat of the bus next to Néstor Fabbri and Edgardo Bauza. During the journey, at one point I looked out the window and noticed that the bus was followed by an infinity of motorcycles and scooters. Suddenly, next to me, a motorcycle appeared, driven by Carmine Iuliano, the supposed leader of the Neapolitan *Camorra* (the local crime syndicate) and one of the most-wanted criminals in Italy. The curious thing about the fact is that, a few metres from Iuliano, who was driving without a helmet, several police motorcycles were circulating, guarding our bus. The uniformed men did not realise – or did not want to realise – the famous person who accompanied them in that caravan.

We got to the stadium, we went down to the changing rooms and in one of the corridors I ran into Ciro Ferrara and Fernando de Napoli. We greeted each other and Ciro told me:

'Listen, *Fer*: tell the *capitano* not to spoil this to us, that today we have to win.'

He told me that they had made five different suits for each Italian player, for the different celebrations that were planned for when they became champions. One was white, to visit the Palazzo del Quirinale, where the president of Italy was going to receive them. In addition, I had read that the merchandising companies had planned to raise more than $600m from the sale of t-shirts and all kinds of articles if the *Nazionale* lifted the World Cup, and that the publishing industry had planned the launch of several commemorative books. There was a lot at stake in that semi-final, and the home team had the most to win ... but also to lose.

I saw the game from the press section. From there I was struck by the elegant black and white jackets of the Italians, which contrasted with the clothes of the Argentine team, which went out on to the pitch with only the shirt, directly dressed to play. I think that was Argentina's best game in that World Cup. The South American squad controlled the midfield and did not have too many shocks on defence. However, it began losing by an early goal from Salvatore Schillaci, who would become the *capocannoniere* (top scorer) of the championship, at 17 minutes, and only achieved equality at 22 minutes of the second half, through a header from Claudio Caniggia and a wrong move from the goalkeeper Walter Zenga.

After the draw, Italy stayed back, probably for fear of suffering another goal from the *Bird* in a counterattack. The local team did not even dare to seek victory when referee Vautrot sent off Ricardo *Gringo* Giusti. Before the extra time ended, I went down to the changing room and found Giusti and Julio Grondona, president of the Argentine Football Association, sitting on one of the benches looking worried.

'You don't have to ask more to God. With what they have done, it is already well,' said Grondona with his unmistakable voice.

As Giusti could not go out on to the pitch to witness the penalties, we went to the television studio that the RAI had set up in one of the stalls and asked the journalist Giampiero

Galeazzi for permission to see the shoot-out on his screen. They authorised us and there we saw the two shots stopped by *Goyco* and the four light-blue-and-white conversions, including Diego's. When Sergio contained Aldo Serena's shot, the *Gringo* jumped up and ran on to the field. The Italians were tremendously sad. I was embarrassed, I apologised but, two steps after leaving the studio, I started running towards the playing field, as happy as I can be! Upon reaching the pitch, I found Diego and we merged into a hug.

'This was the game!' I said in his ear.

A few minutes later, a tumult broke out at the entrance to the tunnel to the dressing-rooms, where Italian goalkeeper Walter Zenga was out of control, berating a couple of players.

'Argentini di merda! [Argentinian shits],' he was screaming, overheated.

Suddenly, *Moncho* Pedro Monzón appeared, who stretched his shirt and tore it like the Incredible Hulk. When Zenga saw Monzon – who was a mountain of muscles, eyes shooting rays – approaching him, the goalkeeper ran off. He hid in his locker room while several security personnel tried to stop the defender, without much success.

That same night we returned to Trigoria in a state of grace, singing and enjoying the three hours that the trip lasted. I don't think anyone had taken into account that we had obtained a Pyrrhic victory, because the red card to Giusti and the yellow cards to Caniggia, Olarticoechea and Batista had left the team decimated for the last game.

The next morning, the Italian press distilled hatred on every page. The sports newspaper *TuttoSport* ran two big headlines on its cover: one was 'End of a dream!'; the other,

'Maradona is the Devil'. Somehow, Argentina had become the team to beat, but not on their own merit, perhaps, but 'because of Diego'. That meeting in Naples was the last straw that broke the camel's back and wore out the patience of Italian power. At Napoli, he had already ruined several parties for the supremacy of the north; with the light-blue-and-white shirt, he destroyed a sports and financial business. The World Cup left a very large bill, and someone had to pay it.

During the period prior to the final, there were at least two curious events. First, with *Lalo* Maradona. Raúl arrived one morning at the gates of the Trigoria sports complex in one of Diego's Ferraris and, when he asked to be allowed to pass, a police officer refused. *Lalo* got out of the vehicle and began to yell at his older brother. Diego appeared and an incident was generated in which some slaps flew.

The second happened the day before the final. I was in my room and I heard Bilardo go back and forth shouting that the Argentinian flag that had been raised on one of the poles nailed near the entrance had been burned. It seemed strange to me, since the security operation mounted around the place was as strong as it was efficient. Not a mosquito entered there. I remembered that, once, Bilardo had told me that, when Estudiantes de La Plata played the second leg of the Intercontinental Cup against Manchester United in England in 1968, coach Osvaldo Zubeldia had expressed great concern:

'Carlos, I see the team a little bit listless. We have to do something to lift their spirits.'

They went to the sidewalk and threw stones at the windows of the rooms, to pretend that it was an attack by local fans. Then they came in and said:

'We have to go through these criminals tomorrow.'

As Estudiantes became intercontinental champion, Bilardo took note of this resource and reserved it for use on a special occasion. The burning of the flag was a riot to embolden the players. I'm sure he had a lot to do with it, at least as an ideological author.

Many times we talked with Diego about the final with Germany, played at the Olympic Stadium in Rome. We were always struck by the fact that the Mexican referee Edgardo Codesal did not award a very clear Lothar Matthäus penalty against Gabriel Calderón, being three metres away from that play, but he did so firmly whistle the alleged foul of Néstor Sensini to Rudolf Völler. We wonder how he managed to award it from about 20 metres and blocked by other footballers. Codesal's rulings have fuelled doubts about the probity or credibility of some actors and the political interest in football. Perhaps, without the suspected pressures 'from the top', things would have been different. But things were as they were. Also in the memory is the action in which Pedro Monzón thrashed the German Jürgen Klinsmann through the Roman airs, which deserved one of the reddest cards I saw in my life, and the first sending-off in a World Cup Final since the first edition, Uruguay 1930. Eight years later I met Jürgen at the Genoese club Sampdoria, and he told me that this had been 'the most ruthless and brutal kick that I received in my life'.

In a way, I think it's even better that the light-blue-and-white squad lost that final, for the good of Argentine football. There are triumphs that delay the advance more than the defeats, because the winner is copied and taken as a good example. The national team was a gang in a World Cup of very poor level. From a distance, I am more and more convinced that, for different reasons, Argentina got much more than it deserved. The team was forged from a base plagued with injuries, and luck was undoubtedly smiling on them against Brazil, and in the two penalty shoot-outs, against Yugoslavia and Italy. Also, do not forget that the South American squad qualified from their group in third place. After the 1998 World Cup in France, that situation became impossible, because only the best two from each group continue in the race.

Football has those mysteries. It is as Marcelo Bielsa says: what is achieved is rewarded and not what is deserved. However, I must also underline the courage that the boys had, which compensated for their physical deficiencies, and admit that I am left wondering what would have happened if Caniggia, Batista, Giusti and Olarticoechea had not been suspended for the final.

After the game was over and the awards ceremony completed, I waited for Diego inside the tunnel that connected the field with the changing rooms. He came sobbing and I hugged him. I asked him in his ear why he was crying. Through tears, he told me that it was the World Cup that he wanted to dedicate to Dalma and Gianinna.

'Stop kidding! They don't need you to raise another cup, but rather spend more time with you, which is what they don't have. All you can give them, although for them it will always be little, do you understand? So stop fucking around. You know that if it hadn't been for our luck, we would have had to go home after the first phase.'

Diego reacted. He stopped crying immediately and entered the locker room assuming his role as captain and team leader: he congratulated each of his team-mates and encouraged them to continue fighting for the white-and-light-blue colours. Afterwards, he took off his shirt and asked me to take it to Lothar Matthäus, who in turn gave me his. After bathing, he faced the press with nobility:

'I wanted to be champion. I am very sorry to have finished second. Anyway, I am proud to be the captain of this team.'

A journalist asked him if Italy 1990 meant his farewell to the World Cups.

'Yes, it was the last.'

'Won't you play for the national team anymore?'

'I think not,' he answered. 'I don't think I can accept another challenge like this, being so old.'

We know that the story ended differently.

Chapter 8

Losing control

DIEGO'S AFFAIR with drugs began in Barcelona. I am convinced that the romance began the night he celebrated his transfer to Napoli. I already related that, after the signing of the contract with the Italian team, at the El Prat airport, we returned to the house in the Pedralbes neighbourhood and there began a wild party that even dyed the pool water champagne pink. I didn't stay long at that celebration, but apparently, as the hours passed and the bubbly French drink was drunk, the merriment led to someone showing up with cocaine and inviting Diego. That would have been the first time he ever used, as far as I know. During the first leg of his time in Napoli, he never consumed again. I would have noticed, because we lived in the Royal Hotel and we were together every day.

The drug issue is very complex. Nobody had prepared Diego to reach those heights. He said a famous sentence:

'With a kick I went from Villa Fiorito to the top of the world. There I had to take care by myself. Nobody explained to me how the things were.'

I told him that if he had been born in Avenida del Libertador and Tagle (the richest Buenos Aires neighbourhood), he would have been a polo player. But he was born in Fiorito. There, the horses are eaten, because there is a lot of hunger.

Diego was the world's first product of globalisation. He was the most famous man in the world, without a doubt, and that led him to look for something that would put him in a position to respond to everything that was expected of him. Many times I noticed him extremely stressed, confused, and distraught. He found in the cocaine a kind of crutch to help him, without knowing that many times this path is only one way, it has no way of return.

One of the most painful moments for him was the birth of Diego Sinagra. That was an obstacle that he could not overcome, and that he only accepted, almost resigned, after 30 years. From the diffusion that the subject had in the media and, logically, inside the department of Via Scipione Capece 3/1, the first signs of abandonment appeared. Diego began to need more of the help of cocaine to cope with everything that tormented and anguished him. Apparently that gave him moments of escape, I suppose. Peace, in the face of pressure from leaders, sponsors, people and journalism. Sometimes I say to myself, 'Thank goodness Diego found the cocaine.' If he had not run into it, the decision he would have made, perhaps, would have been irreversible, as happens to so many who end up committing suicide. If many of the people who kill themselves first had come across cocaine, they might have bought time for therapists to come with help. They don't come across drugs and the end comes. One should not speak so irresponsibly and irreverently about addicts. What is preferable, that a child starts taking cocaine, or shoots himself in the head for not being able to cope with the vicissitudes of life? I am a father and I would choose that, first, they find the cocaine and give me time to get professional help, because the other is irreversible. Diego, after that, lived 35 more years.

One afternoon I received a call from Mary, his sister.

'*Profe*, Diego says if you can come home, because he wants to talk to you.'

I got into a taxi and went to the house where Mary lived, which was in a condominium next to the Parco della Rimembranza. When I arrived, she received me and sent me to her room. The door was closed, I knocked and it was opened by Diego's brother-in-law, whom we all knew as *El Morsa* (The Walrus). Inside there were about five people, and Diego was sitting on the double bed, leaning against the backrest. I said hello and he asked the others to leave us alone.

'I have to talk to the *Prof*,' he explained.

They all came out and I sat on the edge of the bed.

'What's up, *Die*?'

He began to speak, without a clear direction, going around, until he finally got to the point: he invited me to take some cocaine.

'This makes us talk,' he assured me.

However, I noticed that he immediately began to struggle to find the right words that he wanted to express. What's more, he suddenly became speechless. I looked at him without making a single sound.

'So? What are you saying?'

'I say no.'

'Why?'

'Because when I am happy, I want to know why; and when I'm sad I also want to know why. When I need to speak, I speak. I don't need anything to do it.'

'OK, that's fine ...'

'That was all?'

'Yes.'

'OK, bye. See you tomorrow.'

I left the room, greeted the others, and went home. It was the only time he proposed something like that to me. He never tried again.

After the Italian World Cup, Napoli strengthened itself with the intention of winning the title that was missing from its showcases: the European Cup. The club's board took on goalkeeper Giovanni Galli, who admitted to having accepted the Neapolitan proposal fed up with conceding goals from Diego. 'I played many times against him, he has scored many goals against me and, in order not to suffer more, I decided to play for his team,' agreed the goalkeeper who had been a victim of Diego in the Italian league and also in the 1986 World Cup in Mexico. Diego, Antonio Careca and Ricardo Alemão continued to form the foreigners' trident.

The preseason in Macerata was, once again, an ideal opportunity for Diego to test his new toy: a red Ferrari F40. We left from Naples, we passed through Rome and, when it was starting to get dark, we went up to the Autostrada del Sole. In that section, the highway becomes undulating, with ups and downs that offered the *Ten* the opportunity to verify his new car in all its glory. The irresponsible guy stepped on the accelerator and, in a descent, the Ferrari reached a speed of 300km per hour. The car was making a tremendous noise. Diego yelled at me:

'*Blind*, you're all screwed up!'

I looked at him with a serene countenance and replied:

'No, not at all. Didn't I ever tell you about the gypsy?'

'No,' he yelled.

'Ah, once a gypsy woman who read my hand predicted that I was going to have a very fiery accident with a red car, and that I was going to be the only survivor.'

Diego suddenly released the accelerator, a scared look, and the Ferrari stopped.

'Motherfucker!' he shouted, enraged. The rest of the trip did not exceed 120km per hour.

As happened every time Napoli travelled for pre-season, the chosen city was filled with fans, especially southerners. The club managers took advantage of the massive pilgrimages to negotiate with the mayors a reduction in hotel rates – or their total cost – in the selected localities in exchange for a match against a local team, of a very low category and generally amateur, in which an entrance fee was charged for the commune to compensate for that expense. But, on this occasion, a problem arose that nobody had foreseen: Diego had not fully recovered from the injuries suffered during the World Cup, so he refused to participate in the game agreed to against the Maceratese club, fearful that his ailments would be aggravated. Faced with this spontaneous inconvenience, local managers, terrified that when the absence of the *Ten* was known an avalanche of returns would be triggered – the tickets were sold out several days before – took an unusual measure: they enabled the entry of the fans to the training sessions in which Diego was, but only to those who had already purchased their admissions for the Maceratese–Napoli duel.

The Serie A season started very badly for the champions. At the winter break, Napoli had achieved just four victories, along with seven draws and six defeats. Diego scored just three goals, all from the penalty spot. The cocaine had twisted his arm and the effect was beginning to show on the pitch …

and off it as well. He was lacking in unconcentration, he did not accept that reality that he had to live. He first began to misalign himself, then to skip training – when the addiction became very strong, there were days when he couldn't get out of bed – and he made ridiculous excuses. He called the club's sports director, Luciano Moggi, and gave him justifications that seemed typical of a schoolboy who must explain to his teacher why he did not do his homework: one day he told him that he had eaten something in bad condition and he was sick; another, that he had the flu. Then, that his knee hurt, that he had a contracture, and I don't know how many more justifications. One morning I came to his house very worried. He had eluded his umpteenth training.

'What's going to hurt you today?' I asked.

Diego considered his answer.

'We can say that Dalmita felt ill.'

'No, stop, in no way am I going to use Dalma as an excuse. How are you going to get her in the middle of this?'

I turned around and left, angry that he was already resorting to any kind of excuse to hide, because he did not allow himself any weakness. It was a sign that the deterioration was having a serious effect. Of course, his addiction problem was known to President Corrado Ferlaino, Moggi and the team doctor, Emilio Acampora.

Another day, I went to look for him to train and he didn't want to get up, he had taken a lot of cocaine. At one point I treated him half badly, and he replied:

'Don't yell at me, because if one day I got into a fight with my old man, I don't see why I won't fight with you!'

'Do you know why you don't fight with me? Because, just as you are now, I'd slap you and leave you spinning like a top!'

Diego didn't expect my reaction. He looked at me with wide eyes, surprised.

'Who the hell do you think you are? Maradona? Maradona is the wrinkles on your dad's face and hands! That's Maradona! Because, if it had been someone else, when I came home exhausted from working to feed so many mouths, as you told me once, instead of accompanying you, he would have kicked you in the ass and sent you to work. That's Maradona!'

I held on to a story that he had told me years before. He always related with great pride that, in his days in lower divisions in Argentinos Juniors, Don Diego arrived exhausted from work, ate something fast and accompanied his son to training. Sometimes, in the middle of a game, Diego would look to the side and see his father asleep standing up, clinging to the woven wire.

His deterioration made me very sad, because I had met another Diego, a lucid, funny and generous guy, with beautiful gestures of tenderness. Once, Napoli thrashed Bologna and left them on the verge of relegation. The match ended and the *Ten* approached the Emilia-Romagna team coach, Luigi Maifredi, and gave him his shirt. Why? Because he remembered that, several years before, his partner Eraldo Pecci had told him that Maifredi admired him very much. Diego, a little saddened by the bad sporting moment that the coach was going through, made a generous gesture to lift his spirits.

Diego associated his addiction to his difficult life in Naples. For me, it is the least boring city in the world, the most confusing, warm, because its people have incredible creativity and because the climate, the landscape, the company, the food, the way of life of the Neapolitans, give a unique atmosphere to it. But he, in that same context, suffered. He couldn't stand suffocation, not being able to leave his house with his daughters in freedom, to go to the movies, to a park, to lunch.

'I want to be free like all the fathers in the world, but in Naples it is impossible,' he confessed to me once, bitterly. For Diego, birthdays, Christmas and New Year's parties always had the same setting: his house. His private life was condemned within four walls. He could not even go out to the balcony, because immediately cars and motorcycles stopped and people who appeared from everywhere, even under the sidewalk and the asphalt, started to shout at him, take pictures, ask for autographs.

At the beginning of November 1990, Napoli had to travel to Moscow to face Spartak for the round of 16 of the European Cup. The first leg, played at the San Paolo, had ended goalless, and the rematch at the frozen Lenin Stadium looked extremely difficult. However, at the time when the bus with the delegation had to leave from Soccavo to the Roman airport of Fiumicino, Diego did not appear. Fed up with the repeated absences of the *Ten*, Ferlaino, Moggi and coach Alberto Bigon asked three players, led by Ciro Ferrara, to please go to the house on Via Scipione Capece 3/1 and try to convince the captain to join the team. The boys couldn't even talk to him: Claudia attended them and she explained that he was locked up and didn't want to see anyone. In truth, not because he did not want to, but because he could not, due to the fact that at that moment he was suffering an episode of insecurity and anguish. Finally, the team flew to Moscow without its *capitano*. However, the next day, Claudia called me to tell me that we were going to Moscow because her husband was fine and wanted to travel.

They hired a private flight and we left for the Soviet Union with Diego, along with Claudia, his representative Marcos Franchi and a collaborator. We arrived at the Moscow airport and, as we descended, a 'pleasant' temperature of 22 degrees below zero enveloped us. Already in the hotel, very beautiful, set in the time of the tsars, the leaders did not welcome the biggest star of the team: they were offended. Resentful of the frigid welcome, in keeping with the Moscow climate, Diego became infatuated and at nine o'clock at night he told Marcos that he wanted to visit the Red Square. Franchi made some inquiries, but did not get much:

'They tell me it's impossible, it's already closed.'

Diego began to shout that he wanted to visit it anyway, which forced Marcos to move heaven and earth and, around 11 o'clock at night, we entered the Red Square. One thing only the *Ten* could accomplish. We were only there for five minutes, because it was terribly cold.

The next day, we arrived at the Luzhniki Olympic Stadium and discovered that the pitch was covered in a thick layer of snow, about half a metre high. In an hour, special machines lifted the white blanket and it was like a wall of ice around the playing field, although the grass was frozen. The players had to wear boots with special caps, sharper, to hold on better, because they could not stand. Diego was not a starter, he entered the second half with shirt number 16, replacing Gianfranco Zola. Spartak and Napoli drew without goals and the home team prevailed in the penalty shoot-out, in which Diego, at least, converted his shot from 12 yards.

On the return trip, while we were flying over Hungary, the plane had a turbine failure, so we had to make an emergency landing in Budapest. We spent two hours outside, in the middle of a terrible cold, because the airport was closed, until the local technicians repaired the engine and we were able to return to Naples.

That game in Moscow was a point of alarm for the club leaders, who were very concerned about the elimination and loss of several million, but much more because of the behaviour of the team captain. One day, coming back from training, he was in very bad shape. I never thought of throwing in the towel, to quit never crossed my mind, but I did feel a huge concern because the stage was overtaking me.

'Look, Diego, let's say things as they are: you no longer need a physical coach. You needed it when you were a player, but now you are no longer a player. You are not anymore. You would have to look for people who know how to help you, because the world is full of people who want it, and maybe I am the first. But I did not study to recover addicts. Here we need people who know about the subject, because this situation is very serious. You have to accept that you can no longer handle this condition.'

'You don't know the force I'm dealing with,' he replied.

He made me the gesture of rowing, as if it was difficult for him to move forward. He knew he had a problem, that the drug was spoiling him, but he couldn't face adversity, even though he wanted to. However, sometimes he does not reach only with will: in that degree of addiction, therapy and medication were needed.

We had that talk a week or two before the famous game against Bari. The game in which the Napoli leaderships decided to throw the lemon in the trash, because it no longer gave any more juice. The team's campaign was very poor: outside of the European Champions Cup much earlier than planned, with just six victories in 24 Serie A games, the squad was too expensive and on its horizon was not the sun but dark clouds.

Diego was not going to play against Bari. He had spent two or three days very bad, most of the time shut up in his room, depressed, taking drugs. He hardly slept. On Saturday afternoon I went to his house and we started talking. I remember that a Spanish movie, *Las cosas del querer* ('Things of love'), was going to be televised that day. I proposed to him to watch it, but he didn't want to, so we continued chatting. At one point I asked him:

'What are you going to do tomorrow?'

'Nothing. I'm not going to play. And you, what are you going to do?'

'I'm going to go to the stadium. There is not much to do on a Sunday. Besides, I want to see what the team does without you,' I provoked him.

We said goodbye and I went home. At eight in the morning the phone rang. It was Claudia, with a very cool, radiant voice.

'*Profe*, Diego says can you take his boots to Soccavo.'

'To Soccavo?'

'Yes. Today he got up at 6.30, very good, he showered and went to Soccavo.'

She told me that he had climbed into his white Rolls-Royce Corniche – as if he wanted to go unperceived – and had left for the pre-meeting to join the team. I had breakfast, went to Scipione Capece, got the boots and took them to Diego. When I arrived at the sports complex, the entire team was in a large courtyard that bordered the sector for the rooms, everyone chatting, laughing. I stayed a while and went home. In the afternoon I went to the field. As always, before starting the game, we meet Diego in the locker room. He warmed up by dancing, as he liked, as he had done for many years.

Napoli won 1-0. After the match, I went down to the dressing-room area and found Diego chatting with Gianfranco Zola – the scorer of the only goal of the match – the Romanian Florin Raducioiu and another player from Bari, while the four waited to be called from the room where a doctor would take urine samples for doping control.

'*Profe*, wait for me to do the anti-doping and let's go,' he asked me.

Before entering the room, Diego, wrapped in a white towel, approached the door of the dressing room and shouted for Luciano Moggi, Napoli's general manager.

'Luciano, come here. Do not leave me alone.'

The leader came out and the two talked for a couple of minutes. A few seconds later, Moggi returned to the dressing room and Diego complied with the procedure for the urine test.

The following Sunday, the *Ten* scored a penalty goal in Napoli's defeat against Sampdoria, at the Luigi Ferraris stadium in Genoa. Two or three days later, a fax from the Italian Federazione Giuoco Calcio arrived at Diego's house informing that the test for the match with Bari had been positive, with which he was immediately suspended from competing in Serie A. Against the Genoese, Diego played his last match in the light-blue jersey, after 259 official games in which he scored 115 goals.

There is no doubt that thanks to the *Ten*, Napoli won the only two *Scudetti* in their history (1986/87 and 1989/90), in addition to their exclusive international title: the 1988/89 UEFA Cup. However, his farewell was far from what the southern team's top hero should have had. Ferlaino, ungrateful, related in a report published by the Argentine sports newspaper *Olé* in 2000, 'Our doctor, a specialist in drug addiction, told me that Maradona acted in a manner opposite to that which characterises a cocaine addict. Neither did his colleagues notice anything strange, that's why I was calm. Of course, if now I start to think that many times he did not come to practice, that he disappeared for several days, that when he travelled to Argentina it was an uncertainty when he returned, it was clear that he was hiding something.

'The truth came out little by little. Knowing that on Sunday he could get the anti-doping control, since Thursday he did not consume cocaine. For a long time he knew how to control himself, then he could no longer'.

Although the team president remarked that Diego 'always wanted to win, in games and in training. He was a leader. He never got angry with team-mates who made mistakes on the court. He was perfect. But at one point his contradictions', a few years later, in 2003, Ferlaino launched a bomb complaint that hurt Diego and a lot of people ... and also hurt himself with the splinters. In an interview with the Neapolitan newspaper *Il Matino*, Ferlaino claimed to have 'saved at least ten times' Diego from testing positive for drug controls. How? The former manager specified that he used to give the *Ten* a rubber container, with a format and tone similar to that of a human penis, filled with clean drug pee from another person, to avoid the analysis ordered by the Federation. Ferlaino – who incriminated himself in a serious crime – described that, at the end of each game in which Diego was chosen for analysis, he received the container in the dressing room before going to the room for the examination, generally from the hands of Moggi. He would hide the gadget in his pants or under the towel and, when he was inside the room for the procedure, instead of urinating into the bottle, he would dump the contents of the fake member into the jar delivered by the doctor in charge of the test and covered by a fairly lax regulation, which led to this kind of thing happening. Today this procedure has evolved to minimise possible cheating: footballers must remove their pants when depositing their sample, under the watchful eye of a supervisor.

I don't know how much truth there is in those Ferlaino words. According to the former president of the Neapolitan club, on the day of the control Moggi 'forgot' the container, and 'asked him if he was in condition' and he replied, 'Yes, I am, everything is fine.' The fact is that cocaine addicts lie to themselves. But he also lied, because that day Moggi would have told Diego that, if something irregular happened, Ferlaino would solve it later at the Federation headquarters with his supposed influences. Which he did not do. Asked by an Italian journalist, Diego's lawyer, Giovanni Verde, considered that the *Ten* was the victim of 'a conspiracy. I am convinced that Diego was betrayed. He believed that he could never be caught at the control. They tricked him into terminating the contract [with Napoli], which included such a clause in the event of a suspension for doping.' In his autobiography *Yo soy el Diego* ('I am Diego'), he said that the episode had deeper roots: 'I got drug control and ... the vendetta was fulfilled. Revenge was written, and at last it came ... That doping control was revenge, vendetta against me because Argentina had eliminated Italy, and they had lost many millions.'

I do not have proof or the certainty that there has been that rubber penis that Ferlaino spoke of, but it could be, everything could be. What I do know is that, as I said a few lines ago, the lemon no longer had any juice and they wanted to reject it. The power of football had given a thumbs-down to Diego. On 6 April 1991, the Disciplinary Committee of the Italian Football League suspended him until 30 June 1992. Although many newspapers had demanded a greater sentence – the maximum contemplated by the regulations was two years – the court justified its conviction by stating that it had not been possible to prove that Diego had used cocaine to improve his athletic performance. The second part of the committee's ruling is consistent with a beautiful text written by the Uruguayan narrator Eduardo Galeano: 'Diego Maradona had never used stimulants, on the eve of the games, to multiply his body. It is true that he had been involved in cocaine, but he was doped at sad parties, to forget or be forgotten, when he was already cornered by glory and could not live without the fame that would not let him live. He played better than anyone despite the cocaine, and not because of it.'

The court, on the other hand, acquitted Napoli, who had been denounced for 'strict liability' in the same case. It seems that Ferlaino's influences did work there.

After the suspension, the operation to return to Buenos Aires was arranged in a hurry. I took Claudia, Dalma and Gianinna to the Fiumicino airport in Rome to take the flight to Buenos Aires. The next day Diego travelled. Various local media reported that he had escaped from Italy at night. At night! All the planes that leave for Argentina do so at night, there are no flights during the day! As always happens, many of the things that the press published were true, but others were not; they functioned as the yeast of lies. Furthermore, if Diego had worn the Juventus or Milan jerseys, the media would have protected him differently. But he played for Napoli, and the whole press in the north had a crush on him. We all have miseries.

With Diego we said goodbye and I stayed in Naples, to solve many things that had remained pending, from assembling a container with the infinity of things they had and paying bills, to shipping the cars to Argentina. I also represented him during the hearing in which the second doping test was made.

I travelled to Rome with the lawyer Vicenzo Siniscalchi, who during our journey to the Eternal City told me that he had represented many important figures, such as the Sicilian gangster Salvatore *Lucky* Luciano, when he settled in Naples in the early 1960s. Surprised by the lawyer's résumé, I asked him:

'Of all the celebrities that you met, which was the one that impacted you the most?'

'Without any doubt, your friend Diego.'

At the institute where the second test was carried out, we were joined by the German chemist Manfred Donike, a professor at the University of Cologne who, in those years, was the world's leading expert on doping. Donike had created a system to detect banned substances that, at the Seoul Olympics, discovered the drugs used by Canadian sprinter Ben Johnson.

As expected, the retest came back positive. After the process was finished, Siniscalchi, Donike and I went to lunch. During the midday meal, the German specialist asked me:

'What is the plan that will be addressed in Argentina for Diego's recovery?'

'According to him, a group of doctors and therapists will be organised to assist him.'

'That's like giving a candy to a cancer patient.'

The specialist extracted a personal card from his jacket and, on the back, he wrote the name of an addiction treatment centre that was in Colourado Springs, United States, which had had actress Elizabeth Taylor and boxer Sugar Ray Leonard as patients, among other celebrities.

'This is the ideal centre to admit Diego,' he assured me. But sadly, the *Ten* never followed the advice.

Meanwhile, in Buenos Aires, a brutal, unjust and inhuman act happened. On 26 April 1991, a few days after Diego's return to Argentina, a group of agents from the Superintendency of Dangerous Drugs of the Federal Police broke into an apartment on Franklin Street, in the Caballito neighbourhood, the geographic centre of the city of Buenos Aires. The procedure ended with the arrest of Diego and two of his friends, in addition to the confiscation of drugs for personal use. The detention was broadcast live and direct on various television channels, and recorded on the cover of every newspaper in the world the following day. The magazine *El Gráfico*, the most important sports media in Latin America at that time, published in its issue 3734, of 30 April, a surprising and yellowish description of Diego's capture, entitled 'Maradona's drama'. 'Only *El Gráfico* accessed this secret report,' was asserted in one of the subtitles of a note that did not save on details to destroy the image of the man who had been captain and star of the national team in the two previous World Cups. The chronicle included exaggerated, fabled descriptions, and suggestive comments in very bad taste about Diego's private life.

The scandalous procedure even made the cover of the US magazine *Newsweek*, with a photo of Diego leaving the apartment surrounded by plain-clothes officers and the phrase 'Maradona's crash'. It attracted a lot of attention. Several news channels had arrived at the place of detention together with the police – some witnesses assured that a couple of TV trucks appeared even before the presence of the first police vehicle – to broadcast the footballer handcuffed. Diego was detained for about 35 hours and was released after the payment of a bail that, according to the press, amounted to $20,000. The federal judge in charge of the case, Amelia Berraz de Vidal, ordered Diego to undergo rehabilitation treatment.

I never had doubts that Diego was a victim of a trap. Above all, when I learned of a very suggestive detail: to give him the famous diplomatic passport and appoint him ad honorem advisor to the government 'for sports matters and dissemination of the Argentine image abroad' the day before the match with Cameroon at the Giuseppe Meazza stadium of Milan, Carlos Menem had previously signed a presidential decree. Do you know when that directive expired? The day before the raid took place in the department of Caballito! A new decree, number 811, dated 25 April 1991, annulled the previous diplomatic designation exactly 24 hours before Diego was handcuffed and exhibited before the world press. What a coincidence!

What happened to Menem was brutal: he cut off Diego's head because he needed a smokescreen to cover several tricks of his government, especially a scandal due to the supposed coming and going of diplomatic bags that, according to several complaints published in the newspapers, they would have delivered through the Ezeiza Airport from New York loaded with drug money for laundering in the country. One of the people involved in this court case was Amira Yoma, sister-in-law of the Riojan president, for which the case was baptised by the media as *Yomagate*. Other 'coincidences' that force me to think that the black hand of power was behind Diego's arrest was that Berraz de Vidal was also in charge of the *Yomagate* case, in which Amira was dismissed. In addition, two years later, the magistrate was awarded for her 'equanimous' performance by Menem himself, who promoted her to judge of the National Chamber of Criminal Cassation.

A lot of people asked me many times if I questioned Diego's 'environment', a word that, by the way, I detest. To be honest, no. Never, never would I have allowed it. He was always with the people he wanted to be with. Who was I to tell him who to meet with and who not? He didn't mess with my friends, I didn't mess with his. Yes, I have made suggestions several times, as I also did with other friends or as Diego himself told me. But you can't change a person's environment. Argentines always have our pockets full of solutions for others, but we never find measures for our own inconveniences. In that we are world champions. Once a French journalist asked me:

'Can you imagine what Maradona would have been with Platini's behaviour?'

'Yes: he would have been Platini, nothing more. Maradona is something different,' I replied.

While that nefarious spider web in which Diego had been trapped unfolded, I continued taking care of his affairs in Italy. I took the two Ferraris to Barcelona, to a very large garage that served as a warehouse there; the Rolls-Royce, to Switzerland, to the house of Gabriel Calderón, who played in that country. I took two BMWs (an 850 and a Z1) to Cologne, Germany, to ship them to Argentina.

I moved the Ferraris with the help of an Argentine friend, Luis Ruzzi, who had worked with the national team in the 1990 World Cup in Italy. First we passed through Monte Carlo and I took the opportunity to circulate at night through the streets where the Monaco Grand Prix is run and that I wanted to drive. From the Principality we moved to Saint-Jean-Cap-Ferrat, very close to Nice. There I met Giulio de Angelis, father of former Formula One driver Elio de Angelis, who died during a test at a circuit on the French Riviera. Ruzzi had been the driver's manager and had also collaborated with Giulio, a former motor-boating champion and construction entrepreneur, when he was kidnapped by a Sardinian mafia group. The poor guy was held captive for four months and had his ear cut off to send it to his family and, with that proof of savagery, speed up the payment of the ransom. While we ate at Giulio's house, he asked me how much Diego loved the five cars he had left in Italy. I didn't know, so he made me a proposal: a million dollars for all the vehicles. I called Marcos Franchi by phone, from that same house. I transmitted the offer to him and the representative suggested that I should consult with the *Ten*. He asked me to call him back in a while. After the deadline, I contacted Franchi, who replied:

'Diego says that, for that money, he prefers to set them on fire.'

A shame. Later, due to the high cost of transporting Ferraris to Argentina, Diego ended up selling them for coins.

While working in the Via Scipione Capece department, I received a call from the Diadora representative in southern Italy: Stefano Capriati, the father of American tennis player Jennifer Capriati, wanted to speak with me. They were in Rome because the young woman had to compete in the traditional Open that is played in the Foro Italico. I travelled to the capital to meet them and, since I was there, to see Gabriela Sabatini, who won that edition of the tournament play. Stefano offered me to work as a physical trainer for his daughter and as a supervisor in a school they had in the city of Tampa, in the state of Florida. I had to say no, because I was still engaged to Diego. I had never signed a contract that tied me to the *Ten*, but the handshake that we had given each other in Barcelona was still in force. There are things that happen on the other side, and also I had assured Diego that I was going to finish what had been pending in Naples. It took me almost a year to finish it all!

With my task accomplished, I finally left the beautiful city, not to return to my country, but to return to Spain. When Diego's suspension for positive doping against Bari was about to end, the newspapers began to associate his name with different teams: Real Madrid – it was said that the *Casa Blanca* (White House) wanted him to replace Romanian Gheorghe Hagi – Olympique Marseille again and a new candidate, Sevilla Fútbol Club. The entry of the Andalusian squad had to do with the previous hiring of a coach who, along with Diego, had won the 1986 World Cup in Mexico and reached the final in Italy 1990, Carlos Bilardo. 'I have never, since 1965, dropped from fourth place, and here I want to continue like this,' said Bilardo during the press conference in which he was introduced as a new Sevillian coach.

Diego did not want to return to Naples. One day he went to the River Plate stadium to see a friendly between

Argentina and Australia, and he crossed paths with Bilardo's brother.

'Why don't you tell Carlos to take me?' he asked him.

Bilardo liked the idea and proposed it to the president of the Spanish club, Luis Cuervas. The coach and the manager contacted Corrado Ferlaino, and began a very long negotiation to define the cost of the transfer, since Napoli still owned the rights of the *Ten*. In his autobiography, *Doctor y Campeón* (Doctor and Champion), Bilardo said that 'Ferlaino was very angry with Diego and did not want to give him up, so I spoke with João Havelange, the president of FIFA, to try to get him to mediate in the conflict. In conversations, Havelange asked me: "Carlos, is Maradona going with you?" I answered yes. "Then, I will try to help you," he promised. FIFA intervened and finally the pass was finalised.' According to what was commented at the time, Havelange would have asked the secretary of the entity, Joseph Blatter, to intercede with the rectors of the federations of Spain and Italy, Ángel María Villar and Antonio Matarrese, to facilitate the cut of that Gordian knot.

Diego was greeted with great enthusiasm by a squad that included his compatriot Diego Simeone and Croatian striker Davor Šuker. The *Ten*, immediately anointed captain, made his debut in Seville on the fifth game of the season, 4 October 1992, against no less than Athletic Club at the San Mamés stadium in Bilbao. The visiting squad took the lead thanks to a free kick taken by their new star: the local goalkeeper saved the ball and Marcos de la Fuente took the rebound and sent it to the net. In the second half, Diego was again the target of a very tough tackle from a Basque defender, Andoni Lakabeg. The kick looked like a replay of the blow that another Andoni, Goikoetxea, had given him almost a decade earlier: Lakabeg threw himself at him from behind while Diego had the ball in his own half of the pitch, and injured his ankle operated on in Barcelona. The Aragonese referee Emilio Soriano Aladrén – who a minute before had annulled a second goal for Sevilla, scored by Ignacio Conte after a masterful pass from Diego, for an alleged offside that had not existed – barely showed the yellow card. Lakabeg continued playing, while the Sevillian captain had to leave the pitch, replaced by Alfonso Cortijo. Without Diego, Athletic Club turned history around and won by two to one.

After the meeting, when interviewed by a journalist, Diego highlighted a nice gesture that Andoni Goikoetxea had with him: the Basque went to visit him at the Bilbao hotel where the Andalusian team gathered while waiting for the game in San Mamés. 'What Andoni did is something that good men do. Only grown guys have that kind of gestures,' he declared.

I personally knew Goikoetxea in Madrid, many years later. One night I went to dinner with Cesar Menotti and Ángel Cappa at a restaurant. While we were eating, two big guys came into the room. Cesar distinguished one of them, the former Basque defender, whom he had had as a player at Atlético de Madrid.

'Old fellow, what are you doing here?' he greeted him as he stood up to shake his hand.

Menotti introduced us and I welcomed Goikoetxea with a smile:

'You don't know how long I waited for this moment to thank you for what you did for me!'

Menotti related to the former Basque defender the beginning of my story with Diego, as a result of the fracture. Goikoetxea celebrated my occurrence with laughter.

After that game, Diego called me and asked me to continue working with him as his personal fitness trainer. We met again in the house that the club had gotten him, which had belonged to the bullfighter Juan Antonio Ruiz Román – known as *Espartaco*, one of the most famous in Spain – located in the Simón Verde district and close to the Guadalquivir river. In our first talk, I suggested that we start with a battery of studies to find out how his body was. He agreed, so I got in touch with a renowned scientist from the Department of Physiology at the University of Seville, named Juan Ribas Serna, who also practiced his specialty at the University of California, Los Angeles (UCLA). We met in the bar of a well-known hotel in the centre of Seville. I suggested to Ribas that I wanted the essential analysis to be carried out to determine what state Diego was in and what recommendations he would suggest to improve him. A few days later, we went with Diego to the University of Seville. As Ribas had unexpectedly travelled to the United States, the studies were led by one of his closest collaborators, Juan Fernández. The specialist put him on a treadmill and filled him with electrodes.

Diego endured the efforts required with a contagious enthusiasm, which generated any kind of competition, even if it was against himself. Then, we moved to an athletics track, where for the first time he was subjected to a test aimed at evaluating the biomechanical characteristics of his career, with the support of several video cameras that captured his movements and sent the images directly to a computer. The video cameras captured his movements from different angles: forward, backward, right and left. While Diego worked, I found that his condition was far from ideal to withstand the requirements of high competition. He was once again 'a Rolls-Royce covered in dust that needed a feather duster', as Dr Rubén Oliva had once defined him.

A week later, we were at Diego's house and the university specialists arrived. Fernández, accompanied by two of his assistants, began to communicate his conclusions to me: he told me that of everything they had evaluated, the first thing that stood out was Diego's very bad running technique. He opened a laptop and an image of him taken from behind his back appeared on the screen, showing his knees out with each stride. According to Fernández, this characteristic in Diego's gait meant a huge loss of efficiency in his movement, since when his legs advanced they produced a divergent movement with respect to the longitudinal axis, with the consequent wastage of force at the crucial moment of acceleration. Consequently, he considered that we should urgently correct this style, so harmful from the athletic point of view, for a better optimisation of the use of his energy and therefore of his efficiency. When Fernández completed his conclusions, I replied:

'Juan, Diego is 32 years old and his saddlebags are full of precious trophies won, among other reasons, thanks to his very personal and inimitable run technique. Without wanting to contradict you, let me tell you with absolute conviction that we can change Diego's earring, maybe his hairstyle or the watch he wears, but never the way he runs, which is dazzling.

The guy started to blush.

'Juan, don't get in trouble: Diego is going to keep running on a football field, not on an athletics track.'

Fernández nodded his head. He looked at his companions and finished:

'Damn, you're right, I feel like an asshole!'

After the setback in Bilbao, the team quickly rose to the top, thanks to four wins and two draws in six games. Diego quickly got into shape and on the 15th matchday he achieved a legendary performance against a Real Madrid side of stars such as the Croatian Robert Prosinečki, the Chilean Iván Zamorano and the Spanish Fernando Hierro, Martín Vázquez and Luis Enrique. Sevilla won at home, the Ramón Sánchez-Pizjuán stadium, 2-0 and the *Merengue* team surrendered at the feet of the exceptional South American footballer.

In mid-February 1993, the *Ten* once again starred in a new example of commitment and love for the Argentine colours by repeating a marathon odyssey between South America and Europe to perform in two games with the light-blue-and-white team, interspersed between three very important Iberian league matches. On that occasion, he was accompanied by another star of the national squad: *Cholo* Simeone. The two Diegos played at the Sánchez-Pizjuán against Valencia on 14 February 1993 – a 2-2 draw with both goals from Davor Šuker, both after assistance from the *Ten* – and left that same day, at night, for Buenos Aires to face Brazil in a friendly called 'Centennial Cup of the Argentine Football Association'. The *Ten* returned to wear the shirt of his country after almost 30 months, since the final of the 1990 World Cup in Italy, against Germany. On 18 February, on the River Plate pitch, the great South American duel ended 1-1. The two players returned to Spain and on the 21st they went out on to the Las Gaunas stadium to play against Logroñés. Diego had a poor performance and the Andalusian team was defeated 2-0. The setback enraged the Sevillian president Cuervas and Bilardo himself, who tried to stop the departure of their two stars for the second international match, against Denmark. However, Julio Grondona, the president of the AFA, interceded because the duel with the Nordic side corresponded to an official tournament instituted by FIFA: the Artemio Franchi Cup destined to pit the South American champion (Argentina had won the last Copa América in the edition of Chile 1991) against the European champion: Denmark, surprising winner in the Euros Sweden 1992. 'We spoke with Grondona and he told us that we should travel. We told him that Cuervas did not want to, and that it was a difficult situation, but he told us that we are obliged to travel,' Diego said to a journalist. The *Ten* was right to get out of the way of a conflict that had to be resolved, and it was resolved, in high places, because Sevilla, according to official regulations, could not refuse to give up their players for an official FIFA competition.

Protected by international regulations, the Diegos travelled an hour by car from Logroño, in La Rioja, to the Foronda airport, on the outskirts of Vitoria, the capital of the autonomous community of the Basque Country. There, the players boarded a small plane that the *Ten* had hired to arrive on time for a flight that was leaving that night from Madrid's Barajas air station to Buenos Aires. The Sevillian duo landed in Ezeiza and boarded another aircraft bound for Mar del Plata, a seaside city located about 400km south of the Argentine capital, the site of the intercontinental meeting. On 24 February, goalkeeper Sergio Goycochea once again saved two penalties – the match ended 1-1 and was resolved with a shoot-out – which gave Argentina a new title, the last one that Diego would claim.

The boys rested one day and returned to Spain, in time to join the team that, on the 28th, beat Athletic Club de Bilbao by three to one. Diego's performance was diametrically opposite to what he had offered in Logroño. The *Ten* was greeted at the Sánchez-Pizjuán by some whistles, coming from the most demanding sectors of the Andalusian fans, but due to a performance as brilliant as it was effective, the whistles were buried under a huge ovation. The Argentines' display was so unusual that Athletic coach, German Jupp Heynckes, told the press that he would buy his players 'a ticket to Argentina, to see if they come back with that desire'.

A couple of trips against possibly inferior teams and two hard falls at the Santiago Bernabéu and the Camp Nou blurred the campaign of the squad led by Bilardo. On 13 June, for the penultimate date of the tournament, Seville received Burgos, a club who had already been relegated to the second division some games earlier. In the first half of the season, Bilardo's squad had beaten the same opponents as visitors 2-0 in the small ground called El Plantío. The victory was essential to seize one of the places in the UEFA Cup the following year, and things started well: 34 minutes into the first half, the home team opened the scoring with a ball to the net from Ramón *Monchu* Suárez del Valle. I don't know what happened, but ten minutes before full time, Bilardo decided to remove Diego and send José Carvajal to replace him.

My God! The *Ten* took off the captain's band, threw it to the ground and left the pitch swearing at his coach. He went through the locker room in a fury. I went down with Marcos Franchi and we found him kicking everything that crossed his path, punching the metal lockers. We let him vent and then we went to the residence. Diego didn't even take a shower.

Burgos drew a minute from the end, which practically destroyed Sevillian aspirations to play a continental tournament: although in the last match they defeated Sporting de Gijón, they remained in seventh place in the table, with the same points as Atlético Madrid but outside of the UEFA Cup for having a worse goal difference than the red-and-white club.

At the end of the duel against Burgos, the journalists asked Bilardo what he thought of the insults Diego had given him. 'I don't know, I don't know, he didn't tell me anything,' replied Carlos, who apparently hadn't noticed the reaction of his compatriot. He would find out a long time later, when he turned on the TV at home.

That night, while Diego was in a room on the first floor watching television, sitting on one of the two armchairs, alone, Marcos, the lawyer Daniel Bolotnicoff and I were talking in an office next to the front door of the mansion. Suddenly, the bell rang, and I answered through the automatic entry phone.

'Who is it?'

'It's Carlos, it's Carlos. Is Diego there, is Diego there?' he said, duplicating each phrase.

'Yes, come in, Carlos.'

I opened the door and he quickly walked over to the office.

'Where is Diego, where is Diego?'

I noticed he was disengaged, very excited.

'Upstairs,' I indicated.

Bilardo went to a staircase that connected the ground floor with the first floor and ended just in front of the room where Diego was watching television. After a few seconds, we began to hear a very loud discussion, shouting, with insults launched by both Diego and Carlos. Suddenly, we feel a blow and, immediately, silence. I went up quickly with Marcos and Daniel, very worried, and we found a scene that seemed to be taken from a Federico Fellini movie ... or Pedro Almodóvar, to reference an artist from that country: Diego was standing on one of the armchairs of the room, bare-chested and wearing only tight boxer shorts, looking like a boxer, but very nervous. Bilardo, sitting on the floor, had his back against the wall and his eyes wide. When he saw us, he relaxed his expression a little, surely relieved that we had come to rescue him. Later we would learn from Diego that the dispute had been settled with a single blow. Bilardo left the house at a faster pace than he had used on his arrival, without even whispering a 'good night'. We asked the *Ten* what had happened, but he only reproached his coach. We left him alone and went back to the office. After a while, I proposed to Marcos and Daniel that we go see Bilardo. 'How is he going to hit him like that?' I asked. They agreed and we went there. Gloria, Carlos's wife, received us.

'Hi, Gloria, is Carlos here?'

'Yes,' she answered very kindly. 'He's upstairs. Come in. This man [her husband] is getting crazier every day!'

We went upstairs and Carlos was in his room, sitting on his bed, with his back against the backrest and his legs bent, and he was still upset by the incident. He had a pill of an anxiolytic medicine in one hand and a glass of cognac in the other. We tried to reassure him, but we withdrew after a long time without having achieved our goal.

That same week, Diego and Sevilla broke relations. The club issued a harsh statement in which it accused its player of 'systematic failure to attend training sessions', 'bad image on and off the pitch' and 'disorderly life, because of his poor performance in recent months'. In addition, a curious rumour emerged: that President Cuervas had hired a private investigator to pursue the *Ten* throughout the city. The press gloated over countless stories, most of them made up.

Diego decided to travel to Buenos Aires. I suggested that he meditate on his future.

'If this is the price you have to pay,' I said, referring to the stupid banquet served by the press, 'don't play football anymore.'

He arrived in Ezeiza and, at the same airport, agreed to speak with the many journalists who were waiting for him. He unloaded with everything:

'My decision to stay away from high competition is final, so I don't want any more offers.'

According to the press, clubs in England, Japan and other countries rubbed their hands to sign him. But Diego had other plans.

'I want to be with my family and watch the final stage of the Copa América on television. Nothing more.'

A journalist asked him about his interdict with Bilardo.

'It's all cleared up. We discussed the matter as two men.'

After Diego's decision, I agreed to work for a few months in football clinics that were held in Japan. I came back on 5 September. I remember that, on a stopover at the Madrid airport, I watched the famous 5-0 that Colombia gave to the Argentine team led by Alfio *Coco* Basile, in the qualifiers for the 1994 World Cup in the United States. Diego was at the River Plate stadium that day, where his ears were filled with a popular clamour: 'Please, come back!' And he did!

Encouraged by the *Gringo* Ricardo Giusti, his former partner in the World Cups in Mexico and Italy, Diego agreed to join Newell's Old Boys of Rosario. A little because he was seduced by the club proposal. Also because he wanted to return to the national team, who had to face the South America–Oceania intercontinental play-off against Australia, for the last place at the World Cup. The presence of the *Ten* in the city located on the left bank of the Paraná River unleashed a phenomenal madness, at the height of the Neapolitan ardour: the brand-new incorporation was officially presented on Monday, 13 September 1993 in an open practice in the Colossus of the Independence Park, attended by 50,000 people!

Invited by Diego for his debut with the red–and–black jersey, a friendly match against the Ecuadorian club Emelec, I arrived in Rosario the day before the match, scheduled for 7 October.

I appeared in the suite on the top floor of the Hotel Riviera, where Claudia received me. Diego appeared later, dressed only in a black slip, very tight. His figure surprised me, because he was very skinny.

'Who are you going to play for, for the Versace team?' I shot.

He laughed.

'Look, football is not a matter of aesthetics, but of performance.'

'But I feel good!' he retorted.

He explained to me that he was following a special diet that a Chinese doctor had organised for him, and that he was training with a bodybuilder named Daniel Cerrini.

'As you are now, the rivals will break you … or you will break alone,' I warned him.

Diego had not worn the light-blue-and-white shirt for several months, since that match against Denmark in Mar del Plata. After lifting the Artemio Franchi trophy, he had a strong argument with *Coco* Basile and he excluded himself from the 1993 Copa América in Ecuador and the World Cup qualifiers for the United States tournament. After the memorable 5-0 and the request of the fans, Diego and *Coco* smoked the peace pipe and the *Ten* prepared himself for the duel with Australia, which was resolved with a draw in Sydney and an Argentine victory by a meagre 1-0 on the River Plate pitch, in Buenos Aires. With qualification assured, a door was also opened for Diego to return to the main sporting scene: the World Cup.

In May 2011, almost 18 years after that suffered repechage, Diego threw a grenade in the middle of a dialectical war with Julio Grondona. The *Ten* assured that in that double game both countries agreed that anti-doping controls should not be carried out on the members of both squads. Based on this amendment, Diego continued, the South American players were given *speed coffee*, a euphemism suggesting that stimulant drugs were introduced into the infusion consumed by the athletes, in order to improve their performance on the pitch. During a television interview, Diego demanded that Grondona be asked 'why there was no doping in the game against Australia, if we had had doping in all the games. Because they gave us speed coffee and that way you could put the ball at one angle! They put something on the coffee. You could run more.' When his interviewer asked him if he was indeed sure that the Argentinian football players had been given prohibited substances, he insisted: 'If they do ten anti-doping tests and in the game that Argentina goes to the United States there is no anti-doping control, you have to be very stupid. There was the trap and Grondona knew about it.' After the acid complaint, Alfio Basile replied that Diego's accusations were 'all bullshit'.

The AFA, meanwhile, issued a statement to address the serious complaints. 'It has been generated in recent days,' the text indicated. 'A tiny personal controversy, the result of a former player believing that with his inaccurate and ill-intentioned words he was violating or attempting to violate the sportsmanship of a dramatic qualification against Australia. We think of all those men who played the qualifying games and we say that they were all worthy, decent, honest and total sportsmen. And, for the peace of mind of them and their families, they are exempt from giving answers to the abstract. There was no anti-doping control simply because it was not a regulatory obligation for such matches.'

Unfortunately, I was not wrong with the phrase I had said to Diego in the Rosario hotel: because of those crazy things that he was subjected to with supposed magic diets, or to which he allowed himself to be subjected, for the first time in his entire career he suffered a fibrillar tear in the hamstring. The injury occurred during his last official game with Newell's, on 2 December 1993, against Huracán. Almost two months later, on 26 January, Diego played a friendly against the Rio de Janeiro club Vasco da Gama. It was the last time he played in the red-and-black jersey, and a new entry into the tunnel of uncertainty, with a World Cup just around the corner.

Chapter 9

The stab in the back

*One searches full of hope the way that dreams
promised to his desires ...*

*One knows that the fight is cruel and a lot, but
struggles and bleeds out for the faith that stubborns ...*

*One goes crawling among thorns, and in his eagerness
to give his love, suffers and breaks until understands
that has been left without a heart ...*

('One' – famous Argentine tango)

COMPOSER ENRIQUE Santos Discépolo died almost ten years before Diego's birth. However, the lyrics of his tango 'Uno' ('One'), premiered in 1943, perfectly portrays the bitter passage of the *Ten* through his fourth World Cup: United States 1994.

The path of dreams began on Friday, 1 April 1994. That day I received a call on my cell phone. I answered with some disdain, since I did not know the number that appeared on the mobile screen.

'Hello?' I asked laconically.

'What are you doing, *Blind*?' come from the other side his unmistakable voice, sparkling and cheerful as rarely before.

'How are you doing, *Die*? I see you're very happy ...'

'I'm very happy, *Blind*. I just made a decision ... and I want you to help me.'

'Well, tell me what it's about.'

'I'm going to play in the United States.'

'But, Diego, we've already talked about it twice and ...'

'Yes,' he cut me off, 'but now I'm convinced. This time it will be my last World Cup, but the first in which Dalma and Gianinna can see me play.'

'You're sure?'

'Very sure.'

In those two conversations that we had had, between February and March of that year, I had suggested to him to completely discard the idea since, in my opinion, that almost unattainable peak had already been achieved eight years ago in Mexico. I was of the opinion that, given the infinity of blows of all kinds that he had suffered throughout his exaggerated life, that last effort would surely bring him more problems than solutions. For me, his career in the national team had ended with honours having collaborated with the qualification for the World Cup in the play-offs with Australia. However, his euphoria was contagious.

'Well, OK, you convinced me,' I replied at that moment, overwhelmed by the force of the argument.

'Go on, great! So, come home tomorrow at five in the afternoon, that's when we organise everything.'

The next day, at the agreed time, I rang the automatic entry phone on the seventh floor of the building located on the well-known corner of Segurola and Habana (in the

Villa Devoto neighbourhood, in Buenos Aires city), which has become a place of worship for all Maradonians. After the affectionate greetings with him, Claudia and Marcos Franchi, I insisted his idea could cause more inconvenience than happiness. He was firm in his desire. The Argentine team had just left a pale image in Brazil (they had lost 2-0 against the *Verdeamarela*, without Diego or Claudio Caniggia) and the *Ten* was delighted to strengthen the team and, along with *Cani*, Diego Simeone, Fernando Redondo, Gabriel Batistuta, Oscar Ruggeri and Abel Balbo, among others, make it a powerful contender to win the World Cup. I announced to him that I agreed to accompany him in this new adventure but with one exclusive condition: he had to accept my terms. Curious, he asked me what they were.

'To get you ready, we need to work very hard during two weeks, and alone. No distractions.'

Diego agreed. The first step was to find a place to prepare. I made it very clear to him that, to reach the goal he set for himself, he had to 'leave the sordid neighbourhood looking for heaven', as the lyrics of 'El Choclo' say, one of his favourite tangos. We analysed three possibilities that Marcos had provided and I chose a ranch located 40km from the city of Santa Rosa, in the middle of the Pampean meadows and about 500km from the city of Buenos Aires. The other two fields belonged to very famous people, who used them to receive a lot of guests, and we needed privacy.

'It is the ideal place, we will be away from the swarm that always buzzes around you. We need the maximum peace of mind and privacy possible in those first days, OK?'

'If you say so, that's fine with me,' he certified.

'Who is the owner of this ranch?'

'A man I met when I went to spend a few days on a beach in Oriente [a quiet Buenos Aires seaside resort, near Bahía Blanca]. He gave me his phone number in case I ever needed something.'

'Perfect, that day arrived. Let's call him right now.'

I dialled the number, a female voice answered me that identified itself as the secretary of Mr Ángel Rosas. She immediately connected me to him.

'Who speaks?' The tone of my new interlocutor seemed to me between annoyed and reluctant.

'Good afternoon, Mr Rosas, how are you doing? My name is Fernando Signorini and I am Diego Maradona's personal trainer.'

Don Ángel was silent for a few seconds, until he replied:

'Hey, man, I ask you please: stop this shit. It is enough! I'm busy, don't waste my time.'

I was speechless. Marcos rescued me, listening to the conversation over the loudspeaker.

'Ask him who won the last hand of *truco* [a very popular playing card game in Argentina] and how,' he said in my ear. I repeated Franchi's words precisely.

'Ah!' shouted Rosas, relieved. 'So then it's true.'

The man confided in me that when he returned to Santa Rosa after his vacation on the Buenos Aires coast, he had told his friends at the club that an unexpected and exciting event had happened to him on those deserted beaches: meeting *Dieguito* Maradona and his family. As the story had seemed implausible to those close to him, one of his companions demanded a photo that testifies to the miraculous encounter. Ángel, between ashamed and sad, lamented:

'I don't have any, I hadn't brought the camera.'

Starting that night, and for several weeks, his friends took turns calling him at his office and also at his house to make phone pranks on him, posing as Diego. That was the reason why Don Rosas took my telephone call with indisputable weariness. But, with the ice broken and the real purpose of my contact revealed, we immediately defined the details concerning our stay at his establishment.

On the morning of 9 April, we left in a Mercedes-Benz car with Don Diego and two friends of the Maradona family, Germán and Rodolfo, both from Corrientes, heading to Santa Rosa. We arrived at the house of Don Ángel, who, with his wife, happily received us.

After making our stay official and receiving the keys to the house where we would stay, we went through a supermarket to stock up on a series of things that would be essential to us throughout our Pampas adventure. Shortly before six in the afternoon, we finally arrived at the gate of the 'El Marito' ranch. The sun, which was setting on the horizon, seemed to ignite the infinite plain with its last rays. Quickly, we divided up the tasks to prepare the dwelling that would serve as our home for 12 days. The first thing we did was light several logs in the fireplace in the main room, to heat the picturesque house while outside the cold began to freeze the thermometers. Exhausted from travel and extended housework until midnight, I fell asleep right away. Don Diego woke me up, who, with his sweet voice, whispered to me an offer impossible to refuse:

'*Profe*, would you like a maté?'

'Don Diego, you are in charge of waking up the roosters, right?' I replied as I reached out my hand to accept the pumpkin freshly charged with loving kindness.

Outside, the field had been covered in a merciless frost. It looked like a ski slope. The first activity of the day consisted of approaching, with Don Diego, the house of the caretaker of the field, which was about 80 metres away, with the intention of introducing ourselves. I clapped my hands from the fence and immediately the silhouette of a very tall and thin man, with abundant white hair, dressed in the Creole style and unmistakable Nordic features, appeared at the end of the corridor. After a loud and cordial greeting, he came over to shake hands. I held out mine, explained who we were and the reason for our presence. Then I turned to Don Diego, who was standing a few metres behind, and I introduced him:

'The man is Don Diego Maradona.'

Our host called his wife and, while she approached smiling, he, looking fixedly at my companion, raised one of his hands to his head and, while pulling his hat backwards, exclaimed with a tone that melded confusion and surprise:

'Maradona, I thought you were skinnier!'

With Don Diego we exploded with guffaw. When I recovered from the uproarious laughter and tears that had covered my eyes, I explained:

'No, no! This man is Don Diego, the player's father. Diego will arrive today after noon.'

The old man, clasping his hands in a prayer position, exclaimed:

'Ah, he seemed too chubby to me, what the hell!'

The man apologised and told us that his confusion had originated in the fact that he did not have a television or receive newspapers or magazines, so that the image that had been made of Diego had been based only on descriptions of the radio commentators.

After noon, Germán and Rodolfo went to the Santa Rosa airport to look for Diego and Marcos Franchi, who had taken a commercial flight. Knowing the place where he would stay and train, Diego felt somewhat surprised. Much more when he discovered that his room had a small television whose antenna barely captured a channel in the capital of the Pampas, although with more rain than clarity of images. He opened the bedroom window and yelled at me angrily:

'Where did you take me, you son of a bitch?'

I was arranging my work items on a table in the gallery, while Don Diego lit the fire next to the grill to prepare one of his famous barbecues. My answer, in the same tone, knocked him out:

'I brought you to Villa Fiorito!'

I looked at Don Diego and winked at him:

'Who will this boy be the son of, Anchorena [Patriarch of one of the richest families in Argentina]?'

The old man, divine, looked up at the diaphanous sky and exclaimed:

'This is a paradise!'

Diego had asked me to include Daniel Cerrini, the bodybuilder who had advised him during his brief stint at Newell's, who arrived at the ranch a day later. The guy made him eat a series of pills with vitamins, amino acids, herbs to lose weight and other concoctions, several times a day. It worried me.

'You will arrive perfectly on bread and water. You don't need any of those things.'

He was firm, so that, before leaving for La Pampa, I had suggested that, if he wanted to consume all those things, at least we first consult a doctor specialised in nutrition. With his endorsement, I made a lightning trip to meet in Rome, once again, with the distinguished Antonio Dal Monte, who had already helped us, and a lot, to organise the proper preparation for the World Cups in Mexico and Italy. Diego was 33 years old, and although it was a utopia to think that he could arrive in the United States with a physical state like the one he had in 1986, he could achieve an extraordinary level of quality to which was added his unmatched experience and his undeniable overwhelming personality. Dal Monte not only gave me the parameters to carry out the appropriate training for Diego, who was out of shape and had not engaged in physical activity for several weeks, but he also suggested that I study the question of the pills with a specialist in sports medicine in Argentina, Néstor Lentini, who was the medical director of the National Centre of High Performance Sports (CeNARD).

'In your country there is only one person in whom I absolutely trust, and that is Dr Néstor Lentini,' he assured me.

A couple of days after Diego's arrival at 'El Marito', Lentini came to the ranch. I got together under some trees with him and Cerrini – the *Ten* preferred not to intervene in that meeting – and the doctor meticulously studied the leaflets of each one of the products that Diego was taking, to analyse their composition, usefulness and way of use. Apparently, everything was fine and there was no risk of anything.

My differences with Cerrini were not only concentrated in the pills. I wanted to stabilise Diego at 76kg, since we were preparing him to participate in a World Cup and not in an abdominals competition. Cerrini insisted that he should stay at 70kg, the weight he had been during his time at Newell's.

'Sure, but the rivals touched him and he flew like a leaf,' I protested during a discussion we had in front of Diego. Also, what a coincidence, by being out of his weight, he tore himself for the first time in his life.

The bodybuilder denied that the injury had anything to do with that, and stressed that in sport the issue of body weight was not important.

'You are a phenomenon! So, with that criteria, a flyweight boxer could fight against a light heavyweight.'

The controversy was resolved with a final phrase from Diego, which today I must also recognise as premonitory:

'Cerrini, close your mouth, you don't know anything about this.'

Meanwhile, Diego followed a normal diet, with a variety of dishes. I could not expose him to the brutal sacrifice of taking him out of his routine: he ate a sober breakfast of fruits and cereals, lunch and dinner with carbohydrates, vegetables and low-fat proteins. We also ate some good barbecues prepared by the magical hands of Don Diego, although the *Ten* was controlled. As Jorge Valdano once said, when Diego wanted to do things well, he was the best of all; when he wanted to do them wrong, he was also the best of all.

I had diagrammed a preparation scheme based on the knowledge I had of Diego's physique after so many years in which we had worked together in Barcelona and Naples: series of exercises with which I sought not only to improve endurance, but also power and speed. In the first two or three days of training, I noticed him really out of shape. His movements were very forced and the fatigue limit appeared quite fast. However, towards the end of the first week, his muscles began to hint at the feline elasticity of the best moments.

Every morning, as soon as the alarm clock rang, inside his room the catchy rhythm of Los Auténticos Decadentes (a musical group very popular in Argentina) began to sound at full volume, with moving songs from they first album, which made the rest of us jump out of our beds, in a climate of contagious joy. Diego's attitude changed radically when he began training. His face was serious, and he pursued his efforts with unwavering determination. Many times, during the excruciating choking work, I would yell at him – with swearing of all calibres – to overcome the hated pain threshold and stay there. He did not remain silent, and he unloaded on me curled epithets to discharge his anger and the suffering that the fight caused him.

In the afternoons, we would travel to Santa Rosa to do the second shift, at the gym that former boxer Miguel Angel Campanino had kindly made available to us. There, we performed exercises for joint mobility, stretching, punchbag, punching ball and rope. Diego also went up to the ring to play five or six rounds with Miguel Angel. Before returning to the ranch, we went through another gym, which had a pool with heated water, where Diego relaxed his muscles.

The only free afternoon that we were granted was due to an invitation that Diego received to visit a humble little school that operated about 40km from the ranch, in the middle of the squat Pampean hills. I still remember with emotion the selfless and admirable sacrifice that those worthy rural teachers made to satisfy one of the most basic and inalienable rights of children.

At night, after dinner, we would go for a walk in the park, bundled up like Eskimos. We preferred to converse under the stars than to stay and watch TV on the only available channel, although the antenna had more streaks and rains than clear images. We also played close, disputed, endless *truco* games.

One of the last days, after finishing the hard training in the morning, Diego hung a small mirror on the branch of a pine tree and smeared his face with foam. As he began to shave under the rays of the bright midday sun, he turned his head and, looking at his father, said with a smile on his face:

'Daddy, doesn't this remind you of Fiorito?'

Hearing it, I thought, 'We're fine.' Those were the most unforgettable 12 days of all the years that I spent with Diego. I was moved by his enthusiasm and his determination to achieve a goal that at first seemed very distant, almost impossible, and in no time he was within reach. Even though he was still a prisoner of drug addiction. He fought every day to banish that shit from his body, and when the withdrawal syndrome hit, he had a very bad time. It was very tough and distressing, but that love of wearing the light-blue-and-white shirt and fulfilling his purpose motivated him to put everything aside.

There were a few occasions, during those days, in which the ghost of need appeared to overwhelm him, usually in the dark, in the middle of the solitude of his room. One night, I was reading with the help of a little nightstand that barely emitted a dim light when I heard a noise at the door. In the gloom, I identified Diego: standing by the entrance to my room, he was staring at me. He nodded at me, as if he was saying 'let's go'. His eyes denoted the urge to rid himself of the monster within. We wrapped ourselves up well, because it was extremely cold, and we went out to sweat, to eliminate tension under a sky full of stars and a moon that looked like a reflector. Those moments redoubled my admiration for him.

The road from the door of the house to the gate of the ranch was almost two kilometres. We started jogging to warm up our bodies and, when Diego got into rhythm, I ordered him to do dips, jumps, sit-ups, push-ups, spins ... until in a moment, steaming up through the ears, panting, he announced:

'It's done, it's done.'

We walked back. He was relieved. I was happy because he hadn't brought cocaine to the ranch. If at that moment he had held it close, he would have fallen once more. By not having it, he had to find another argument for the syndrome to pass: an escape of great intensity.

Having completed the 12 days in 'El Marito', we returned to Buenos Aires. Diego embarked for Salta, where on 20 April the national team played a friendly against Morocco, in preparation for the World Cup. I did not travel to the north, because I went to prepare the facilities of another farm, baptised 'Santa María', in the town of Norberto de la Riestra. We prefer it to spend the last week of the pre-season because it was not so far from the sports centre that the Argentine Football Association has in Ezeiza. In mid-May, he had to join the team that would face four friendlies abroad before arriving in the United States to compete in the World Cup.

In 'Santa María', Diego stayed in the main chalet, situated in the middle of an extensive park embellished by a rich variety of trees. The remaining members of the group settled into a comfortable and quaint little house,

which in the past had served as a home for the labourers who
worked in the family's ranches. We spent eight days there,
in which we bravely managed to get the *Ten* ready for their
last appearance at the World Cup.

After a tour with more doubts than successes –
Argentina lost with Ecuador and drew with Chile, beat
Israel and drew without goals with Croatia, a poor harvest
against four teams that had not qualified for the tournament
in the United States – the Argentina national team settled
in the sumptuous Babson College, an educational institution
in Massachusetts, on the outskirts of the city of Boston,
nestled in the middle of a charming wooded landscape.
The complex had an infrastructure that guaranteed all the
comforts to complete the preparation for the debut against
Greece, at the Foxboro Stadium in Boston.

One afternoon that the players had free to relax a bit
from the sports environment, Diego took the opportunity to
visit, with Claudia, his daughters and a friend, the journalist
Adrián Paenza, the Faneuil Hall Marketplace shopping
centre located in the city of Boston, a few kilometres from
Babson College. In the food court of the imposing mall,
the group had pizza for lunch with a former student of
Paenza, Gerry Garbulsky, who lived in the state capital of
Massachusetts. At the end of the meal, Diego asked Gerry
to accompany him to a sportswear store located a few metres
away, Foot Locker, since he needed to buy shoes. Already
in the store – which was decorated in accordance with the
competition, with posters of different football players, none
of them the Argentine 10 – Maradona was amazed by the
great variety of brands and assortment of models, so he
began to try on different footwear, helped by Gerry and the
kind assistance of a young salesman. After choosing eight

pairs, Maradona went to the cashier to pay for his purchase. The employee, happy with the volume of the sale, gave the Argentine a key ring alluding to the World Cup.

'I don't know if you know,' the boy confided in English, 'but the football World Cup is about to begin here in the United States. This keychain has the tournament logo on it.'

Gerry translated the comment, Maradona thanked him for the gift and the two Argentines left the store. Seconds later, Paenza entered the same shop with Claudia Maradona, who had forgotten to ask her husband to also buy sneakers for their daughters. The journalist noticed the football decoration of the place, very appropriate for the proximity of the championship, and asked the happy salesman:

'Do you have any idea who was just here?'

Faced with the refusal of the guy, Paenza continued:

'The best football player in all of history.'

Overwhelmed by the observation, the boy was embarrassed by his ignorance on the matter and by not having recognised such an illustrious visitor. However, emboldened by a sudden impulse, the young man took a paper and a pen and hurried out of the place to run, shouting, to his recent clients. There was no way he could miss out on getting the autograph of such a glittering sports star. When the salesman reached them, he extended the paper and pen and excitedly asked for the signature of ... Gerry!

During training at Babson College, Diego continued his evolution. To the tactical work with the team, commanded by Alfio Basile, we add effort exercises aimed at enhancing the state of his form. The planning was designed to reach his maximum expression at the beginning of the second phase, since we all took it for granted that Argentina would qualify from their group: that was the last World Cup that took place with an initial round of six groups of four teams, of which the first two went to the knockout phase from the round of 16 along with the four best third-place sides. In one of his first training sessions, Diego gave his friend Paenza an interview, in which he highlighted:

'God willing, I'm going to be better than in 1990. We are working as in Mexico and in Italy. I told Dalma and Gianinna about it. Everything I do is going to be for the love of football and because I want to give my last World Cup to the Argentines in a big way.'

The debut game against Greece, on 21 June, was encouraging. The light-blue-and-white squad achieved a convincing performance and four goals: three by Gabriel Batistuta and one by Diego, after a stupendous succession of speed touches that culminated in his lethal left-foot strike to the upper right-hand corner of the Hellenic goal. Nobody imagined that this would be his last strike in World Cup tournaments.

Diego returned to Foxboro on the 25th, for his last game at the World Cup. Argentina began losing to Nigeria, but two goals from Claudio Caniggia sealed the second victory for the team led by Basile. When the Swedish referee Bo Karlsson whistled the end of the match, Diego celebrated euphorically with his team-mates, oblivious to the black clouds that were beginning to form the perfect storm. From the stalls, which I shared with a group of joyful compatriots, I laughed when I discovered him walking hand in hand with a blonde assistant towards the dressing rooms. A broad smile spread across his face as he raised his free arm toward the stands in grateful salute. He did not know that that woman, Sue Carpenter, an employee of the organisation of the championship and co-star of one of the most emblematic images in the dark history of the event, had gone to look for him inside the field to lead him to the room where he would be tested. Anti-doping control. That night I went to sleep thinking that the reasons for being optimistic were justifying themselves little by little.

On the afternoon of 28 June, we went to one of the Babson College gyms to work on stretching and joint mobility. Towards the end of the session, Diego tried to achieve a position that he had not achieved since the previous World Cup. Sitting on a mat and with his legs extended and separated, he began to lean the trunk forward (his hands clasped at the nape of his neck and his elbows following the line of the body), with the intention of pressing it against the ground and also supporting his forehead. He pressed his chest against the floor, counted out loud to three, and rose like a spring, his fists clenched and a happiness that did not enter his face. Afterwards, he squeezed Claudia with a hug and in that sublime state of grace we returned to the building where we stayed. Diego was full of happiness. He told jokes to each companion who crossed his path, he stretched out on the massage table of the dressing room and he poured his heart and soul in between the magical and relaxing hands of Salvatore Carmando, his inseparable Neapolitan masseuse. I took the opportunity to shower and rest for a while in my room, waiting for dinner, while mentally reviewing the day's work. Until three knocks on the door destroyed my musings. Behind my door appeared Daniel Cerrini. He was pale, extremely nervous. He wanted to say something to me, but he could barely move his trembling lower lip.

'It can not be possible, it can not be!' was the only thing he managed to get out before taking his face with his hands.

'What can't be possible, Daniel?' I incited him to continue speaking, since I did not understand what he intended to notify me.

His imprecision lasted a few seconds, until he finally gathered up his courage and announced that Marcos Franchi had just called him to inform him that one of the anti-doping controls corresponding to the game against Nigeria had tested positive. Two players had been analysed: Diego and defender Sergio Vázquez, who had not played in the game against the Africans. But, according to what Franchi had communicated to him, everything pointed towards the light-blue-and-white captain.

'*Profe*, what do I have to do?' He asked me with his eyes overflowing with tears.

'What do you have to do? Take a plane to the end of the world, because Don Diego is arriving and, if he sees you, he will shoot you in the head.'

He paid so much attention to me that I never saw him again.

The adverse news did not take long to reach every member of the delegation. Everyone's eyes asked questions that no mouth could answer. Someone murmured that at the 1986 World Cup in Mexico a Spanish player, Ramón Calderé, had also tested positive but FIFA had pardoned him after the Iberian team doctor admitted that he had made a mistake in giving him a medicine. Many clung to this background as if it were a life preserver in the middle of the ocean, although we did not know which banned substance had been detected in the sample.

The dinner took place in a rarefied atmosphere, a mixture of doubts, nervousness and disbelief. The next day, we travelled to Dallas, where the national team was supposed to play the last match of the first phase against Bulgaria. Towards the evening of 29 June, I went to Marcos Franchi's room to wait with him, Oscar Ruggeri and other friends for Rubén Moschella, the AFA administrative employee who would inform us about the official FIFA decision. Some said they had confidence in Julio Grondona to propose some kind of activity that would solve the problem. Others were not so sure ... and we sensed that the worst was yet to come. The sound of knuckles rapping on the bedroom door put an end to speculation. Moschella's expression left no room for doubt. Even less his succinct words, loaded with infinite sadness:

'Diego is outside,' he announced with an almost imperceptible tone.

With Marcos and Oscar we got strength from I don't know where and we walked to Diego's room to communicate some of the most devastating news of his short but very intense life. The room was dark. I turned on the bathroom light and sat on the edge of his bed. Marcos and Oscar did the same on the other bed in the bedroom.

'What's happening?' he asked us while he moved his arms as if to stretch.

There was a brief silence. None of the three of us knew what to say. As naturally as I could manage, it occurred to me to say to him:

'Come on, *Diegucho*, they killed us! We have to go.'

'How?' he interrupted me, incredulous.

'That's it, they took you out of the World Cup. It's over! Come on, get up, take a shower and come to Marcos's room.'

He got up slowly, went to the bathroom without saying a word, shut himself in and then a heartrending cry was heard. Oscar tried to comfort him on the other side of the door, but I suggested that it was better to leave him alone so as not to interfere with the externalisation of his pain. Almost an hour later he joined us, fragile, vulnerable, in that state of utter devastation in which irreversible events usually leave us.

'Is this why we broke our souls, *Fer*?' he asked me with a thin voice. He was completely demoralised.

Five prohibited substances derived from ephedrine appeared in the urine sample of the Argentine captain. How did that get into his body? Apparently, when the delegation was already installed in the United States, Cerrini ran out of one of his little pills, a fat burner known as Ripped Fast, and went to buy more at a store specialising in proteins, vitamins and other nutritional supplements. As he did not find a product of the same brand, he acquired another one – Ripped Fuel – and did not notice that it contained ephedrine, a substance prohibited in football but curiously enabled for other sports. Also, at the time, it was a supplement suitable for sale without prescription. What could we do?

In highly competitive sports, super-professional, the person dedicated to the athlete's nutrition must be highly trained, demonstrate absolute suitability, and above all be aware of what he is giving to a player. I do not know if Cerrini failed due to negligence or irresponsibility, but it must be recognised that he acted with a high degree of lack of professionalism. His decision ended much more than Diego's dream of reaching a new World Cup Final. The team collapsed after the result of the doping control was confirmed to their captain: they lost the last match of the initial phase with Bulgaria and were eliminated in the round of 16, when they fell to Romania at the Rose Bowl in Los Angeles. Undoubtedly, along with the fracture of his left ankle in 1984, that was the most difficult moment of Diego's career: FIFA immediately banished him and punished him with another suspension for 15 months.

The outstanding Uruguayan writer Eduardo Galeano pointed out that 'when Maradona was finally expelled from the 1994 World Cup, the football fields lost their most vociferous rebel. And they also lost a fantastic player. Maradona is uncontrollable when he speaks, but much more when he plays: no one can foresee the mischief of this inventor of surprises, who never repeats himself and who enjoys puzzling computers. (…) In the frigid end-of-the-century football, which demands winning and prohibits enjoyment, this man is one of the few who shows that fantasy can also be effective.'

On his return to Argentina, Diego received the moving tribute of millions of fans, most of whom attributed what happened to a plot orchestrated against him from the high command of FIFA.

The sanction against Diego not only generated rejections in Argentina. I have read that, in Israel, an 11-year-old boy from the city of Haifa went on a hunger strike and had to be hospitalised after he spent three days without food or drink. In Bangladesh, a group of exalted people took to the streets to demand that FIFA revoke the sentence and burned an image of the entity's president, the Brazilian João Havelange. There, a lawyer, Mohammed Anwarul, filed a lawsuit against Havelange in a court of law, demanding the payment of 1,000 takas (about $25) as compensation for the 'mental disorders' caused by the expulsion of the Argentine captain. In India, workers from a food company boycotted a wedding in protest. Diego's power could also be measured in tickets sold: the 64,000 tickets at the Cotton Bowl stadium in Dallas for the match between Argentina and Bulgaria on 30 June were sold out several days before the game, when before the suspension of the *Ten* had been announced. This huge demand did not occur with the two meetings that took place there previously: on 17 June, Spain–South Korea brought together 56,000 people, and Nigeria–Bulgaria, on 21 June, barely 44,000.

In Buenos Aires, Dr Lentini compared the two products consumed by Diego, Ripped Fast and Ripped Fuel, with very modern equipment that would be used in the 1995 Pan American Games in the city of Mar del Plata to carry out anti-doping controls, and found that, indeed, the second contained the prohibited substance. But no study can reflect the bravery of a man who faced the last great adventure of his life with tremendous audacity and resolution, as Diego did. Nor can it measure the capacity for suffering of a human being who endured a tremendous effort to re-wear the shirt of his country, nor his ability to generate so much joy through the ball. But perhaps it is more appropriate that this dark chapter is closed by Diego himself, with the words he used to say goodbye to the United States in a last interview with his friend Paenza, recorded in a hotel in Dallas:

'I prepared very well for this World Cup, I prepared like never before. They hit me in the head at a time when I can resurface. When I got high, I went and told the judge: yes, I got high, what do I have to pay? And I paid for it. It was two very hard years. But, well, I don't understand. They were wrong about me. I didn't take drugs to play. With what need, if I have Fernando? I didn't run for drugs, I ran for the heart and the shirt. My arms are down, my soul is shattered. FIFA disappointed me, they hit me in the head without disgust. They took me out of football permanently. I don't think I want another rematch. I don't want to dramatise, but believe me, they cut off my legs.'

Chapter 10

The comeback

ON MONDAY, 17 October 2005, I saw the transmission of a striking report: on his own programme, 'La noche del Diez' ('The night of the Ten'), Diego interviewed Maradona. Or Maradona to Diego, I am not very clear about it, because the roles passed from one chair to the other constantly, throughout the conversation between the interviewer and the interviewee, who were ultimately the same person, favoured by the 'magic of television'. In that dialogue, which had a phenomenal worldwide repercussion from the sharp confessions released, Diego declared his love for Claudia, his daughters, his parents and the ball, and his unfortunate relationship with cocaine. He also threw out a phrase that caught my attention: 'The national team is a lifelong dream, but it is far away. It is a very long road. Some managers told me that the doors were always open, but they did not give me the key. It is biggest dream I have.'

At that time, a couple of months ago with Cesar Menotti we had finished our third stage in Independiente – which we alternated with processes in Sampdoria of Italy and Rosario Central – and, the truth, I fantasised about Diego's dream. While enjoying it with him, of course. The *Ten* had had two short and ineffective periods as a coach at the Correntino club Deportivo Mandiyú (he had offered for me to accompany him, but at that time I was in Japan, working in some clinics, and, when I returned, his cycle there was already over) and at Racing Club, during the 15-month suspension due to positive doping in the United States. At *La Academia* we worked together. We started in January 1995, after the president of the club, Juan De Stéfano, proposed to Diego that he train the professional team. He formed a technical duo with Carlos Fren and offered me to take care of the physical preparation of the players. The episode lasted just four months and 11 official matches: two wins, six draws and three losses. True to his style, Diego announced that he would resign if De Stéfano lost the club's presidential balloting and was not re-elected. The winner was finally the opposition list headed by Osvaldo Otero and we did not stay. 'Anyone would die to lead Racing. I am proud to have done it, but I am a man of my word,' declared the *Ten* when he left his position.

When Diego served the FIFA sanction, he returned to Boca Juniors as a player until his final retirement in 1997. In that last period we were not together: I had already started my journey with Cesar Menotti.

A few years later, in October 2008, Chile beat Argentina in the qualifiers for the World Cup in South Africa 2010. That was the first and only Chilean triumph over their trans-Andean rival in official matches since 1916, including World Cups, qualifiers and the Copa América (for statistics, penalty shoot-out wins are considered draws). That light-blue-and-white squad defeat caused the resignation of coach Alfio Basile, and opened a range of applicants for the vacant position that included Sergio Batista (manager of the under-23 team who had won the gold medal at the 2008 Beijing Olympic Games); the River Plate trainer at that time, Diego Simeone; and Miguel Ángel Russo, coach of San Lorenzo who led the Apertura Tournament. Carlos Bianchi, winner of four Copa Libertadores editions as manager of Boca Juniors (3) and Vélez Sarsfield (1), also emerged as a strong candidate.

In those days, I was in my house in Lincoln. The landline phone rang. It was a friend from that city, Luis Godoy who called me, very happy:

'Congrats, Professor.'

'How are you, Luis? Why congratulations?'

'Because I just heard that you are the new physical trainer for Diego's team.'

'But stop fucking around! Where did you hear that bullshit?'

'Just on a radio program.'

'No, I know absolutely nothing. Really!'

'Seriously?'

'I assure. It's bullshit. They've been speculating on that for a long time.'

We said goodbye and, after five minutes, the cell phone rang. When I looked at the screen, the name was ... Claudia!

'And this?' I asked myself, curious. I answered the phone.

'Hi, *Clau*, how are you?'

'Hello, *Profe*,' she replied with a happy, pleasant tone of voice. 'Diego asks if you would like to accompany him in the national team for the World Cup in South Africa.'

'What are you saying?' I answered a little nervous. I was not working: my last adventures had taken place in Mexico, between 2006 and 2007, at the Puebla club, together with Rubén Rossi, and Tecos, again with Cesar Menotti. I had also accompanied Cayetano Rodríguez at Banfield and Ubaldo Fillol and Jorge Higuaín at Racing Club.

'Now I'll pass the phone to him. He is by my side.'

'He still has you as a secretary ... Did he increase your salary, at least?' I joked, maybe to calm myself down a bit. She extended the phone to Diego. In the last 14 years we had seen each other only once: we met at the Ski Ranch on the Costanera (a former bar and disco that was in front of the River Plate) for a few drinks and a long chat.

'What are you doing, *Blind*?' he greeted me affectionately, as if we had seen each other for the last time the day before. I responded with the same courtesy.

'What are you doing, *Die*, how are you?'

'Very happy. Did you know that I was appointed coach of the national team?' his satisfaction gushed out naturally, sparkling.

'Then it was true ...'

It always seemed to me that Grondona had named him in the middle of a strange juncture. The indicated coach at that time, the favourite for the people, was Carlos Bianchi, but I do not know what kind of differences he had with Grondona, who did not want him, in any way. Then, Julio took the easiest way: he named Diego, even though he surely wasn't convinced with him nor did he want him, although he will have thought, 'If he wins, we all win; if he loses, I will bury him head-first and get rid of him forever.'

'Will you accompany me?' Diego invited me, frankly, with the simplicity of someone who scores in front of an empty goal.

'Obviously!' I didn't think about it for a second. He had included me with graceful friendship and transmitted me his happiness.

'They are going to officially present us tomorrow at the AFA sports complex.'

'I'm in Lincoln, but I'm travelling there right now.'

So it was, literally: the next day, very early, I left by car for Buenos Aires to be with Diego on the day of his coronation. Along the way, I heard Mercedes Sosa sing 'Gracias a la vida' ('Thanks to life') a couple of times, feeling that, at least from a professional point of view, Violeta Parra had also written that song for me.

When we met again, I ran into a radiant Diego.

'How do you feel, *Die*?'

'Like the days my two daughters were born. Beating Bianchi is like beating Foreman, Tyson or Monzón [three former boxing world champions].'

About to turn 48 years old, Diego had the opportunity to make history again with the Argentine national team, although on the other side of the line. On the day of his official presentation, the press room of the AFA sports complex was overflowing. Journalists from around the world struggled to gain access to a privileged place. Once again, Diego's magnetism put the predictions contemplated by the organisers of the event in serious difficulties. During the ceremony, Julio Grondona announced with pomp and pageantry that this was 'a very special day for Argentine football'. Diego, triumphant and optimistic, specified that, 'When I entered the complex today I felt the same as when I was a player: my chest swelled. This is a dream that comes at the best moment of my life, because I am regaining the confidence of my daughters, my parents are very good, I regained the happiness of seeing the day and I feel good spiritually. This is like touching the sky with my hands. I would be a coward if I were not sitting here today assuming in this mini-crisis that the national team is experiencing and I stayed in my house,' he finished with his classic style. Carlos Bilardo, who took over as general director of national teams, launched a very controversial phrase:

'Life is for the national team. It is wrong to say it, but first there is the national team and then the family.'

I thought, 'It will be yours; not mine.'

Once the hiring was sealed, I returned to Lincoln the next day and the following weekend I settled in Buenos Aires. We began to meet regularly at the AFA premises to begin to diagram the first match – the *Ten* called them 'international matches' and not 'friendlies' – agreed in Glasgow against Scotland. There, Diego is a great idol: the Scots love him for having scored two goals against England and eliminating the Three Lions from the World Cup in Mexico.

That first experience set us a pattern that had worsened, and much, since the time in which Diego played, and that today remains in force, unfortunately stronger in South America than in Europe: those responsible for a national team are no longer trainers, but coaches, because they do not have a group to train. When do you work with the players? After a long time of not seeing them. The kids arrive exhausted from an intercontinental trip and a match the previous day, and there is no other possibility than to do a single practice before an official match: the first day they rest, the second they do a regenerative treatment, the third they train and the fourth they play. It's all a lie! A great orchestra conductor would never give a concert in an illustrious hall like the Teatro Colón in Buenos Aires, Carnegie Hall in New York or La Scala in Milan with a single rehearsal, with musicians arriving from different countries the day before. It would be crazy! The parallelism is perfect, because in football the proper functioning of a team is also the product of rehearsals, and this takes time. Time that does not exist, as a result of the overloaded calendars of the players and their clubs, designed by a community of senile and obese gentlemen from the overstuffed armchairs of their extremely packed offices. Today, footballers don't even have time to rest, and even if they need it, they don't let them!

Diego wanted to build a stable selection with players from Argentine teams, as Menotti did during a couple of years before the 1978 World Cup, but the teams' leaders and the Argentine Football Association rejected the idea. The most important clubs preferred to reserve their figures to play the league, the Libertadores Cup, the Milk Cup (in Argentina, a tournament without importance). It became very difficult. Several friendlies were organised, but if a club gave you a footballer for one game, they would deny you for the next. In addition, the European institutions released their players only to participate on 'FIFA dates'. In just 18 months, from his debut in Glasgow on 19 November 2008 to the formation of the list for the World Cup in South Africa, made official on 19 May 2010, Diego summoned and tested … 108 different players! Of them, 42 were only summoned once. The system became a mess, and not only in Argentine football: the same is suffered by all teams in South America, who have most of their players in Europe. For those national teams from the Old Continent it is much easier: they meet in an hour and a half. Spain won in South Africa 2010 with 20 of its 23 players in the local league, and seven FC Barcelona boys playing the same game; Germany, in 2014, with 17 players in the German league, and a base of seven from the same club: Bayern Munich. What a coincidence! In 2010, Barcelona was managed by Josep Guardiola, like the Bavarian team in 2014.

In Argentina the leaders and the press demand that you become champion, and when you don't, they kill you. The obligation is not to raise the World Cup, but to give the maximum and go as far as is possible. In football, sometimes you deserve to win by a landslide and you lose, and sometimes you deserve to lose by a landslide and you win. He who does not assume it like that does not understand anything. It seems ridiculous to be carried away by stupid fanaticism and rude nationalism.

For the debut in Scotland, we arrived in Glasgow after a stopover in Madrid, where we met with all the boys who played in European teams (only three had travelled with us from Buenos Aires: Emiliano Papa, Daniel Montenegro and Cristian Villagra) and had a charter flight to our destination. Diego's technicial staff also included assistants Alejandro Mancuso and Miguel Ángel Lemme; a second physical trainer, Javier Vilamitjana; and Bilardo. Lionel Messi was not called because Diego respected a pre-existing pact between the AFA and FC Barcelona, which had yielded his young star for the 2008 Beijing Olympics in exchange for being excused from acting with Argentina in some so-called friendlies on 'FIFA dates' close to important commitments in the Spanish championship or the Champions League. A few days after the game in Glasgow, the *culé* club had a key match for the Champions League, and asked the AFA to allow them to preserve their footballer, a circumstance to which Diego agreed without reproach: 'There is a clause and we have to respect it. We are nobody to oppose it.'

We prepared for the debut in the beautiful sports complex of Celtic, without problems. But, the night before the game in Hampden Park, a delicate unforeseen occurrence. While we were at the hotel, Javier Vilamitjana approached me and said:

'*Fer*, Diego's calling you.'

'What's the matter?'

'I don't know what problem *Kun* has with Gianinna.'

Diego's youngest daughter was pregnant at the time and Sergio *Kun* Agüero was her boyfriend. I went to his room and I found him with Agüero, Bilardo and Mancuso. The *Ten* was upset, on the verge of tears.

'What's the matter?'

'Gianinna is bleeding,' he informed me, his eyes watery. 'What do we do? What do I do?'

I took *Kun* by the shoulder and said:

'You are leaving urgently for Madrid. Let's go talk to Moschella and ask him to get you a ticket. You have to be next to Gianinna.'

I looked at Diego.

'And you're leaving too.'

'Me?'

He had a nervous breakdown, because he wanted to go with Sergio and, at the same time, stay to manage his first game with the national team. That was not the right moment to say anything, but I wanted to say to Bilardo, 'Can you see? The national team is not more important than the family!' Finally, only *Kun* travelled to Madrid.

The afternoon of the match with Scotland, the footballers and the coaches met in one of the hotel lounges for the technical talk. It was a large room with very little light. The players were talking among themselves and suddenly

Diego entered the place with Mancuso and Lemme. He was wearing a navy-blue windcheater. He started giving the talk and I was looking at the footballers. Everyone followed his words with an almost reverential emotion. Carlitos Tevez's tears were falling. It was an indelible moment.

I think that, in that emotional exhibition, Diego used up what little energy he had left. During the match – Argentina won 1-0 with a goal from Maxi Rodríguez – he barely got up from his seat to give any instructions. The Gianinna question had him very concerned. On his return, Diego stayed in Madrid to be with his daughter. Fortunately, her condition improved and her pregnancy continued calmly.

In February, the planets aligned. For the first time, Diego and *Leo* coincided. The meeting took place in the French city of Marseille, where Argentina had agreed an international friendly against France. Messi not only admired his new national coach for everything he achieved in the World Cups in Mexico 1986 and Italy 1990, at six years of age, the guy from Rosario, a Newell's fan, had gone with his father Jorge to see Diego's debut with the red-and-black jersey, on the afternoon of 7 October 1993 at the Colossus of Parque Independencia, against the Ecuadorian club Emelec.

That trip to the French Riviera was one of the ones Diego enjoyed the most during his time as the light-blue-and-white coach.

'You don't know how I envy you,' he told the boys in the locker room, as they changed to face the French. He wanted so much, or more, to go out and play. Throughout his career as a coach, Diego always maintained a very affectionate relationship with all of his footballers. His excellent humour, loaded with contagious spirits and good vibes, conveyed calmness and confidence both on and off the pitch. During the first practice in France, on 9 February at the Gemenos Municipal stadium, Diego was fascinated with *Leíto*: despite the intense cold, he savoured every minute of training as if he himself were going to join the team.

That night, after dinner, the members of the coaching staff met to reflect on the working day. Diego was overflowing with happiness.

'Can you believe how that dwarf is playing?' he commented, ecstatic.

I laughed.

'What are you, an NBA player? You two are the same height!'

The relationship was forged between mutual admiration, Diego's protection, and the reverential respect of *Leo*, who was still a 22-year-old boy, for the former *Ten*.

They both talked a lot. The most significant anecdote of that trip occurred the night before the game, when we went to examine the playing field of the Vélodrome stadium, the stage of the international duel. After Diego ended the session, characterised by the cold and strong winds, and most of the players began to walk towards the locker room to protect themselves from the low temperature, some forwards stayed with goalkeeper Juan Pablo Carrizo to practise free kicks on goal. I looked at them from the centre circle. On Messi's turn, at that time the star of Barcelona, he placed the ball two metres outside the area, almost in a straight line, and hit it with his left foot looking for the right angle of the frame defended by Carrizo. The shot went high and wide, to the left. *Leo* spun on his heel and made a gesture of undoubted annoyance, moving his arms like a windmill. Then he started a walk to the locker room. When he passed near me, I took him by the shoulder and said:

'You are not going to tell me that you, who is on your way to being one of the best in history, are going to go to sleep after such crap, right? You're going to have nightmares, *Leo!*'

Messi smiled mischievously, but did not stop. A second later, he heard Diego's voice calling him to turn around and return to the edge of the area.

'Come on, *Leíto*, come on,' he said as he put an arm around him, like a hardened father to his inexperienced son. 'Come here.'

Diego asked Carrizo for a ball and placed it in the same point from which Messi had shot at the goal. For me and for the other players who were on the pitch at that time, the world had stopped.

'You're rushing too hard. When you kick the ball, don't take your foot away so fast. It must accompany it more because, if not, the ball does not know what you want, nor where you want it to go.'

While he provided his explanation, he took two or three running steps.

'You have to do it like this, look!'

He ran to the ball and landed a deadly left foot, just like old times. The ball struck violently into the net, two centimetres from the junction between the right post and the crossbar. Carrizo flew, but was unable to deflect the missile. *Leo* looked at me as if to say: 'Look what this guy did!'

'You see? This is how you have to do it. Accompany the ball more.'

It was a luxury class from a great teacher towards his admired disciple. Don't believe me. If you review the statistics, you will discover that *Leo's* free-kick goal average increased exponentially from 2010. By the way: on 11 February, Messi played with the 18 on his back and scored a Maradonian goal that contributed to an Argentinian victory, 2-0, over the French team.

Shortly before Diego's official debut as coach of the Argentine team, against Venezuela in the qualifiers for South Africa, on 28 March 2009, the members of the coaching staff met with some administrators of the AFA – among them Daniel Pellegrino, a man from Grondona's confidence – to coordinate the schedules of the different activities prior to a game of these characteristics, such as training sessions, lunches and dinners, snacks, rest periods, video sessions, technical talk and transfer from the Ezeiza sport centre to the Monumental stadium in the north of Buenos Aires. The meeting took place in a room that had been set up for this type of session, with a large round table. When the administrators asked Diego what time he wanted to leave for the River Plate stadium, I asked:

'What are we going to travel on?'

'On the official AFA bus,' Pellegrino answered, with an intonation that sounded mocking.

'I think we should take another one as well.'

'Another bus? For what?,' inquired Pellegrino. His tone of voice had gone from irony to arrogance. Diego looked at us in silence, weighing the situation.

'I believe that, at that time, the General Paz avenue [a highway that serves as a political boundary between the city of Buenos Aires and the province of the same name] will be full. If something happens to the bus, how do we continue to the stadium?'

Pellegrino looked at Diego and returned to ironic mode.

'Something like this never happened, it would be absolutely unusual.'

'I know it has never happened, but there is always a first time. A thing like this cannot happen to the Argentine team, and even less if the coach is Maradona.'

Diego, nodding his head, finally got into the discussion.

'Daniel, another bus.'

'Well, Diego, OK.'

Pellegrino wrote down the coach's order in his notebook.

The day of the game arrived. We all got on the bus and went to River Plate stadium escorted by four police motorcycles, two in the front and two in the back. We advanced along the Riccheri highway and, when we reached the General Paz avenue, we ran into a sea of cars. The road was packed with fans heading to the coliseum to cheer on the Argentine team, which would play for the first time officially since Diego's appointment. With the support of the police motorcycles, we advanced but very slowly, with constant starts and stops. Near the Avenida de los Constituyentes, I noticed that the driver began to force the gear stick, which had stuck. The bus broke down! I was sitting next to Diego in the first seat, he on the side of the window and I on the aisle. After a few moments in which the driver tried to resume in vain, Diego stopped and shouted:

'Come on, everyone downstairs, to the other bus.'

The people in the cars that surrounded us began to honk their horns, but when they threatened to descend to hug the players or ask for their autographs, we were all on top of the substitute bus, again on our way to the stadium. Returning to the march, Diego approached my ear to say:

'You're a son of a bitch. You are very lucky!'

241

'Very lucky?' I retorted. 'As I told, it could happen …
and it did!'

That day, we won 4-0, with great forcefulness. In
the second half, Diego told Juan Sebastián Verón to start
warming up to replace Carlos Tevez. When Verón, who
was on the bench because he had a problem with his ankle,
began to trot to the edge of the playing field, whistles and
murmurs of disapproval rained from the four stands. The
fans were still bitter over the elimination from the World
Cup in South Korea and Japan 2002, in the first round,
and Verón had been pointed out by many people for several
years as the person responsible for that failure. Facing the
reaction of the public, Diego left the bench and made a
gesture with his hands, as if pushing down. Everyone shut
their mouths, and seconds later, no one disapproved of
Verón's entry.

Four days later, Argentina travelled to the city of La
Paz to face Bolivia. A month before, I had gone with Dr
Donato Villani, head of the AFA's medical department,
to choose the hotel where the Argentine squad was
going to stay in Santa Cruz de la Sierra, a city with
geographical parameters similar to those of Buenos Aires.
Why didn't we go directly to La Paz? Because, among
all the suggestions we had received, the most successful,
apparently, consisted of staying on the plain and travelling
to the height the same day of the game, to play before the
effect of the altitude, some 3,500m above sea level, would
begin to have an effect on the players' bodies. On that
trip, we had a meeting with a delegate from the Bolivian
federation. After booking the hotel, we began to talk
about the problems of organising a sports competition in
that context.

'Why don't they play here? There is no advantage for anyone here,' I asked the representative, referring to Santa Cruz de la Sierra.

'No, we reserve the right to choose the place that most affects the opposing team,' replied the guy, arrogantly.

'But that's not sport. This position violates one of the main principles of sport, which is equal conditions when competing. With the same criteria, we could choose the base that we have in Antarctica, and you could not get off the plane: it is 30 degrees below zero there. That would not be fair.'

We arrived on a charter flight to Santa Cruz de la Sierra and I started drinking coca tea and chewing coca leaves, which I had bought from a street vendor on the previous trip, to be better prepared for the effect of the altitude. The next day, we left for La Paz: we arrived at the international airport of El Alto, at 4,000m, and from there we went directly to the stadium. It was hot! We went into the locker room and I went to the pitch. I had never been to La Paz or at such a height. To get to the pitch from the locker room, you had to climb 22 steps. I remember counting them. When I stepped out on to the track that surrounds the playing field and approached the sideline, I felt shaken. I took my heart rate: while on the plain, under the same normal circumstances, I usually have 60, 65 beats per minute; at that time I was at 110. I went downstairs and there were two police officers on the first landing. I took out my pack of cigarettes, took one, and invited the uniformed men. I could barely gasp twice: I threw the cigarette because I was choking! I went to the changing room and Diego was in a small room reserved for the coaching staff, while the players changed.

'And?' he consulted me.

'It's terrible.'

'Do not say anything!'

'I won't say anything, but they will notice it soon.'

We went out on to the pitch to warm up and I met up with the boys.

'Pay attention to me: most will be affected by this. Be careful, it's not a joke. Make efforts now, as if to look for the drowning and to know what is going to happen to you.'

I preferred that they were scared before the game and not during, so that they would not fall into insecurity. Carlitos Tevez made a sprint from the small area to a couple of metres before the midfield line, where I was. He came with his mouth open like a fish.

'I can't breathe!'

'Well, that's what will happen to you during the game.'

The match started, a few minutes went by and the rival No.10, Alex da Rosa, a boy born in Brazil and a Bolivian national, took the ball on the left, ten metres into the local field. He advanced a little, he crossed the central line carrying the ball and I, in that hundredth of a second, I thought:

'Will he shoot? No way ...'

Sure he shot, and how! He took out a cannon shot and Carrizo almost tore himself to get it out.

'Whoops, fuck, what is this?' I reasoned.

Shortly after, Marcelo Martins opened the scoring, Lucho González tied and Bolivia scored two more goals before the end of the first half. In the second, we got three more in our net. We lost 6-1, but when we saw the match again, we counted that they had 16 chances. If they had been a bit lucky, they would have hit us for ten or 12 goals. The best performance of Argentina was

Carrizo's, widely, despite having conceded half a dozen goals. That day, the Bolivian Joaquín Botero was Messi; and Messi, Botero. If there had been an agent interested in buying players, he would take Botero and leave Messi. The only Argentine who played almost without problems was Ángel di María.

The principles of physiology suggest that, to achieve optimal performance at altitude, one week of adaptation is needed per thousand metres. You have to have the players in La Paz three or four weeks before the match, but no team is going to give them to you a month before for a game that, in the long run, could be inconsequential. We had made a plan: to bring a suitable youth team in Jujuy, as was done in 1973 with what became known as 'The Phantom Selection': that team beat Bolivia in La Paz 1-0 in the tie for the 1974 World Cup in Germany. Grondona did not authorise us. The logic in the AFA did not exist.

'Bolivia surpassed us in all aspects of the game. We made mistakes and we paid for them. Bolivia played good football, we did absolutely nothing of what we had been doing,' Diego acknowledged in the post-game press conference. 'Each Bolivian goal,' he remarked, 'was a dagger to the heart.' In the home dressing room, one of the footballers, Joaquín Botero, celebrated as if he had won the World Cup. Why? Days before the game, the Bolivian federation had offered the players $11,000 for each goal they scored. Botero, in an unforgettable afternoon, had just scored three goals for which he added 33,000 reasons to celebrate; green, like his national team jersey. Leaving the stadium, there were hundreds and hundreds of kids dressed in typical Altiplano clothes. They were beckoning us with their fingers, showing us five of one hand and one of the other. Diego overheated, but I told him:

'That's it, *Die*. Look on the bright side: at least we gave these kids a joy, who never have the chance to be happy with football.'

He did not agree very much, but after all, 6-1, 1-0 or 17-1 is the same: we lost all three points. However, this result had become Argentina's worst in a World Cup context, including the qualifying round, together with the beating that, for the same score, Czechoslovakia gave to Argentina in the 1958 World Cup in Sweden. By goal difference, it is equivalent to Colombia's 0-5 of 1993, although in that case the disgrace was greater because it had crystallised in Buenos Aires. The particular conditions of La Paz justify such a defeat, or at least provide an excuse.

On the return trip, on the scale of Cochabamba, Fernando Gago, who had played the 90 minutes, suffered a decompensation. The height had affected him greatly. In these circumstances, one should not play: not only is this principle of equal conditions being violated when competing, but the health and lives of players who are not adapted are put at risk. Anything could have happened. A few years later, in 2013, an 18-year-old youth named Yair Clavijo, a footballer for Sporting Cristal de Peru, died during a reserve match at the Estadio Municipal of Urcos, located 3,100m above sea level.

A year before our defeat, on 7 March 2008, Diego had participated in a 'demonstration' game with Bolivian President Evo Morales, in response to a FIFA initiative to veto international football games at more than 2,500m high. The *Ten* supported Morales for ideological reasons, not sports. What does Evo know about physiology? It is one thing to express an opinion out of patriotism, another to risk health and transgress sportsmanship. Bolivian football leaders must not be hypocrites: they want to win in any way, even at the risk of the lives of foreign players. You cannot prioritise a result when the health of a human being is involved. For me, you have to give them the points and that's it. When Yair Clavijo died, all the football leaders looked the other way and nobody said anything. I don't understand what the scientific community expects from the federations. Doctors sometimes have to do something. They never say anything and they are the ones who have to speak. Those from FIFA watch the games on television, leaning back on their thrones, with air conditioning and smoking a cigar.

In May, Argentina organised an international match against Panama in the city of Santa Fe to test various players from the local league. During the preparation for that match, Diego led a practice open to the press at the AFA sport centre against Tristán Suárez, a team from the town of Ezeiza, a neighbour of the national team, who at that time was performing in the Metropolitan B, the third category of professional football. The light-blue-and-white team won 1-0 with a goal from José Sand, forward of the Lanús club. As soon as the game ended, Bilardo, quite disturbed by the result, approached the national team's press officer, Andrés *Coco* Ventura, and ordered him to inform the press that the team had won 4-0.

'But, Carlos, how am I going to say that? The journalists were watching!'

In June, Argentina beat Colombia in Buenos Aires and lost to Ecuador in Quito, 2-0. That match could have been won: Tevez missed a penalty when the score was blank, and Gago and Messi missed two incredible goals. When Diego's team got tired, Walter Ayoví hit a shot and, a while later, Pablo Palacios increased the score. Despite the fact that the match was held in Quito, 2,800m above sea level, Argentina played very well and deserved to win. Football never ceases to amaze us. But it is also fair to point out that, while in Bolivia we played at the time when the sun beats the strongest, in Quito it rained and the sky was always covered. The meteorological conditions offered a different, less aggressive context.

In the double match week of September, the table was very complicated. To host Brazil, it was decided to change the scene and play in the Rosario Central stadium, which had been the scene of a goalless draw between the same teams during the 1978 World Cup.

A few days before the South American classic, while we were doing the last training session at the Rosario field, I was talking with Alejandro Mancuso, and Bilardo approached us, too nervous:

'We have to lower the crossbar,' he suggested with a trembling voice.

'Why, Carlos?'

'The Brazilians have made a lot of goals shooting to the top of the goal.'

Of course, nothing was done about it. What Bilardo proposed did not make any sense, since in each international match a delegate controls that the pitch is in perfect regulatory condition. Also, as if to destroy that ridiculous idea, we lost 1-3 with three goals with the ball entering the goal … skimming the ground!

'Did you see, *Mancu*? We should have raised the floor, not lower the crossbar!' I commented sarcastically.

Four days after the fall to the *Verdeamarela* squad, we lost again against Paraguay, in Asunción, 1-0. Argentina was in fifth place in the table, outside the automatic qualification places but with the possibility of participating in a play-off with a CONCACAF team: Costa Rica. A sector of the press tore Diego to pieces: he was criticised because he had taken over with the team in third place and, after just one victory – against a weak Venezuela – and three consecutive defeats, passage to South Africa at that time depended on the intercontinental play-off. But the matter could get even more complicated, as Argentina led the dangerous Uruguayan team by just one point.

To relax a little and detox from so much reproach, Diego went for a few days to the Hotel Palace Merano, the energy regeneration centre and Spa to which he had already gone a couple of times in his days as a Napoli player, in the Italian Tirol. The rest could not be complete: Italian treasury agents raided his room and seized his diamond rings, valued at about €4,000, from an alleged tax debt that the former player had since his time as captain of the southern team. The officials acted after the complaint of a deputy linked to Prime Minister Silvio Berlusconi, Maurizio Fugatti. The legislator took advantage of his influence to demand that the tax affairs body proceed against Diego and thus gain some tabloid credit. According to some newspapers published, the *Ten* owed €37m in taxes. Crazy! He can't have won that much money in his eight seasons with the Neapolitan team.

Back in Argentina, Diego and the national team faced very brave moments. The penultimate game, against Peru on the River Plate pitch, was a suffering from the start to the end. The Andean team, which had been in the last qualification for several rounds, went out to play without pressure, and complicated their rival, to the point of turning goalkeeper Sergio Romero into a real star. After a first goalless half, during half-time Diego entered the locker room and called one of the substitutes aside, Martín Palermo – who was about to become the top scorer in Boca's history – and announced that he would come on for Enzo Pérez:

'Go ahead and solve this story, as you solved so many others.'

Martín looked at him.

'How?'

'Play more advanced than *Pipita*,' replied the coach, referring to Gonzalo Higuaín.

Pipita, precisely, opened the scoring two minutes into the second period, but a little while later a storm of water and wind broke out, which seemed to favour the game of the Peruvians. Amid the torrents and gusts, the visiting squad levelled on 45 minutes, thanks to a header from Hernán Rengifo. Equality seemed to stifle Argentine aspirations, but almost immediately, at 47 minutes, the miracle came. After a string of shots and centres to the Peruvian area without a precise destination, Federico Insúa took a rebound and launched a ball that was found by Palermo's left foot and ended up in the net. That key goal, which Diego celebrated by throwing himself on his belly on the flooded grass, helped us to understand that the hearts of Argentines can bear anguish to the limit of the impossible.

The victory radically changed the Argentine situation, who rose to the automatic qualification zone with one game remaining, which would take place at the difficult Centenario stadium in Montevideo.

'We are going to go with total pride,' said Diego, who in the press conference after the duel with the Peruvians said, 'My goals were normal, Palermo does miracles.'

The Centenario was a bonfire, it was packed. Diego arrived calm, convinced that we were going to go to the World Cup. We were confident that, if the qualification was not straightforward, we had a good chance in the play-off against Costa Rica. The main objective was to get passage to South Africa. I remembered that Marcelo Bielsa's team had qualified first, with a wide margin, but then they had come back after the group phase.

The classic from the River Plate was defined in favour of Argentina thanks to a single goal from Mario Bolatti and a lot of anxiety. After the referee's whistle, all the players and most of the coaching staff hugged each other in the centre of the pitch. On the other hand, I walked calmly into the Centenario and went to the home dressing room to greet Diego Forlán, with whom I had worked at Independiente. I asked him not to be angry and I wished him good luck for the play-off against Costa Rica. Forlán had his revenge: Uruguay not only qualified, but he was one of the tournament's top scorers (he scored five goals, like the German Thomas Müller, the Spanish David Villa and the Dutch Wesley Sneijder) and was chosen as the best player at the World Cup.

Diego, meanwhile, confronted the press with some phrases 'made in Maradona', with which he unloaded the tension accumulated in a complex and tricky process. For his outbursts, FIFA punished him with 'a two-month ban on carrying out any activity related to football and a fine of 25,000 Swiss francs'. The sanction included a ban from participating in the tournament draw, held on 4 December in Cape Town.

We returned to Buenos Aires on a charter flight. Diego was happy, and calm. In his head he was already outlining the first steps towards South Africa.

Before the end of the year, the AFA scheduled a meeting for Tuesday, 22 December against the Catalonia national football team led by Johan Cruyff, in Barcelona. It was a game without any relevance. We embarked on Saturday the 19th and, while we were flying with Diego to the first European city in which he lived, we stayed chatting for a while after dinner.

'What are you going to use *Leo* for in this friendly?'

'Why do you ask me?'

At that time, there was a belief that Messi could not be taken out of a game, or that he could not be left out because he was angry.

'Because you already know that he is going to the World Cup. Why don't you try another player? In addition, the kid is exhausted, saturated with matches. What would happen if he suffers an injury?'

Indeed, Lionel had played that same Saturday in the final of the FIFA Club World Cup that Barcelona had won 2-1 against Estudiantes de La Plata, in Dubai.

'What do you want us to do?'

'Tell him that he's not going to play. If it's okay with you, I'll discuss it with him, prepare him, and bring him to you. I will explain the reasoning.'

'Well, go ahead.'

We arrived at the Princesa Sofía hotel in Barcelona in the morning. The players from the European teams had to start arriving around four or five in the afternoon, to have dinner and retire to rest in their rooms. I asked the head kit man to, when *Leo* arrived, ask that before he goes to Diego's room, he stop by mine. At around six in the afternoon there was a knock on my door. I opened it and there was Messi.

'How are you doing, *Leíto*?'

'Hi, *Profe*, how are you?'

'Come in, I have to talk to you.'

When he came in, I looked at his feet.

'But ... what a shame, your ankle is injured! Is it a sprain?'

He looked at me in surprise.

'No, *Profe*, I have nothing.'

'Listen to me carefully: the day after tomorrow is a game for nothing, it has no significance, less for you. The only argument you would have to play is to please the leaders of the AFA, so that they take $250,000 more, of which surely neither you nor your colleagues are going to see anything.' Logically, the organisers of these kind of meetings do not pay the same price if the game is played with a superstar on the pitch or not. The amount with Messi is completely different than without him.

'You,' I continued, 'arrived exhausted from Dubai, without time to recover, and it is crazy to put you on the pitch with a risk of suffering an injury. I already discussed it with Diego. We agree that testing you is unnecessary, as it was in his time having tested him. We believe that the best thing is, at the time the game will be played, you will be in Rosario, eating a barbecue with your family, your girlfriend, your friends or whoever you want. Take advantage and travel, start your vacation!'

Leo didn't say anything, just nodded.

'Diego already knows. Now we go to his room. Dr Villani is going to speak with the Barcelona doctors to write a report in which he is going to suggest that you do not play because you have suffered a sprain in your ankle.'

We went to Diego's room, where he was with Mancuso and Héctor Enrique, who had joined the coaching staff.

I left *Leo* there and went back to my room. The next day, Messi travelled to Argentina, and watched the game on television from Rosario. All the newspapers, meanwhile, announced that the FC Barcelona star had not played due to having suffered a 'grade two' sprain in the match against Estudiantes.

A few days passed, also Christmas and the New Year's Eve festivities and, on our return to Buenos Aires, we met Diego at the AFA sport centre to continue our work. While we were having lunch at the restaurant of the complex, President Julio Grondona arrived. He greeted us, put both hands on the table and said:

'It's the first time I've seen a sprained player with such thin shoes ...'

Of course, he had crossed paths with Messi at the hotel in Barcelona and had been annoyed that we had withdrawn him. He was overheated because the AFA had lost $250,000.

The following months served to define salient details of the organisation, among them closing the agreement with the High Performance Centre of the University of Pretoria, whose facilities served as the base camp for our stay. I was part of the group that travelled to South Africa to visit the options we had – for a week we supervised several places – and signed a suggestion from Carlos Bilardo: that the base camp be mounted on the grounds of that educational institution located about 70km north of Johannesburg. We found the place more than appropriate, with all the comforts for optimal preparation and adequate rest for the players. The only thing we requested was that the curtains be changed, that all the rooms have box springs and that the bathrooms have a bidet. This last requirement caused an incredible situation: the university authorities bought special toilets called Bathroom Bizarre, which offered three drainage speeds and a bidet with built-in hot water. When the incorporation of this artefact became known in the local newspapers, its sales multiplied – how could it be otherwise – tenfold. In the sanitary-product businesses, Bathroom Bizarre took over the window displays along with Argentine flags and clippings of the articles published in the newspapers with funny headlines. Almost everything Diego touched turned to gold, and even a toilet can enjoy an original commercial success favoured by the 'hand' ... or, rather, 'the buttocks of God'. Thanks to these details, the campus accommodation was better than a five-star hotel.

There was a very short period that separated the beginning of the World Cup, on 12 June against Nigeria, with the end of most of the European leagues – Diego Milito, Walter Samuel and Martín Demichelis played the Champions League Final on 22 May in Madrid, the first two for the winners Inter and the third for runners-up Bayern Munich. Due to this and with the idea of saving the discomfort of a flight to our country for the footballers who played in teams from the Old Continent – the majority, 17 of the 23 summoned – with Diego, we decided to carry out a first phase of training in a modern sports centre in the German city of Frankfurt, for about 11 or 12 days, and from there fly directly to Johannesburg to complete the preparation in Pretoria over the remaining ten days, which would also help us acclimatise to the country and to finish putting ourselves in World Cup mode.

The experience of the champions showed that, in 1978, Cesar Menotti had almost all his players about three months before the start of the tournament, and only one footballer, Mario Kempes, who played in Europe – Valencia CF of

Spain – joined 25 days before the debut against Hungary. In 1986, Argentina arrived in Mexico on 5 May. They were the first foreign team to arrive on Aztec soil, almost a month after the first game against South Korea. However, our proposal ended up in a garbage can at the AFA headquarters: the brainy leaders had arranged, on their own, a match on the River Plate pitch against Canada, for 24 May. They justified the friendly saying that this meeting would include different celebrations corresponding to the bicentennial of the Revolution of May (25 May 1810), which constituted the first Creole government and laid the roots for independence six years later.

It seemed a bit strange to me, at least, that people who died before this sport arrived on British ships to the River Plate were entertained with football ... The truth is that, beyond the international date, that match caused inconvenience and loss of time, because all the boys in Europe had to travel to Buenos Aires first. In addition, the three who had played the Champions League Final in Madrid could not play. Neither did Lionel Messi, who had suffered discomfort in practice. As always, the convening power of the light-blue-and-white national team made the Monumental stadium insufficient to house the crowd that came to give their encouragement. From a commercial point of view, the match was a success; from the sporting angle, just a nonsense. Preparation time, already short, was shortened alarmingly. Finally, on 30 June, we left for South Africa, on a flight that also carried about 80 VIP hooligans. We found out when we were already in Pretoria, because fortunately the 'fans' behaved correctly, and also no one approached the delegation.

With the extra fatigue accumulated in the walk through Buenos Aires and the start of the competition at hand, we were forced to evaluate and decide that the daily programme at the High Performance Centre of the University of Pretoria should be divided into two shifts of work. The fundamental, of course, would be the afternoon, in which Diego would rehearse his tactical system on the field. In the morning period, each member of the team could choose between three options: bath or massage sessions and/or kinesic treatment; activities in the gym; movements on the playing field. The footballer had to select one and communicate it to the coaching staff during breakfast. The purpose of not imposing a rigid and common routine for the group was to delegate to each player the freedom and responsibility of their fine-tuning. Even those who had a plan previously laid out by their personal trainers (such as Fernando Gago or Juan Sebastián Verón, for example) were invited to carry it out with absolute independence. This endorsement of their sense of professionalism showed a high degree of honesty and manifest nobility of this magnificent team of young people, who gave me the priceless treasure of a month of unforgettable coexistence in that little piece of Africa. The quality of the relationship achieved between all the members of the delegation – footballers, coaching staff, doctors and physiotherapists, masseurs, kit men, cooks, sparring players, etc. – was the opposite of the gloomy omens launched from most of the journalistic media. All the members of the team put aside any type of personal interest to make themselves available to the longed-for common goal.

The coaching staff turned out to be a very united group: we were together all day and every night; after dinner, we met to draw the conclusions of the day. In a building, the installation of the players had been arranged, and in front there was another, joined by a corridor, in whose ground floor the rooms of Diego, Héctor Enrique, Mancuso and Bilardo were distributed. At the top were Javier Vilamitjana, Rubén Moschella (the administrative officer who, at that time, was working as director of the Ezeiza sports complex) and me.

The players selected by Diego to travel to South Africa were Diego Pozo, Martín Demichelis, Clemente Rodríguez, Nicolás Burdisso, Mario Bolatti, Gabriel Heinze, Ángel Di María, Juan Sebastián Verón, Gonzalo Higuaín, Lionel Messi, Carlos Tévez, Ariel Garcé, Walter Samuel, Javier Mascherano (the captain), Nicolás Otamendi, Sergio Agüero, Jonás Gutiérrez, Martín Palermo, Diego Milito, Maximiliano Rodríguez, Mariano Andújar, Sergio Romero and Javier Pastore. Many media outlets questioned Garcé's inclusion. I think he was a very good defender, although it is also true that an absolutely unusual question weighed in his selection, closer to magical thinking than to a professional opinion: a few days before handing over the final roster, Diego dreamed that he was doing a lap of honour on Garcé's shoulders.

Another striking fact is that *Kun* Agüero, at that time a prominent Atlético de Madrid striker, was the son-in-law of the former *Ten* and the brand-new father of Benjamin, Diego's first grandson. '*Kun* is going to play when I think he has to play. Even if Benja asked me to, I would do it,' he said, with great grace, during the first press conference he gave on African soil. 'But he's not talking yet, so he's not going to ask me,' he joked. Agüero was present in three of the five games: he replaced Carlos Tevez against South Korea, started against Greece and replaced Ángel di María in the game against Germany.

During one of the training sessions in Pretoria, I noticed that Lionel Messi shared an exceptional characteristic with

Diego: the privileged field of vision that the great doctor Antonio dal Monte had told me about during the evaluations we did before Mexico 1986. The players were playing a pick-up game on the side of one of the fields and, in a moment, Diego summoned me:

'*Fer*, call them, we will start right now.'

I yelled and everyone started to approach the centre of the training pitch. *Leo* walked alone along the middle line, pushing a ball gently and his gaze fixed on the spheroid. I approached stealthily, with the idea of taking the ball by surprise, grabbing him by the ear and saying, 'Don't be distracted doing these things, anyone will take the ball from you,' but when I stretched out my right leg to hit the ball … Lionel moved it far from me and I ended up kicking the air! At that moment, I not only remembered Dal Monte: I verified that, like Diego, Lionel has radars instead of eyes.

I think the national team played a very good role in the South African World Cup. In the first phase, they beat Nigeria 1-0, South Korea 4-1, and Greece 2-0. In the round of 16, they defeated Mexico 3-1, and in the quarter-finals they fell to Germany, 4-0. I knew that, as long as the team started winning, we were going to do well, because the kids handled the counterattack wonderfully. The first game we started losing was with Germany. We had beaten this rival 1-0 four months earlier, in Munich, with a goal from *Pipita* Higuaín, but in South Africa the Germans woke us up early and managed the spaces better. This duel was much more even than the scoreboard seems to indicate: their second goal only arrived at 68 minutes, and then the kids became desperate, disoriented, lost order. But, before their second goal, we had several opportunities to tie the score.

In a World Cup, you need many people with a lot of experience, and I think that in South Africa, ultimately, that was the biggest deficit. The World Cup for those kids was going to be the one in Brazil, four years later, as I told Diego. *Leo* Messi, without going any further, was too young to set himself up as a banner. He turned 23 during the World Cup, and he was very withdrawn. Against Greece, Diego decided to reserve some starters, including Javier Mascherano, and appointed Lionel as captain. Upon receiving the armband in the locker room, he had to speak in front of all his teammates and practically said two things and nothing more. Now he has grown a lot in that, he is the owner of the team. But, at that time, there were players with more weight and he did not know if he felt ashamed or perhaps exceeded by the responsibility of being captain.

On the eve of the game against Germany, during the last training session, an event took place that today I rescue as an invaluable pearl from the treasure of my best experiences. Before starting the practice, Diego called Walter Samuel to tell him that, as he had not yet fully recovered from the injury that had afflicted him in the match against Greece, he preferred to reserve him and put Nicolás Burdisso in his place. Walter, most naturally, replied:

'It seems perfect to me, Diego, stay calm. Also, *Nico* is my friend, I'm sure he will play very well. I am here to join forces.'

Diego thanked him for the gesture and then called Burdisso to inform him of his decision. After listening to him, *Nico* made it clear that he liked Walter's philosophy, adding that if the choice had been the other way around, he would have said the same. The next day, in the dressing room and before entering the field for the warm-up, I approached

Walter and then Nicolás to tell them that I had already won my true World Cup for having had the enormous fortune of meeting two people of such moral stature, and that against that any result for me was insignificant.

Then Germany crushed us. After the quarter-final and our elimination sealed, the atmosphere in the dressing room was horrifying. I tried in vain to comfort each of the boys, thanking them for their enormous effort. Diego was heartbroken, very bad. I remember going into the England dressing room in Mexico 1986, where I went to exchange some of the Argentine players' jerseys. Ray Wilkins stood with one foot on a wooden bench, trimming a fingernail with pliers. John Barnes was chatting with an aide with admirable peace. But, in our South African dressing room, a river of unbearable tears and laments ran.

'How are you going to cry for a football game?' I said to several players. I knew that the boys had given everything, that it was a very young group that would play an excellent role in Brazil 2014: I was right, since four years later they reached the final at the Maracanã stadium. But, in South Africa, they could not escape the damn success injected by our football culture: you have to give your life, losing is a drama, all that nonsense that has gotten into our heads. This is how Argentines are, and not only in football.

I also witnessed the almost inaudible voice of the president of the AFA recognising the dedication and commitment of all, guaranteeing that Diego's continuity depended 'on him, on his decision'. Words that were echoing in the dressing room of Cape Town's Green Point Stadium but never crossed the Atlantic Ocean.

On the return trip to Pretoria, the players communicated to Diego their wishes to return to the country as soon as possible. The AFA administrators, with incredible speed and greater professionalism, managed to make what seemed almost impossible a reality. In the early hours of the next morning, the coaching staff, the players and some relatives boarded a direct flight to Buenos Aires. I decided to stay with the kit staff and the boys from the selective directed by Sergio Batista, who had collaborated as sparring partners.

During our final tour of the venue, I picked up an extra joy: upon arriving at the university complex, before the start of the championship, I put together a small library of about 30 books that I had bought to offer the players of the team a different entertainment alternative to the PlayStation or card games. I chose three works by the famous Uruguayan writer Eduardo Galeano – *The Open Veins of Latin America*, *The Book of Embraces* and *Football in Sun and Shadow* – biographies such as those of Facundo Quiroga and Felipe Varela (two Argentine political leaders of the 1800s), and essays such as *The Mediocre Man*, by José Ingenieros. The first few days, I noticed with some concern that the books, placed in the recreation room, seemed destined to collect dust and cobwebs. But, little by little, the volumes began to disappear. When the main group left the sports centre and I accompanied the kit men to check the rooms and check that no one had forgotten personal effects, I was afraid I'd find the discarded books in the back of some closet. However, I was delighted to see that none were left, and that many of the players had decided to take them with them to add to their own libraries in their respective homes. For me, training is also educating and, for this, good books become the voice of essential teachers.

Four days later, we left that wonderful place where we had enjoyed many unforgettable days.

As a coach, Diego had the advantage of his charisma and his career, and the disadvantage of never having developed a method. He believed that it was the same with him inside as with him outside, and it was not the same: there was a huge difference. But it was Diego, and for the players that was a bonus track, something that not just anyone could have.

He had been with Cesar Menotti, with Carlos Bilardo, with a lot of prestigious coaches, and he thought that what he had learned from them, plus what he added, was enough. He had a great deal with the players, but he lacked preparation time. However, he took on his role change very well. In the World Cups of Spain, Mexico, Italy and the United States, he did not have to take care of anything; everyone cared about him. In South Africa, by contrast, he assumed his role as group leader with enormous responsibility. He was on top of all the details.

Diego really enjoyed his time as coach of the Argentine team. In training, travelling, pre-game meetings, I saw him happier than ever. He had regained enthusiasm and freshness. He was the same kid who played for *Los Cebollitas* (his first childhood team) and lived in Villa Fiorito, but he was standing on the other side of the touchline. His plunge on to the soaked pitch on the day of the match with Peru, at the Monumental stadium in Buenos Aires, speaks clearly that he had not lost his enthusiasm for the national team … nor his impudence.

After the World Cup, Grondona came out to say that he wanted Diego to continue, but he had to get rid of some of his collaborators. An infamous malice, because Don Julio – who from the first moment wanted to bury him – knew that the *Ten* was incapable of betraying his people. Diego said goodbye with a very harsh message that went out on all the channels in the national chain, and had repercussions all over the world:

'Grondona lied to me, Bilardo betrayed me. While we were in mourning, Bilardo worked in the shadows to kick me out, knowing that my entire team and I were ready to move on. I defend all my people, from the masseur to the kit-man worker, and I am not going to change: I have values and codes that they do not have. The next coach who assumes in the national team should know that betrayal is just around the corner because there are characters who do not want the Argentine jersey and only think about their personal accounts.'

A shame Diego's legs were cut off again.

Epilogue

Live is life

I SAW Diego for the last time when his father passed away, in June 2015. When *Doña Tota* died, a few years before, I was in Lincoln and I could not travel to accompany him, but Don Diego's departure found me in Buenos Aires. That day, I went to dinner with Cesar Menotti and other friends. At one point, shortly before midnight, Guillermo Blanco asked me:

'*Fer*, are we going to the funeral?'

'No, not the funeral. In any case, let's go to the wake. But let's wait a while, because it's going to be full of people, all the journalists. Let's go later.'

We arrived at about 1.30 in the morning and I reported to the two security employees who were guarding the door of the funeral home.

'Who are you?' asked one of them, with the kindness that characterises most of these guys. I gave him my name, but he didn't recognise me. He kept his face stony.

'Is Claudia there?' I insisted.

'Yes, she's upstairs.'

'Perfect, now I'm calling her.'

I left to communicate with her and to allow me to enter, and at that moment I noticed a group of big men arriving and, in the middle, was Rafael di Zeo (note: leader of Boca Juniors hooligans gang), surrounded by guards as if he were a president. He walked by as if nothing had happened, no one stopped him or asked him who he was. Claudia attended me and told me that she was sending a boy who worked for Diego, who ordered the guards to let me pass. When I went upstairs, I entered a small room where Diego was sitting in an armchair, with his back to the door, next to his secretary Sergio Garmendia, Rocío Oliva and Héctor Enrique. Sergio saw me and informed him that I had arrived. He sat up, all dressed in black. I went to meet him and his face flushed, he raised his right hand and placed his finger on my chest, as if tapping.

'Today I was thinking about you, son of a bitch.'

'Yes? Why?'

He put a hand on each shoulder, pulled me closer to him until I was nose to nose and triggered:

'Because today I was reminded of a conversation we had one night in a hotel in Rome.'

'I don't remember ...'

'We were with the team to play the next day. It was close to midnight and I couldn't sleep. I called you to my room to chat for a while and you came. We sat in the hall, the two of us, against the wall.'

At that point, I thought that the cocaine had been taken by me, because I did not remember anything he said to me.

'We started to chat,' Diego continued, 'and at one point I told you that I loved my old man and my old woman so much that I preferred to die before them, and you replied, "How are you going to say that? So you prefer that your parents suffer the cruellest pain that there can be for a human being, such as the loss of a child? Parents always

266

have to go first, and you will surely go before your daughters because this is the natural order. So you, in order not to bear and assume the pain of their departure, you prefer that they suffer the unspeakable if you die before them!" That's why I remembered you, you son of a bitch!'

He gave me a hug that I still feel. I never imagined it would be the last. I had gotten used to his ups and downs, to the multiple hospitalisations that seemed permanent until he returned with new vigour. One day he did not return. I admit that this did not surprise me. When they did that tribute to him on the Gimnasia club pitch, for his 60th birthday, I noticed a very worrying deterioration. I didn't like his gestures, his empty lifeless eyes. That was not the Diego who looked at you through two balls of fire, nor the one who had reached the top out of conviction, love and sensitivity.

Of all sports, football is the most difficult. It is played with the feet, the part of the body furthest from the neuronal centre, in an uneven field, with divots, sometimes wet or muddy, with wind, or fog, or objects that fly from the stands to the pitch ... or footballers' heads. You get kicked from behind, or elbowed. In that scenario, Diego became eternal. He was much more than a football player; he was an artist who played football. However, over so many years of living together, I learned that two people coexisted within the same body: one was Diego and the other, Maradona. Diego was an adorable boy, generous, with insecurities. Maradona was the character who could not allow himself any weakness, the disguise that he had to invent to meet the demands of the football business and the media. One day I told him:

'With Diego I would go to the end of the world, but with Maradona I would not take a step.'

'If it weren't for Maradona, Diego would still be in Villa Fiorito,' he answered me with remarkable sagacity.

In an interview, one journalist asked me which had been the best Maradona I had ever met – the Maradona from FC Barcelona, from Napoli, from Sevilla, from the national team. I answered that the best Maradona I knew was Don Diego. The son played football better, but the best Maradona was Don Diego. He was a guy with a huge culture of life. Not in the intellectual, but in values, in knowing how to be, in speaking little and saying a lot. He reasoned very slowly, each thing he expressed was read in memory. I loved listening to him. Don Diego did not speak a lot with his son, if he said four words in a row it was already a speech. His means of communication were gestures of approval or disapproval, looks, smiles. Don Diego smiled with his eyes. He was a person of infinite tenderness. Diego suffered greatly from his death.

After being arrested in Caballito by order of the Carlos Menem government, Judge Amelia Berraz de Vidal instructed Diego, among other things, to undergo psychiatric treatment. I had been fixing his affairs in Naples and one day Claudia called me to ask me to travel to Buenos Aires, because the therapists who treated Diego wanted to talk to me. One was a Peruvian psychiatrist named Julio Villena Aragón, the other a psychologist, Rubén Navedo. I flew to Argentina and met with the *Ten* and Claudia in an apartment they had in a building located on Avenida del Libertador and Correa street, in front of the property occupied by the disastrous School of Mechanics of the Navy (note: a place where thousands of people were tortured and killed during the Military dictatorship which governed Argentina from 1976 to 1983). The meeting with the two specialists, a group therapy session, took place in another apartment in the same building that Diego had rented as a space to carry out his recovery process. We sat around a large round table and Villena Aragón took out an agenda in which he began to write down things, while Diego played with his nails, a fairly common attitude for him. Claudia was in a passive situation, looking down. At one point, the psychiatrist raised his head and opened the discussion:

'Well, Diego, today we are going to talk to Fernando, whom you have mentioned so many times. What do you have to say in front of him?'

Diego stated that we had always had a good relationship, that I had helped him a lot and that kind of thing. Me, nothing: I just watched. At one point, Villena Aragón asked him:

'Have you ever invited Fernando to take cocaine?'

'No, never,' Diego answered.

'It's a lie,' I replied immediately.

They all looked at me.

'What's that?' asked the psychiatrist.

'What's what? That he invited me one day.'

Diego kept quiet, staring downward.

'Can you tell us that circumstance?'

I calmly related the situation that I have already specified in one of the chapters of this book: that one day, at Diego's request, I had gone to his sister's house in Naples. That once there, in a bedroom, he had offered me to try cocaine. That I had refused.

'Is this true?' Villena Aragón asked.

'Yes,' Diego answered, somewhat withdrawn. 'I had forgotten that. With the fear that I had of him ...'

'Perfect, we'll leave it there. With this we end for today,' Villena Aragón said.

We got up and went out into the hall to take the elevator. First, the psychiatrist, Claudia and Diego got in. The elevator was small, so I stayed with Navedo waiting for the next trip.

'Sorry,' I said to the psychologist, 'but of all this, I have one doubt.'

'Yes, I know exactly why. You were surprised that Diego said that he was afraid of you.'

'Exactly, because we always had an excellent relationship.'

'The fear that Diego spoke of is not physical fear. No. You, in a sense, represented for him the authority that he lacked. The father was not in Naples, and you assumed, for him, the role of authority. Ultimately, what Diego did at his sister's house was put you to the test. If you had said yes to the drug he was offering you, you would have stopped being who you were, you would have become just another person. Surely you, when you told him that in Naples, you would have feared that, the next day, he would tell you, "I don't need you anymore."?'

'Yes, I thought that.'

'On the contrary: that convinced him that he needed you more than ever. If you had said yes, he would have replied, "I don't need you anymore." Thus, he knew that he could trust you, because you were never going to give in. You were like a stake that he knew he could lean on.'

I regret not having answered the psychologist that his reasoning, although quite correct, lacks a second part: reciprocity. Our relationship functioned like a two-handed avenue. I helped him a lot, but he also helped me. With his charisma and generosity, Diego turned an ordinary life like mine into a wonderful life. I am tall, blond, and with blue eyes, but I owe everything to a little black man born in one of the poorest shanty towns in the world.